The Maya Diaspora

Lèdia
Zoila Ramirez

Adelante —
James

The Maya Diaspora

Guatemalan Roots,
New American Lives

edited by

JAMES LOUCKY AND
MARILYN M. MOURS

TEMPLE UNIVERSITY PRESS
Philadelphia

Temple University Press, Philadelphia 19122
Copyright © 2000 by Temple University
All rights reserved
Published 2000
Printed in the United States of America

♾ The paper used in this publication meets the requirements of the
American National Standard for Information Sciences—Permanence
of Paper for Printed Library Materials, ANSI Z39.48-1984

Library of Congress Cataloging-in-Publication Data

The Maya diaspora : Guatemalan roots, new American lives / edited by James Loucky
and Marilyn M. Moors
     p. cm.
     Includes bibliographical references and index.
     ISBN 1-56639-794-4 (cloth : alk. paper) — ISBN 1-56639-795-2 (alk. paper)
     1. Mayas—Relocation—United States. 2. Mayas—Relocation—North America.
3. Mayas—Guatemala—Migrations. I. Loucky, James. II. Moors, Marilyn M., 1934– .

E99.M433.M39 2000
970.004'974152—dc21   00-026974

An earlier version of Chapter 3, Catherine L. Nolin Hanlon and W. George Lovell,
"Huida, exilio, repatriación y retorno: escenarios de los refugiados guatemaltecos,
1981–1997 (Flight, Exile, Repatriation, and Return: Guatemalan Refugee Scenarios,
1981–1997)," appeared in *Mesoamérica* 34 (diciembre de 1997), pp. 559–582. Reprinted by
permission.

*This volume is dedicated to all those Maya who continue
to struggle to build new lives in strange lands. Their resolve and
their fortitude to be Maya in the face of new racisms and new
exploitation give courage to us all.*

Contents

Acknowledgments

Many people have contributed to the development and production of this volume. We are most grateful to the Guatemala Scholars Network and to Plumsock Mesoamerican Studies for providing vital financial and intellectual sponsorship. Authors are to be thanked for sharing their insights into communities of which they are a part or with whom they have worked. Elisabeth Sirucek Nicholson provided invaluable assistance with translation services and in locating missing people. Shanna Castillo prepared the maps of Belize and Darren L. Strange the maps of refugee relocations. Ina Hicks and Crede Calhoun provided further technical assistance.

We are indebted to Doris Braendel of Temple University Press for her faith and persistence in seeing this book through to publication. We also benefited greatly from the thoughtful reading and helpful suggestions of reviewer Nora Hamilton. And we are grateful for the careful attention given the book by David Updike and Suzanne Wolk in their work for Temple University Press.

Our deepest gratitude is to the Maya people, and particularly those across five countries who shared their experiences and vision with the editors and authors of this book. It is our sincere hope that our efforts will engender wider understanding of the remarkable unfolding developments of these vibrant, diverse, and increasingly dispersed communities.

The editors and contributors have assigned their portion of the revenue generated by this book to the Maya Educational Foundation, a Vermont-based 501(c)(3) organization that provides resources for Mayas in the United States, Guatemala, and Mexico to go to school or university. The foundation's outreach increases the opportunities Mayas have to contribute to their and our future. Readers may obtain more information about the foundation by writing to P.O. Box 38, South Woodstock, VT 05017.

The Maya Diaspora

James Loucky and Marilyn M. Moors

1 The Maya Diaspora: Introduction

WHEN THE Spanish conquered the Maya in the sixteenth century, they brought with them feudal patterns of land ownership, reinforced by a patronizing and racist ideology that in time brought about Spanish control over the Maya and Maya incorporation into colonial society as laborers, primarily agricultural workers. Independence in the nineteenth century and modernization in the twentieth did not change the power structure of the country. European elites ruled with the assistance of *ladinos*, a label applied to non-Indian Guatemalans, to *mestizos* or mixed Indian-European people, and to Maya who no longer participated in their community life. Even today, the great disparity between ladino Guatemalans and the Maya is based on the profits originating in the exploitation of Maya labor, and on the chasm between the two groups created by the racism and fear of the Maya on the part of many non-Maya Guatemalans.

Since the nineteenth century, the major role of the Guatemalan military forces has been to secure the Maya labor force needed for the plantations, to reinforce Guatemalan/ladino control over the Maya, and to suppress any intimations of rebellion against the social order. Through their communities, the Maya have fought incorporation into the Guatemalan state, resisted poverty and forced labor, and rejected the degrading images of themselves put forth by the nation-state. This resistance has taken many forms, including, at times, flight from areas in conflict.

While life for the Maya has been difficult ever since the Spanish conquest, it became even more painful after the CIA-sponsored coup that toppled the elected democratic government of Guatemala in 1954. Under the new military power Guatemala was made a safe haven for United States "interests," and bank loans and international aid accelerated the development of crops for export. This in turn exacerbated the already great disparity of land tenure and increased the need for a larger agricultural labor force to harvest those crops. These pressures were felt differently in various Maya areas of Guatemala, but the lack

1

of land and the pressure to work on the great coffee, cotton, and sugar *fincas* of the Boca Costa and Pacific coastal plain were strongest on the Maya communities of northwestern Guatemala, the homeland of the diaspora people in this book.

The widespread poverty in northwestern Guatemala gave rise to some of the hemisphere's most grim statistics on infant mortality and child malnutrition. One child in five died before the age of five, and 80 percent of Maya children were malnourished. But this poverty was of great importance to the large landowners, who used it to maintain the large, underpaid labor force that had no choice but to work under conditions of extreme duress. Labor arrangements were made through contractors who often used indebtedness to insure a large supply of workers. Working and living conditions on the fincas were miserable. Whole Maya families lived in *galerías,* or large open sheds, breathing in the pesticides that were sprayed on the fields while they worked and drinking water often contaminated by the same pesticides. Workers were often shortchanged in the weighing of their coffee or cotton and were almost never paid the official "minimum wage." Work on the fincas involved the annual migration of whole families during harvest season. In northwestern Guatemala the migration to the Pacific coast was one of the few ways in which money, scarce though it was, could be obtained to buy food or household supplies.

Watching one's children die of diseases stemming from poverty and malnutrition is both heartbreaking and infuriating, often prompting both individual and community action. In the 1960s and again after the 1976 earthquake, self-help and international assistance programs came to this area in the form of development workers, empowering church programs, educational assistance, peasant organizing, and cooperatives. Drawing on traditional Maya concepts of community, shared work, and interrelatedness, these programs achieved much economic change in a short time. Other landless Maya established new communities in the Ixcán area and in the Petén. But these economic improvements threatened both the source of the labor supply and those ladinos who had a monopoly on managing the labor and the interface between Maya communities and the larger society.

By the 1970s, Guatemalan society was wracked by struggles over issues of justice and equity. Individuals who promoted change within these communities were targeted for repression by the state. Cooperative leaders, development workers, peasant organizers, priests and catechists, and teachers were killed outright or disappeared, and their bodies were later found along the roadside. Those who were warned often fled, forming the first trickle of the refugee and migrant flows to come. In the Cold War rhetoric of the time, these people were subversive communists, bent on destroying an entire way of life. The Maya, as individuals and as communities, joined other Guatemalans and began speaking up against injustice and demanding the land that had been robbed from them. Two of the four guerrilla groups that until then had consisted primarily of ladinos incorporated Maya grievances in their demands and Maya personnel in their ranks.

During the 1970s and 1980s the military governments of Guatemala and the military itself, armed and trained under U.S. Alliance for Progress programs, intensified their attacks, ostensibly against a growing guerrilla movement. General Benedicto Lucas worried in early 1982 that the guerrillas were within fifteen days of taking over the country, and he used this fear to justify the imposition of state terror, commenting, "Sadly, peace and tranquillity come to a country only after the spilling of blood" (CERIGUA 1996). Under Romeo Lucas García (1976–80) and Efraín Ríos Montt (1982–83), both of whom were also generals, the focus of the attacks turned to the Maya communities that were thought to harbor guerrilla supporters, and the Guatemalan military's war of attrition, "la violencia," of the 1980s began. Some 440 villages by the army's own count, 626 according to the Comisión de Esclaramiento Histórico statistics (CEH 1999), were totally destroyed. Maya as a group were identified by the army as insurgent allies and targeted for elimination without regard to their civilian status. One hundred-fifty thousand Maya were killed during this period. The horror of the massacres, the brutality of the torture and murder, the pervasive fear that engulfed Maya communities in the Departments of Huehuetenango, El Quiché, and elsewhere, remain vivid to this day among those who lived through that time. From these Maya communities came the survivors, seeking physical safety for themselves and their children. Thousands and thousands sought refuge in Guatemala's cities or by crossing borders to Belize, Mexico, and beyond. This unprecedented flight initiated the contemporary Maya diaspora, which now finds tens of thousands of Maya dispersed across the face of Central and North America from Costa Rica to Canada.

Military policies in the highlands after the worst of the massacres in 1981–82 continued to push Mayas into flight throughout the 1980s. By a decree of the Ríos Montt government, men and boys who remained were forced into "voluntary" civil patrols, giving twenty-four to forty-eight hours of service per week under the supervision of the local military commissioner. In the civil patrols, they were forced to work for the army without pay, questioning all strangers at village checkpoints, serving as front-line patrols for army sweeps in the forests for guerrillas, and naming local "subversives." Compulsory civil patrol duty was very demanding and left little time or energy for the men's own subsistence work.

Survivors of massacres in communities that the army considered suspect were relocated into compact "model villages," rapidly and poorly built housing within sight of a local army base. These villagers had to obtain permission to leave, even to go to work in their fields, now at some distance from their homes. Services such as water, electricity, education, and health care for these villages were slow in coming at best and sometimes never materialized at all. When captured, those deemed the most resistant of the indigenous people were placed in reeducation camps, where every movement was monitored and where Spanish and citizenship lessons and patriotic *actos* were compulsory. Most Mayas feared the local civil patrols, and many refused to participate in army-run society, opting instead to flee.

Mayas who sought to leave Guatemala had several options. The major refugee streams moved north across the Mexican border: Q'anjob'al-, Mam-, Kekchi-, and K'iche'-speaking people from the northern portions of the Departments of Huehuetenango, El Quiché, and Alta Verapaz, where the massacres were most frequent. Kekchi-speaking people close to the border of Belize moved in that direction. Still others sought safety in cities and towns where they hoped to remain unknown.

Many joined relatives and fellow villagers who had begun migrating northward during the 1970s in pursuit of agricultural jobs or urban opportunities. By the mid-1980s, substantial numbers of Maya were living in Florida, California, and Texas. From these major ports of entry migrants have engaged in secondary migrations to find work—to Kansas, Alabama, North Carolina, Colorado, and in Canada from British Columbia to Prince Edward Island. Today there are few areas of the United States and Canada where Maya are not found.

This book provides the first comparative view of the formation and transformation of this new and expanding transnational population. It is presented from the standpoint of the Maya migrants themselves, as well as from sociological and international perspectives. Taken together, this collection of essays provides unique and ethnographically grounded insights into the dynamic implications of uprooting and resettlement, social and psychological adjustment, long-term prospects for continued links to a migration history from Guatemala, and the development of a sense of shared ethnicity among peoples of Maya descent.

The literature on migration has grown in direct proportion to public debate over unprecedented levels and implications of global movements of people. New insights have emerged into the causes of uprooting and variations in resulting immigrant experiences. Common assumptions that immigrants are welcomed by, and in turn wholeheartedly identify with, adopted countries no longer seem valid. A research focus on individual motivations and economic calculations of adaptation and impact appears increasingly simplistic. Typologies are more ambiguous, changes more varied, and policy decisions less clear-cut than ever.

The diasporic experience of the Maya gives us a compelling and timely opportunity to understand the complexities of the migration experience. We can begin to determine how historical and structural conditions combine with cultural factors to enable one of the newest and most distinctive groups of immigrants to reshape their own individual and collective destinies within a wide range of physical settings, from Central America to Canada.

The contributors to this book recount the events that followed the massive uprooting during the early 1980s, which involved both vicious atrocities in highland villages and Cold War politics abroad. Even as the violence subsided, there remained marked disparities in human security and opportunities between communities of origin and those of destination, and these disparities stimulated continued emigration. Evolving migratory networks and immigrant communities spurred still further migration, and today Maya continue to leave the Guatemalan highlands for new homes with relatives and friends. One goal of this book, then, is to provide a political-economic perspective on the migration process, to show how military and human rights pressures, emerging ties between Guatemala and places of exile, and unfolding globalization phenomena both shape and are shaped by migration.

A second theme involves how migrants adapt to new challenges, and the conditions within which they do so. Maya decisions to migrate are strongly conditioned by the political and economic situations within and between places of origin and destination, just as relative integration or assimilation is influenced by migration regulations and policies of the receiving societies. Given the involvement of the United States in Central American conflicts, Maya now living in the States have been particularly affected by the intersection of foreign and immigration policies. In addition, the disparate North American settings in which Maya now live enable us to better understand how indigenous networks develop and how institutions evolve in response to needs for employment, housing, safety, and overall well-being.

Because the Maya diaspora encompasses several countries, it is also possible to examine how the links between homeland and new home are both altered and preserved. As people work, raise families, and interact socially, their conception of ethnicity becomes less rooted in physical location and more a matter of cultural transformation over time. How do they, and in turn we, understand the meanings of "Maya" as the diaspora unfolds? Will the sense of being Maya come to outweigh that of being Guatemalan, or will it too eventually be dispersed by powerful global forces, perhaps even as rapidly as the physical dispersion itself? Such questions regarding how lives are structured and identities transformed are crucial in an era of increasing globalization, making the remarkable transnational experiences of the Maya significant for understanding the nature and issues of contemporary migration.

This book is composed of case studies of Maya communities in the United States, Canada, Mexico, and Central America based on continuing primary research. This introductory chapter traces the historical context and the theoretical implications of the current diaspora. The concluding chapter reexamines both distinctive and common elements across the various sites of migration and provides insights into how interactions between structural, cultural, and individual factors determine the emerging overall destiny of the Maya people.

Since both the archaeological and historical records reveal earlier Maya population movements, "Survivors on the Move: Maya Migration in Time and Space," by Christopher H. Lutz and W. George Lovell, provides an ethno-historical examination of Maya migration under Spanish rule and beyond. Lutz and Lovell explore the issue of survival in the face of various economic and political forces, as well as the causes of voluntary migration, and draw parallels between Maya migration in colonial times and the present.

In "Flight, Exile, Repatriation, and Return: Guatemalan Refugee Scenarios, 1981–1998," Catherine L. Nolin Hanlon and W. George Lovell give an overview of the refugee situation in Mexico, providing information on the reasons for migration, the refugees' lives in the camps, and the dynamics of return or repatriation.

Antonella Fabri's essay, "Space and Identity in Testimonies of Displacement: Maya Migration to Guatemala City in the 1980s," discusses the re-creation of cultural identities, both individual and group, through intimate and even heroic ethnographic research among the large Maya refugee population in the barrios surrounding the Guatemalan capital, combining descriptions of displacement as cultural estrangement with accounts that reveal both visible and invisible strategies of resistance. Her work shows how the formation of Maya organizations of the displaced developed out of the necessities of urban survival.

"Organizing in Exile: The Reconstruction of Community in the Guatemalan Refugee Camps of Southern Mexico," by Deborah Billings, examines, through interviews with refugees in Chiapas, how the common experiences of flight, camp structuring under the Comisión Mexicana para Ayuda a los Refugiados (COMAR) and the United Nations High Commissioner for Refugees (UNHCR), and struggle to survive and eventually return home prompted community organizing that cut across village and ethnic boundaries, creating a larger consciousness of Maya identity that aided in those organizing efforts.

Clark Taylor's "Challenges of Return and Reintegration" follows the experiences of one group of Maya refugees as they return from Chiapas to their home community of Santa María Tzejá in the Ixcán and take up their lives as Maya in Guatemala again. Domingo Hernández Ixcoy's "A Maya Voice: The Maya of Mexico City" recounts the experiences he and his friends had on arrival, their problems with immigration, and the strategies they developed for economic adaptation and political and cultural integration in the largest city in the world. Ixcoy's essay illustrates the problems of living and working in a "global city," where sheer numbers of people and social atomization required the Maya to adapt their social organizations, and even their collective meanings, to the practical purposes of economic and family survival.

Michael C. Stone's essay, "Becoming Belizean: Maya Identity and the Politics of Nation," examines the politics of identity in rural communities in Belize affected by Maya immigrants and looks at how refugees comprehend their futures in the face of national ideology and international development projects.

Although they now inhabit nearly all parts of the United States, Maya continue to be concentrated in the Sunbelt, stretching from California to the Carolinas. Within this region sizable Maya communities have taken root in major urban centers such as Houston and Los Angeles. Significant communities have also emerged in rural areas and small towns, both because of the availability of agricultural work and because smaller towns remind Maya more of home and are therefore preferred to big cities. Although there are many border crossing places, Nancy J. Wellmeier's "La Huerta: Transportation Hub in the Arizona Desert" presents an ethnographic study of one of the main points of entry into the United States. This essay looks at the refugees upon arrival and examines their relation to transport agents and volunteers who assist them on their way.

"Indiantown, Florida: The Maya Diaspora and Applied Anthropology," by Allan F. Burns, gives an account of the ten-year presence of the Maya in south Florida, focusing on their adaptation to a multiethnic migrant community, the growing competition for housing and jobs that exacerbates interethnic tensions, and the prospects for maintaining Maya identity. Jerónimo Camposeco adds his thoughts about Mayas living in Florida in "A Maya Voice: The Refugees in Indiantown, Florida."

Leon Fink and Alvis Dunn's article, "The Maya of Morganton: Exploring Worker Identity within the Global Marketplace," looks at a secondary migration of Florida-based Maya that provided a chicken-processing plant in North Carolina with a Maya labor force. It investigates how these migrants have used their Maya identity and roots to understand their role as exploited workers in a modern U.S. sweatshop.

Nestor P. Rodriguez and Jacqueline Maria Hagan, in "Maya Urban Villagers in Houston: The Formation of a Migrant Community from San Cristóbal Totonicapán," provide a report of ongoing ethnographic fieldwork in a community of one thousand Maya in Houston. They look at the replication of social networks, self-help efforts, and cross-national connections afforded by recent changes in U.S. immigration policy. From Vancouver, British Columbia, Zoila Ramirez recounts her experiences as a stranger in a strange land in "A Maya Voice: Living in Vancouver."

In "Maya in a Modern Metropolis: Establishing New Lives and Livelihoods in Los Angeles," James Loucky applies an anthropological perspective to the dynamics of community cohesion among the largest Maya concentration in the United States, focusing on efforts to maintain and renew cultural activity in the face of pressures experienced by families living in inner-city neighborhoods. The concluding chapter by Marilyn M. Moors attempts to pull together the various themes and issues of the Maya diaspora, and Victor D. Montejo's poem "Elilal/ Exilio" provides a bittersweet conclusion to the book.

Throughout their travels, the diaspora Maya have maintained ties to their home communities through letters, visits, and audio- and video-tapes. They have made use of Maya values and community work patterns in re-creating Mayaness in a strange land. They have faced all the problems that accompany illegal status—coping with "la migra," finding work and a place to live, learning a new language, and educating their children in an alien culture.

The war in Guatemala was part of a larger picture of uprisings and rebellions in Central America in the 1970s and 1980s. The United States provided funding and military support to repressive governments in El Salvador and in Nicaragua prior to the Sandinista victory. After 1979 the United States supported a contra war in Nicaragua and counterinsurgency wars in El Salvador and Guatemala. In Central America, two problems needed rapid solutions. First, each country in the region had a large population of the others' refugees, and CIREFCA (Conferencia Internacional sobre Refugiados Centro Americanos/International Conference for Central American Refugees) was formed to prod negotiations on the repatriation of refugees. Under CIREFCA the Guatemalan government's CEAR (Comisión Especial para la Atención a Repatriados, Refugiados y Desplazados/Commission for Assistance to Repatriates, Refugees and the Displaced) opened negotiations with ACNUR/ UNHCR (Alto Comisionado de las Naciones Unidas para los Refugiados/UN High Commission of Refugees) and COMAR about the refugees in Chiapas, only to find the refugees organized and demanding a place at the negotiating table.

The second problem was how to end the warfare. The Central American Peace Process, initiated by Costa Rica's president, Oscar Arias, provided a framework within which each of these conflicts could be settled by negotiation. The negotiations between the united guerrilla groups, the URNG, on one side and the Guatemalan government and military on the other took four years to reach fruition. The Guatemalan Peace Accords were signed in December 1996, promising a different relationship between indigenous and ladino people, a smaller army less concerned with internal issues, constitutional reform, indigenous rights, and new patterns of economic development. In the four years since the signing of the accords, not many of these promises have yet been implemented, but those who know the Maya are not discouraged. The resiliency of the Maya, as individuals and as communities, is the sustaining core of their advancement and endurance.

CHRISTOPHER H. LUTZ AND W. GEORGE LOVELL

2   Survivors on the Move: Maya Migration
    in Time and Space

ON 22 March 1991, at a ceremony held in a snowy Ontario town
more than four thousand kilometers from the village in which he was
born, a Q'anjob'al Maya named Genaro Tomás Castañeda became a
proud new citizen of Canada. Genaro's experience during the decade
prior to becoming a "Q'anjob'al Canadiense" mirrors the disruptive lot of
countless thousands of Guatemalan Mayas who had to flee their communities because of the country's civil war (Morrison and May 1994;
Nolin Hanlon and Lovell 1997). The personal circumstances surrounding
Genaro's situation represent a happier outcome than most, for the majority of the 1 million or so Guatemalans now believed to live and work in
the United States and Canada do not enjoy the security and stability
afforded by legal citizenship (Jonas 1996). The Maya diaspora to which
Genaro belongs today has a transmigrant dimension dizzying in its scale,
complexity, and local and national impact. Migration as a cultural phenomenon, however, has deeper roots than most people realize, and in one
form or another constitutes a recurrent theme in the shaping of Maya history. Archaeologically, Maya origins begin with migration, the most distant ancestors being among the nomadic bands that trekked across the
Bering Land Bridge millennia ago to enter the New World from the Old.
Ethno-historically, the *Popol Vuh* tells us of what might best be thought of
as semi-mythic migrations on the part of more recent ancestors, who are
said to have entered Guatemala from the Gulf Coast of Mexico. These primordial migrations, epic though they may have been, concern us less
than do population movements that occurred during colonial times (1524
to 1821) and, secondarily, during the national period, from 1821 on. Our
aim is twofold: first, to establish a framework within which the migration
experiences of Maya peoples in Guatemala may be understood and
explained; and second, to illuminate admittedly general categories and
considerations with more grounded case specifics.

Migration, we believe, is a crucial element in the story of Maya survival. We view Maya migration as a rational, multidimensional reaction

11

to the daily challenge of survival, whether the challenge arose last year, a decade or a century ago, or in the wake of the Spanish conquest almost five hundred years ago. Continuity in certain key patterns of survival comes as a surprise only if we fail to identify, analyze, and at least try to unravel the complex web of past and present migration experiences. Migration, in fact, is such a ubiquitous feature of Maya life that it would be possible to envision a cultural history that harnesses the theme as its principal organizing concept, as David Robinson (1990) has observed for colonial Spanish America in general.[1] Here we must settle for something far less ambitious: first, the presentation of several basic notions that help us conceptualize the phenomenon of migration; and second, an examination of some of the historical factors most responsible for allowing us to link Maya survival so closely to Maya migration.

ROBINSON'S MIGRATION MATRIX

In his overview of migration in colonial Spanish America, Robinson (1990:5) provides us with a useful typology, one in which he considers three dimensions to be critical—those pertaining to space, time, and migrant ethnicity. Beyond our limited focus on Maya migration, Robinson incorporates into his scheme of things the distinct ethnic groups that constituted colonial society—Europeans, Blancos, Mestizos, Mulatos, Negros, and Indios. Within a three-dimensional matrix (see Figure 2.1) Robinson depicts graphically the interrelationship between the dimensions of space, time, and ethnicity in the process of migration. While we do not concern ourselves here with the multiethnic dimension of his matrix, Robinson's breakdown of space and time is pertinent to what we have to say. Robinson identifies four variations of population movement in space: rural to rural; rural to urban; urban to rural; and urban to urban. In terms of time, he divides migration into three categories: periodic, temporary, and permanent. Periodic migration, in turn, is subdivided into four types: circular, which Robinson (1990:8) defines as "migration that results in a return to an origin," daily, monthly, and seasonal. Robinson's essay warrants a close reading by anyone seriously interested in the topic, no matter their temporal focus. In fact, research on the national period as well as on colonial times, most notably the work of Castellanos Cambranes (1985), McCreery (1983, 1994), and Woodward (1983, 1993), reveals migration on the part of

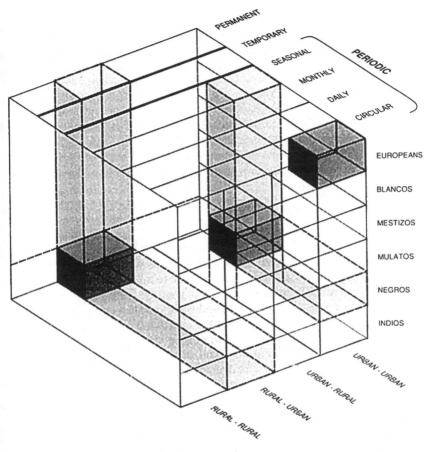

Fig. 2.1 A Matrix of Colonial Migration. (Robinson 1990. Reprinted by permission of Cambridge University Press.)

Maya Indians in Guatemala to have been continuous and widespread. Even though we cannot do justice to all the different aspects of Robinson's ideas, we believe that his schema does allow us to conceptualize Maya migration with some insight and a degree of rigor.

MIGRATION CATEGORIES

In conceptualizing Maya migration, especially for the colonial period, it is important to consider its forced and voluntary characteristics, as Robinson does. Under the first category we examine (1) the post-conquest enslavement of Indians and their removal from their homes to locations where their new masters thought their labor would be most appropriate or lucrative; (2) *servicio personal*, the mobilization of Indians in the quarter-century after conquest to work in diverse locations for the benefit of privileged Spaniards (*encomenderos*) who held them in a tribute grant known as an *encomienda*; (3) *servicio ordinario*, a form of cheap labor, and the *repartimiento de indios*, a form of *corvée* labor; and (4) *congregación*, a policy of resettling dispersed peoples into nucleated places in order to exploit their labor more efficiently.

In addition to these overt forms of forced migration, we also consider the part that migration played in the obligation of every adult Indian (women were exempted only after 1754) to pay tribute either to encomenderos or directly to the Crown. For an untold number of Indians, especially male tributaries, tribute payment meant the obligation to travel, often long distances, to obtain goods specified for payment or to earn cash.

Robinson divides voluntary migration in colonial times into several categories. He notes that persons were attracted to other places, especially to urban ones, by the promise of a better-paying job, an easier life, or even the appeal of the unknown. Indians were also drawn to nonurban centers of Spanish economic activity, including cattle ranches (*haciendas* or *hatos*), wheat farms (*labores de panllevar*), sugar estates (*ingenios*), indigo plantations (*ingenios de tinte añil*), and areas of cacao production. While, as Robinson indicates, there was a negative side to migrating to these operations, part of the attraction for Indians was security, protection by a seemingly powerful *patrón,* and, in many instances, the avoidance of onerous tribute, repartimiento, and communal labor demands back in their communities of origin. Not all migration to these estates, however, was entirely voluntary, for movement could be fueled by necessity, indebtedness, or the lure of a cash advance that was given under contract, thereby requiring the debtor to travel to the place where the creditor wanted him or her to work for a specified period.

Another form of voluntary migration involved Indians abandoning settlements for areas beyond the reach of Spanish jurisdiction and therefore Spanish control. There the immigrant might settle in an unsubjugated area free from obligations to encomenderos, landowners, parish priests, or their own leaders (Conchoá Chet, n.d.). Farriss (1978, 1983, 1984) offers many such examples in the context of colonial Yucatán, where she differentiates between processes of flight, fugitivism, dispersal, and drift.

Besides being pulled or attracted toward opportunities for work, voluntary migrants were also pushed from or came to reject their native communities for personal, familial, societal, and institutional reasons. We suspect, from looking at colonial tribute lists, that Maya men more often sought this escape route than did Maya women. Occasionally, however, couples would leave together, either to escape local conditions or simply to seek a new life elsewhere.

Forced Migration in Colonial Guatemala

Forced migration, as noted above, will be discussed in the institutional context of (1) slavery; (2) encomienda and servicio personal; (3) servicio ordinario and the repartimiento de indios; and (4) the policy of resettlement known as congregación (see Figure 2.2).

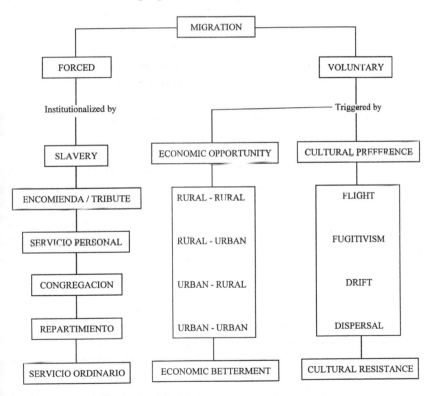

Fig. 2.2. Migration in Colonial Guatemala

Slavery

From the beginning of the conquest, Mayas and other native peoples were enslaved by Spaniards as a result of capture in battles or acts of rebellion. These slaves were called *esclavos de guerra*. Other slaves, already captive and owned by Indians or Spaniards, were often sold to persons willing to pay the price. Indian slaves were so plentiful and so relatively cheap that in the 1530s one could be purchased for two pesos, about the same price as a full-grown pig (Kramer 1990a). Whatever the manner in which slaves were obtained, they were certain to be uprooted and, frequently, forced to move repeatedly in the course of their lives.

Maya slaves performed a variety of functions for Spaniards, but the most common were those of agricultural laborer, household servant, and gold miner. On land around Santiago in Almolonga, the first permanent colonial capital, Spaniards had their slaves produce foodstuffs, especially wheat, for their households and for sale in the urban market. In the vicinity of Santiago in Almolonga and its successor as the colonial capital, Santiago de Guatemala, some three to five thousand slaves lived and worked on Spanish estates called *milpas* and in their masters' urban households. Sixteenth-century sources indicate that the slaves in question came from all over Guatemala, even from as far away as Oaxaca (Lutz 1982:95; Lutz 1994a). When President Alonso López de Cerrato liberated these slaves around 1550, the great majority, having grown accustomed to living in their adopted lands for almost a generation, never returned home. Once emancipated, however, the lives of these ex-slaves seldom improved, for they soon found themselves subjected to the demands of servicio ordinario (see below).

Some of Pedro de Alvarado's slaves were settled around Santiago after their master died in 1541; they were actually liberated by Bishop Marroquín before Cerrato's arrival, but until then they had a much more grueling life than did their milpa and household counterparts. Their fate, along with that of other captives, was to mine or to pan for gold for their Spanish masters in mountainous parts of Guatemala and, especially, in more mineral-rich Honduras. Relatively little is known about this episode, which spanned the years 1525 to 1549, but there are indications that those sent off to Honduras went for eight months at a time. This shift of work was known as a *demora*, and lasted from early October until early June, thus coinciding with the *verano* or dry season in Guatemala. The mortality among the luckless folk who spent a demora in Honduras must have been very high indeed. But this did not cause their Spanish masters much worry, as long as slaves were cheap and their supply still plentiful. We suspect that some of the survivors of these annual migrations settled, after emancipation, in the small pueblos, milpas, and barrios clustered around Santiago.

Other slaves involved in gold-placer mining within Guatemala may not have had to leave or, at least, travel so far, but the level of hardship they suffered was comparable to that of those who migrated annually to Honduras. Thanks to a detailed document dating from the mid-1530s, we know relatively more about a *cuadrilla* or gang of slaves from Huehuetenango. Unlike the slave gangs sent to Honduras or those working around the capital, who could be thrown together to form a heterogenous mix, the slaves at Huehuetenango hailed from there or from nearby settlements; the placer mining they were forced to carry out was thus within a day or two by foot of their homes. While the work was arduous, these slaves did not have to suffer severe changes in altitude or travel long distances; if they survived, they were likely able to remain in or close by their native communities after emancipation (Kramer, Lovell, and Lutz 1991; Kramer 1994).

All slaves, even second-generation slaves born into their status, were eventually freed. But large numbers of slaves from Guatemala, and considerably more from Nicaragua and Honduras, ended up far removed from their places of origin (Newson 1986, 1987; Sherman 1979). Some were dragged off with Spanish masters who, dissatisfied with the limited economic opportunities of Guatemala, sought to make their fortunes in Mexico, Panama, or in the conquest and exploitation of Inca Peru (MacLeod 1973). Other slaves were sold for profit by their owners and "exported" to these distant parts (Jopling 1994). Few if any of those Mayas forced to migrate so far were ever able, even if they so desired, to return to Guatemala. We know that Pedro de Alvarado carried off hundreds of Indian slaves from Guatemala to Peru in the 1530s (Sherman 1979:56; Cieza de León 1998:331–37) and that others lived in conspicuous numbers in the city of Antequera, Mexico, in the early seventeenth century (Chance 1978). A sampling by Lockhart (1968:200) of slave-related documents for the years 1531–43 suggests that over two-thirds of Peru's foreign Indians were of Nicaraguan origin, "with the rest divided quite evenly between Mexico and Guatemala."[2] Documentary evidence from sixteenth-century Panama likewise demon-

strates that some liberated Guatemalan slaves ended up in that jurisdiction (Jopling 1994). Whether or not they survived, as did those who
dwelled in Antequera, is unknown.

Encomienda and Servicio Personal

In the period 1524 to 1550, Indians held in encomienda paid tribute in
a variety of prized items such as cacao, salt, and cotton cloth, as well
as commonplace products like maize, wheat, and turkeys. Like
slaves, they also had to perform a variety of chores. Payment for
ordinary produce or the carrying out of labor services within their
communities—planting crops or herding pigs, for example—did not
require them to journey far from home. It was, however, the obligation to furnish more exotic items of tribute and the need to work away
from home that caused Indians to move about, often over considerable distances.

After Spanish enterprises of mining gold and exporting slaves, the
most sought-after commodity in sixteenth-century Guatemala was
cacao, a lowland crop grown almost exclusively by Indians primarily on
the Pacific coastal plain and, to a lesser extent, in other lower-lying
regions. Even though it was a lowland crop, because cacao was a highly
valued export item for Mexico and Europe, many highland communities were required to supply specified amounts of it to their Spanish
encomenderos. Cacao had been much in demand even before the Spanish conquest, and highland peoples such as the K'iche' and Kaqchikel,
among others, had sought successfully to gain control over some cacao
lands before 1524. Thus the highland Maya had established networks
through which they could continue to obtain the product, either by
exchange or purchase. Nonetheless, heavy Spanish demands, combined
with the disruptions brought about by outbreaks of disease and heavy
mortality, placed a high premium on cacao, which made it consequently
even more difficult and costly for Indians to obtain. Spanish
encomenderos who only held highland pueblos, intent on getting their
hands on cacao, demanded that part of their annual tribute be paid in
the lowland crop. This meant that their tributaries, collectively or individually, had to acquire enough cacao to meet the twice-yearly payments, which in turn meant that it was necessary for Indians to trek far
away to get hold of it. Due to epidemic disease and population loss,
cacao regions suffered early on from a chronic labor shortage. Evidence

exists of highland Maya migrating to the lowlands to fill some of these jobs (MacLeod 1973).[3] At least some of this long-distance migration, from as far away as Verapaz, was motivated by the tributary demands of encomienda.

Even in the later decades of the sixteenth century, when tribute items were more regimented and such exotic items as feathers and jade had been removed from town assessments, Indians still had to pay tribute in maize, chickens, and cash. How, in the context of a subsistence economy, tens of thousands of tributaries came up with the necessary cash points to hundreds of creative solutions. Many of these must have involved the sale of labor and crops, as well as the trade of artisan goods, all activities that imply some degree of migration.

Aside from migration involved in getting hold of the requisite goods and cash to pay tribute, every Indian community or pueblo was required to deliver its tribute, whether it be to a Spanish encomendero or to treasury officials in Santiago. Imagine thousands of Indians descending on Santiago twice each year from all over Guatemala, their own backs or those of their animals laden with maize, wheat, chickens, cotton cloth, cacao, and coins. The bearers from a particular pueblo were accompanied by one of their *cabildo* officers, an *alcalde* or a *regidor*. These delivery trips, made every six months in June or December, took from one or two days to several weeks to complete, depending on the distance from any particular town to the Spanish capital. If a pueblo was small, the amount of tribute to be hauled would not require many bearers. That of a large town, however, would require upwards of forty to fifty bearers. Like other labor tasks shared by able-bodied men or tributaries, delivery of tribute items rotated among the entire population, one's turn coming up again sooner in a smaller, depopulated pueblo than in a larger one. Bearers were paid for this task, but not handsomely. The same could not be said for those Indians who faced the burdens of servicio personal.

Servicio personal, the unpaid forced labor supplied to one's encomendero, had a short but painful history for Maya Indians, if not for their Spanish masters. Encomenderos in Santiago were furious when Cerrato and his officers almost totally abolished servicio personal on top of having emancipated Maya slaves and cutting the actual amount of tribute in goods and cash that Spaniards received. Maya voices are largely silent or, more accurately, absent regarding the hardships involved. Still, despite all the other unmitigated pain they suffered, the reform of servicio personal must have offered some relief. The Spaniards, on the other hand, could not have disagreed more. They made their feelings explicitly known in Spain, complaining loudly of the unfairness and the ruin that would soon befall the colony (Sherman 1979). Examining the details of two cases of servicio personal furnishes some idea of why the institution was loathed by Indians and much valued by Spaniards.

For the 1530s, evidence for the encomienda of Huehuetenango and some adjoining towns held by Juan de Espinar indicates that he had access to the labor of between two and three hundred Indians under the terms of servicio personal. These Indians worked alongside his slaves, both men and women, as navvies and cooks, having to travel some ten to fifteen kilometers to the Río Malacatán, where Espinar had established a gold panning operation. While many others were forced to work within the boundaries of the encomienda itself, large numbers (forty every twenty days) were sent to work as servants and laborers in Espinar's house in Santiago and on his rural estate nearby. When the tour of duty of one group of forty was over, another group the same size was sent to replace it (Kramer, Lovell, and Lutz, 1991; Kramer 1994).

A town to the east of Huehuetenango, Sacapulas, had a different experience. Having its own source of salt, Sacapulas was required for its servicio personal to provide the pueblo's two encomenderos (they split the tribute paid) with four *fanegas* (about 460 pounds) of salt each month. A group of Sacapultecos, however, had to haul the salt by tumpline to their encomenderos' houses in Santiago, almost one hundred kilometers to the south. These tasks ended in mid-1549, but often one hardship was replaced by another. Sacapulas, for example, henceforth had to substitute fourteen substantial loads of cacao for locally produced salt. The travel necessary to obtain cacao, fetched in distant Suchitepéquez and delivered to the capital, required more time and distance than carrying salt to Santiago (Lovell 1990:113–14).

While servicio personal underwent some changes in the course of the sixteenth and seventeenth centuries, especially with respect to Indian movements undertaken to perform it, other forms of forced labor were quickly devised to replace the services lost. What Spanish authorities proffered with one hand, they took away with the other.

Servicio Ordinario and the *Repartimiento de Indios*

In many ways, servicio ordinario took up the slack after Cerrato tried to eliminate some of the more blatant abuses of servicio personal. Servicio ordinario was supposed to apply only to Indians who lived within five leagues of Santiago and was targeted at those who had been emancipated from slavery late in the 1540s and who lived in the milpas or in the barrios of Santiago. Unlike servicio personal, a service given only to encomenderos, servicio ordinario was intended to benefit all Spanish residents of the capital. Under its terms of reference, Indians carried out a multitude of tasks and provided labor for a pittance. Jobs that had to be done included weeding city streets, cleaning out latrines, sweeping public buildings and plazas, providing wet nurses, and making tortillas. Other Indians were forced to work in the *matadero* (slaughterhouse), procure hogs from wherever they could buy them, and provide pork and lard at regulated prices. Indians living in the countryside close to Santiago were required to supply loads of firewood for Spanish kitchens as well as fodder for animals, all at cheap, massively subsidized prices.

Before repartimientos de indios were well established, servicio ordinario served as a mechanism for supplying Spaniards with labor to plant, weed, and harvest their grain crops (Lutz 1996). Relatively little is known about servicio ordinario after the late sixteenth century, but it continued to exist in and around the capital until late in the colonial period (Lutz 1982; Webre 1986). Unlike a free labor market or free sale or exchange of commodities, the Spanish authorities created and maintained a system that forced large numbers of Indians to be on the move constantly in order to satisfy the demands placed upon them.[4]

Another means of procuring and hence displacing Indian labor was the repartimiento de indios.[5] Though better documented in terms of archival sources than is servicio ordinario, the repartimiento de indios still remains poorly studied. Like its predecessors, servicio personal and servicio ordinario, the repartimiento de indios existed solely for the benefit of Spanish colonists. Unlike servicio personal, it did not exist solely for the enrichment of encomenderos and so its impact, while most heavily felt in and around the colonial capital, spread to all parts of Guatemala where Indians could be mobilized. The repartimiento de indios, as its name implies, was designed to distribute Indians to those

Spaniards who needed their labor at reduced salaries within about a day's walking distance from the pueblo of the assigned Indians.

Who was subject to the repartimiento de indios and what kinds of jobs and services did they perform? Evidence exists from all over Guatemala of repartimiento Indians having been allocated to work on wheat farms, on cattle and sheep ranches, and in mining operations. Most extant data, however, are concentrated in the Valley of Guatemala, which contained some seventy Indian pueblos and barrios, and pertain mostly to the distribution of Indian labor to the region's hundred-odd wheat farms and, secondarily, to a handful of large sugar estates. Indian pueblos also provided common laborers and at times skilled workers in the building trades to construct and repair public and private buildings in Santiago. In times of disastrous earthquakes, the city's demand for repartimiento labor greatly increased. Spanish owners of bakeries, producers of the staple bread for the Spanish population of the city, also received allotments of *panaderos* from San Juan Comalapa.

Data on the distribution of Indian labor to the wheat *labores* and sugar estates exist for the late seventeenth century as well as for other periods. If we were to map this data, it would show that, during almost the entire year, thousands of Maya were forced to hike five to ten kilometers, some more, some less, to work for a week at a time on a Spanish wheat farm. The pay was always low, varying from three to five *reales* for a six-day week, a rate of payment in place from the sixteenth to the early nineteenth century.

It was the wheat farms in the Valley of Guatemala that demanded the largest numbers of repartimiento Indians week in and week out, usually for forty-nine weeks of the year. Repartimiento obligations were usually suspended for three weeks of the year, at Christmas, Easter, and the annual celebration of a pueblo's patron saint. Thus, for example, San Juan Comalapa and San Juan Sacatepéquez would have had the week around 24 June, St. John's Day, free. However, as the patron saint's feast day coincided with the due date of the first tribute payment—the other was at Christmas—at least some people had to be prepared to carry tribute to Santiago. About one-quarter of all Indian tributaries at any given time were allocated repartimiento duties. Since the obligation was assigned on a rotating basis, this meant that roughly once a month every able-bodied tributary had to take a turn. If a town was required to supply repartimiento labor for the maximum period of forty-nine weeks hen an individual tributary would have to serve about twelve weekly shifts, some three months in total, performing low-paid duties.

Migration induced by the burden of repartimiento must have put a tremendous strain on town economies, including the planting, weeding, and harvesting of individual and communal lands. In terms of family life, it must have caused many inconveniences and hardships to have one-quarter of a town's men of tribute-paying age away at any given time. While, no doubt, Indian communities far removed from Santiago but near other places where Spaniards lived had to contend with reparimento disruptions, the pressure was felt most keenly by those pueblos in close proximity to the capital city.

Congregación

Encomiendas encompassed, in varying spatial degrees, one or more communities that Spaniards referred to as *pueblos de indios,* Indian towns in the municipal sense of central place and surrounding countryside, segregated areas where non-Indians in theory were not supposed to reside. Upon arrival in Guatemala, Spaniards observed that, morphologically, Maya settlements were decidedly more dispersed than nucleated, with what little urbanization as had developed restricted to defensive hilltop sites not in the least conducive to proper and efficient administration. The policy of congregación was designed to deal with this anarchy, and pueblos de indios were the result of its widespread implementation (see Lovell and Swezey 1990).

As promulgated by Spanish law, congregación was a means whereby Indians dwelling in scattered rural groups were brought together, converted to Christianity, and moulded into harmonious, resourceful communities that reflected imperial notions of orderly, civilized life. To the church, especially to members of the Dominican and Franciscan orders, fell the difficult job of getting Indian families down from the mountains and resettled in towns built around a Catholic place of worship. The mandate to create these new settlements and the rationale behind it are spelled out clearly in a royal order issued on 21 March 1551:

> With great care and particular attention we have always attempted to impose the most convenient means of instructing the Indians in the Holy Catholic Faith and evangelical law, causing them to forget their ancient erroneous rites and ceremonies and to live in concert and order; and, so that this might be brought about, those of our Council of [the] Indies have

met together several times with other religious persons . . . and they, with the desire of promoting the service of God, and ours, resolved that the Indians should be reduced to villages and not be allowed to live divided and separated in the mountains and wildernesses, where they are deprived of all spiritual and temporal comforts, the aid of our ministers, and those other things which human necessities oblige men to give one to another; therefore . . . the viceroys, presidents, and governors [are] charged and ordered to execute the reduction, settlement, and indoctrination of the Indians. (Simpson 1934:43)

The rhetoric of congregación belongs very much to what Carlos Fuentes (1983:33) calls the "legal country," a colonial fiction distinctly at odds with the "real country" that came into being. In the overall vision of empire, few single endeavors differed in outcome so markedly from original intent as did congregación, prompting contemporary observers to express outrage, astonishment, and despair that such a grand plan could amount to so little. But congregación did, from early on, leave an enduring mark on the landscape. In fact, pueblos de indios created by regular and secular clergy in the course of the sixteenth century persist today as *municipios*, or townships, which Sol Tax (1937:44) considers "the primary (and possibly final) ethnic units" appropriate for anthropological inquiry. No sooner, however, had Spaniards resettled Indians where they deemed suitable than many drifted back to the mountains they and their families had been moved from. Why did this happen? What caused the grip of congregación to become undone?

Foremost is the fact that congregación was carried out not by persuasion but by force. The displacement of entire families against their will made it unlikely that members who found the experience disagreeable would stay put. Indians repeatedly fled to outlying rural areas to escape the exploitation they suffered while resident in town or nearby. There they could be free of compulsory demands to furnish tribute, provide labor, work on local roads or the parish church, and serve as human carriers. They also sought the refuge of the mountains when disease struck, its occurrence in (and impact on) pueblos de indios correctly perceived to be less disruptive than arms-length subsistence in the hills. Furthermore, Mayas farmed the highlands more efficiently by living not in large, agglomerated centers but in small, dispersed groups close to the lands they believed to be inhabited by the spirits of their ancestors. Congregación, in terms of the two basic categories in which migration can be discussed, thus represents a process in which forced displacement in one direction could eventually result in voluntary movement in the opposite.

VOLUNTARY MIGRATION IN COLONIAL GUATEMALA

Even if Spanish imperial ambitions had not established such a thoroughly institutionalized system for extracting surplus labor, goods, and cash from Maya tributaries, many natives would still have migrated, in one way or another, as they had in pre-Hispanic times. Certain colonial objectives actually hindered migration or made it more difficult, but others opened up opportunities that had never existed before. Below, we examine several options available to a would-be migrant by considering Robinson's four categories of movement: rural-rural, rural-urban, urban-rural, and urban-urban. Wherever possible, we provide examples of these migration flows by presenting brief life histories based on archival and published sources.

Under the very noses of Spanish authorities, Indians in Guatemala, as elsewhere in southeastern Mesoamerica (Wasserstrom 1983; Farriss 1984), engaged in a host of voluntary migration activities, including trade, seasonal movement to utilize faraway fields, and religious pilgrimages that carried a spiritual reward. Most of these movements, however, were economically motivated and usually of a temporary nature. Given the tensions that could exist in Maya-Spanish relations, many individuals and indeed groups or families used their collective historical experience with migration as a creative response to the colonial order. Robinson (1990:10) observes: "One thing is very clear: migration from adversity, or to opportunity, became one of the most important 'solutions' for colonial Indians." While many forms of voluntary migration were temporary, when the "adversity" factor became intolerable or an "opportunity" more than just appealing, people moved permanently. In the scenarios we reconstruct, both temporary and permanent forms of voluntary migration are evident.

Rural-Rural Migration

Rural to rural migration was probably the most common form of population movement in the colonial period, a phenomenon related to the fact that Guatemala then constituted an overwhelmingly agrarian society. We noted above a Maya predilection to live in dispersed rather than nucleated forms of settlement. Suffice it to say that one solution to Spanish demands was to abandon one's obligations entirely, maybe ever deserting a wife and children and fleeing beyond the limits of Spanish control to live a fugitive life among others who had also fled oppression. This solution was more practical for Indians living adjacent to northerr frontier zones, less so for those living closer to the watchful eye of officialdom farther south.[6]

For the latter, especially those living in or near the Valley of Guatemala, one migratory option was to seek refuge from the demands of life as a tributary by becoming a resident laborer on a Spanish estate. Since many such migrants were attempting to hide their past, it is difficult to trace their origins. Further, landlord interests in securing permanent workers clashed with those of Spanish authorities committed to the efficient functioning of the tribute system. Indian leaders charged with assisting Spanish bureaucrats in collecting tribute were anxious to see those who might have fled return and pay their share. In 1716, for example, the native representatives of San Juan Amatitlán complained of the "continual flight" of their tributaries to work in Santiago and other parts. They noted, on the basis of discreet inquiries, that over 100 of San Juan's 280 registered tributaries had left for the capital and its environs and that others sought refuge on Spanish haciendas or in Spanish settlements. Successful migrants must have learned how to disguise their past identities; doing so was one way to avoid being dragged back to pay unpaid tribute debts and meet unfulfilled labor obligations (Lutz 1982:288, 164–76; Lutz 1994a). At times compromises were negotiated whereby an absent tributary paid his share, or his patrón did, in exchange for being allowed to remain unharassed on a Spanish estate or in an urban household (Lutz 1982:296 n. 11).

Rural-Urban Migration

While we often think of the migration of Indians from the countryside to the city as a more recent phenomenon, it was also a feature of colonial Santiago. Indians migrated to the colonial metropolis, a city in its heyday of about thirty thousand inhabitants, to escape tributary obligations, as did those who fled from San Juan Amatitlán. Others, however, upped and left to take advantage of commercial opportunities.

Such was the case of a group of nineteen tributaries from Chichicastenango who moved to Jocotenango in the mid-seventeenth century, many marrying into a K'iche'-speaking *parcialidad* of that suburb of Santiago. There they made a living by selling woven clothing, *ropa de la tierra*, in the city's market. Despite their long residence in Jocotenango, these Maxeños paid tribute in their native town and helped to pay for religious festivals honoring its patron saint, Santo Tomás. In 1672, Spanish authorities formally recognized the migrant group's residence in Jocotenango over the objections of "hometown" officials back in Chichicastenango. Unlike other rural-urban migrants, this group maintained a strong sense of identity with its place of origin, even though its move to Santiago was permanent. Precisely because they constituted a group, members had the strength to resist the pressure exerted on them either to return to Chichicastenango, where traditional elders believed they belonged, or to become more socialized to the urban ways of Santiago. There was thus cultural solidarity and not just greater physical security in numbers (Lutz 1982:296, n. 12; Lutz 1994a). In terms of size, however, one of the largest groups of immigrants in Santiago was comprised of the nearly continuous flow of young Indian girls and women who moved to the capital to work in Spanish and ladino households, whether in a stately mansion in a wealthy neighborhood or in a more modest situation in a poorer district. The line between voluntary and coerced labor, it must be said, is often blurred when it comes to the business of categorizing domestic labor, then as now. Spaniards and ladinos often had commercial contacts or family ties with someone who served as a priest in an Indian community, both reliable means of securing a maid or even a child (Lutz 1982:286–87, 295 nn. 4–6; Lutz 1994a). In native settlements where young men were absent, a shortage of eligible husbands meant that domestic labor in Santiago might be looked on favorably by young women; rather than remain unwed and live without prospects with aging parents, a move to the city could conceivably increase the chances of marriage.

Urban-Rural Migration

Just as some Indians fled to the city to escape their tributary lot, so also did others flee from it for precisely the same reason. Urban Indians, including some "Mayanized" Mexicans whose ancestors came from Tlaxcala, were often far more acculturated to Spanish ways, and had a much better knowledge of the language, than their rural counterparts. An option for savvy, city-based tributaries was thus not just to move out

to the countryside to escape tax obligations but to try and pass themselves off there as ladinos. In short, for some Indians migration was a
means of traveling across ethnic as well as physical space. However
while documentation exists on urban tributaries fleeing their barrios, it
is difficult to find evidence of where they ended up. This, of course, was
precisely because they could more successfully melt into Spanish-
ladino society than other Indians could. To make oneself invisible in this
way was the desired goal of many migrants.

Urban-Urban Migration

Colonial Guatemala being such a rural society, there were limited
options for Indians to migrate from one urban place to another. A number of Santiago's tributaries did venture out, however, to purchase mer-
chandise for sale in the city or to carry goods bought there for sale in
other towns. These petty vendors always ran the risk of being accused
of *regatonería*, or acting as intermediaries, and therefore, in the eyes of
Spanish authorities, of interfering with the flow of trade. Despite strict
regulations, these hispanized urban vendors, Indians and ladinos alike,
managed to buy maize, cotton thread, and other commodities in order
to do business in Santiago.[7] Those involved in a long-distance venture,
say traveling to Quezaltenango or Totonicapán to buy wheat, often
received official sanction for their movements back and forth, as supplying wheat to Spanish residents of Santiago was looked on with
approval (Lutz 1982:341).

There were, no doubt, other kinds of urban to urban migration, but
they fail to show up in the historical record. The ambulatory ways of
Antonio Natareño, an Indian tributary from Quezaltenango, are an
exception. Natareño first went to Santiago de Guatemala to deal in ropa
de la tierra; like many migrants he would have disappeared without a
trace had it not been for the fact that he was apprehended for conducting an illicit relationship with an Indian woman who, like himself, was
married (Lutz 1994b). When the authorities ordered that his ropa de la
tierra be seized, it was discovered that Natareño had an impressive
inventory packed in huge bundles "that the said Antonio sells in the
public plaza of this city." In the four bundles found, which together
weighed more than 550 pounds, was unearthed an array of woolen
cloth or *jerga*, presumably from the workshops of Quezaltenango and
neighboring towns. The quantity of cloth in Natareño's possession sug-

gests that he was a merchant of considerable standing. In Santiago he owned a house that, even though it had a thatch roof, boasted a patio and wooden doors with keys. The house was furnished with tables, chairs, boxes, and a bed, as well as pottery, crockery, and other utensils. For livestock the merchant had a mule, four Castilian hogs, sixteen chickens, and one rooster. The search of Natareño's house also revealed that the vendor of woolen cloth had at least one servant.

The woman with whom Natareño had an affair was an Indian from Santiago. She also sold clothing in the plaza and was married to a fifty-eight-year-old man, like Natareño a Quezalteco. Her husband, again like Natareño, had a house on the northern edge of the city and was by profession a weaver. Due to the "serious inconveniences" caused to both marriages, Natareño was ordered to leave the capital for his home within four to six days and lead a "married life" there with his legal wife. A judge in Santiago ruled that one of his colleagues in Quezaltenango should be apprised of the situation in order to ensure that Natareño, in future transactions, only visit Santiago for eight days at a time, after which period he should leave. For his indiscretions, Natareño was fined the sizable sum of fifty pesos. This is all we know about the case, but surely there were numerous other vecinos of Quezaltenango and, most likely, other large towns, who regularly migrated back and forth as a part of their day-to-day routines.

MIGRATION DURING THE NATIONAL PERIOD

As a result of more sustained research on the colonial period, we actually know more about Maya migration trends in Guatemala between 1524 and 1821 than we do for much of the post-Independence era. After the demise of Spanish rule, we see four key themes having an impact on migration trends: (1) population growth; (2) the emergence of plantation agriculture; (3) widening socioeconomic disparities; and (4) the eruption of civil war (see Figure 2.3).

The demographic factor is a crucial one. Maya numbers, with some fluctuations, have increased to the point that by the 1950s they approached the total estimated population of approximately 2 million that we reckon inhabited Guatemala at the time of Spanish contact (Lovell and Lutz 1995). Despite the violence, death, and dislocation associated with the recent civil war, a Maya population of between 5

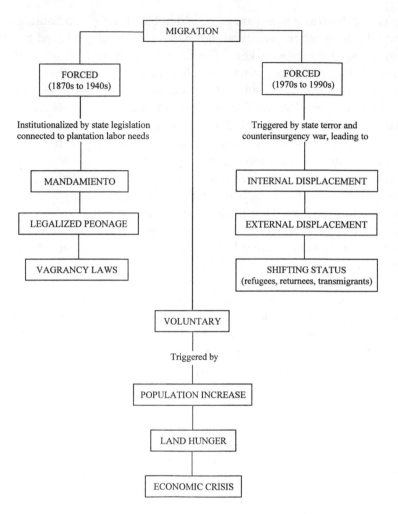

Fig. 2.3. Migration in Postcolonial Guatemala

and 6 million today constitutes about half of a national population of between 11 and 12 million.

Maya population—slowly rising until about fifty or sixty years ago and then accelerating rapidly since—has increased substantially since nationhood (Early 1982; Lovell and Lutz 1996). Guatemala's non-Maya population has also increased, following more or less the same temporal pattern, but even more rapidly. This long-term population growth has increasingly meant that more and more people, of all ethnicities, are in competition for the use of a fixed amount of land and ever-shrinking amounts of other resources, including such domestic essentials as wood and water.

Simultaneously, as both Maya and ladino populations have grown, internal and external economic stimuli have caused an ever-increasing concentration of agricultural lands in the hands either of ladinos or of whites of largely European descent. Changing patterns of land ownership, like population growth, is a complex process with roots in the late colonial period. Among others, Pinto Soria (1989), Castellanos Cambranes (1985), Davis (1997), McCreery (1994), and Carmack (1995) have begun to demonstrate the extent to which Maya lands were appropriated by both legal and illegal means for the benefit of a tiny minority of agro-export entrepreneurs, for the most part ladinos but also those of more recent foreign descent (see Lovell 1995). Beginning soon after independence, land began to be redistributed in order to modernize Guatemala. Some of these development schemes failed and many smaller national recipients of redistributed lands soon lost their holdings to larger, better-connected national and foreign landowners with access to capital, technology, and foreign markets.

What drove this redistribution of land first were crops that had a long history in the region, especially the dyestuffs indigo and cochineal. But this was just the beginning. Coffee cultivation, beginning in the mid-nineteenth century under Rafael Carrera and continuing and intensifying, with the so-called Liberal Revolution, under Justo Rufino Barrios, was the driving force behind non-Indian land accumulation. More recently, other large tracts of land, generally in lower-lying regions, have been appropriated by foreign companies and individuals (national and foreign) for the cultivation of bananas, sugar cane, cotton, cardamom, and the raising of beef cattle (Williams 1986).

Directly and indirectly, this long history of land seizure and accumulation has resulted in the displacement of Maya from hereditary lands in the highlands, the Pacific piedmont, and coastal regions. In the nineteenth century, the Maya population had not yet regained the numerical strength it had at the time of Spanish contact, and consequently the loss of such lands might not have seemed so crucial. At the time, ladinos and others saw Maya communities as wasting Guatemala's primary natural resource, its land, by letting it sit idle.

This, at any rate, was the justification for appropriating huge tracts of Maya lands for export agriculture.

Even though the Maya lost great quantities of land, they still, until perhaps a half-century ago, had sufficient resources and low enough population densities so that what Castellanos Cambranes calls the "coffee state" had to force large numbers of highland Indians to migrate to piedmont and coastal plantations. Under a state-operated system of institutionalized recruitment, Mayas were compelled through devices of forced labor, or *mandamiento*, debt peonage, vagrancy laws, and generalized rural repression, to provide cheap, subsidized labor to the agro-export sector and to the state for such tasks as road construction (Castellanos Cambranes 1985; Handy 1984:94).

Virtually all regions of Maya Guatemala felt the impact of Liberal agrarian policy. Even the highlands, largely untouched by land losses, were nonetheless affected by the state-run mobilization of coffee *finca* labor. McCreery has calculated that by the 1880s "at least one hundred thousand" highland workers migrated to coffee fincas each year (McCreery 1983:758). Lest one think this figure insignificant, in the demographic context of the times it represents roughly one in twelve Guatemalans, one in eight Indians, and as many as one in five highland Indians.[8]

As mandamiento was gradually phased out in the late nineteenth century, debt peonage became the primary instrument used to force large numbers of Maya to migrate annually in order to furnish their labor. It was under Jorge Ubico in 1934 that debt peonage ended but was immediately replaced with an even more onerous vagrancy law. As Whetten (1961:121) notes, "under the old law the laborer could be idle, legally, if he could manage to stay out of debt. Under the new law he must work or be punished as a vagrant." Jones (1940:162) makes a similar point.

Under the "revolutionary" presidencies of Arévalo and Arbenz (1945–54), the vagrancy law was abolished. Serious land reform efforts began under Arbenz, but this program came to a halt with his overthrow in 1954 (Handy 1984; Gleijeses 1989). Scattered figures for the post-1954 period demonstrate continued growth of labor migration. The data do not provide a clear breakdown by ethnicity but it appears that the vast majority of migrants were Maya. Some 200,000 migrated annually in the 1950s, more than 300,000 in the late 1960s, and approximately half a million in the 1970s (Lovell 1990:28).

Caught in the grip of rapid population growth and a shrinking land base, the great majority of Indians found themselves in desperate situations that the upsurge in violence in the early 1980s only exacerbated. The population displacements of the war years, for the hundreds of thousands of families involved, constitute a tragic form of forced migration, the repercussions of which will afflict Guatemala for some time to come.

Meanwhile, as did their forefathers centuries ago, Guatemalan Mayas continue to migrate in order to survive, responding to adversity or lack of opportunity in ways that force us, again and again, to reappraise our conventional, at times erroneous representations of them in the literature. No longer, for instance, can we consider a highland town in Huehuetenango or a coffee plantation in Escuintla to constitute the sole reference points in a fixed spatial universe, for Mayas now live and work far from their places of origin. They are especially numerous across the southern United States, in California, Texas, and Florida, where Mayas from Guatemala fled during the violent years of the civil war. Concentrations of Guatemalan Mayas, however, may also be found much farther north, in the cities of Chicago, Boston, and Providence, and even in parts of Canada. Static portrayals of Guatemalan Mayas as rural, village-bound "men of corn," to use the term of the Guatemalan writer Miguel Angel Asturias, must be reconciled with myriad, ongoing improvisations, for survival hinges, as ever, on doing whatever it takes to make ends meet, including testing the waters of an unfamiliar North American urban setting thousands of miles from home.

While the Guatemalan Maya diaspora began as a response to violence and repression, political refugees have since been joined by a flood of people seeking economic and social improvement. An estimated $500 million are presently sent or taken back to Guatemala each year in the form of family remittances, the impact of which, at the level of individual communities, can be considerable (House 1999). For example, the Guatemalan newspaper *Prensa Libre* reported on 13 November 1996 that in 1995 the Q'anjob'al community of Santa Eulalia alone received $3 million dollars in family remittances, dispatched by the more than six thousand Mayas from Santa Eulalia who live and work in the United States, most of them in California. Coming to grips with migration networks in a transnational realm that extends to the United States and Canada, as well as neighboring Mexico, is today as much a reality of Maya life in Guatemala as confronting the demands of encomienda and mandamiento was in bygone eras. A historical perspective on Maya migration reveals them indeed to be survivors on the move.

NOTES

1. Robinson (1990:2) notes that "one of the most interesting aspects of preparing an overview of colonial migration is the discovery that almost every study concerned with colonial Latin America published in the past, be it on administrative structures, the Church, landholdings, taxes, population fertility—all have some component or other related to migration."

2. Lockhart (1968:200) notes that the estimates of Nicaraguan slaves may have been exaggerated, as "the Spaniards had a tendency to name the whole after the largest part." This tendency was also apparent in sixteenth-century Guatemala, where the ethno-linguistic designations "guatimalteca" and "utlateca" were used as catch-all terms when identifying mixed groups of Indian slaves.

3. Gasco (1991) has unearthed evidence that shows that in eighteenth-century Soconusco, communities were inhabited by "foreign Indians" from forty-three towns who spoke as many as thirteen different languages. See also Lovell and Lutz (1995:68–69).

4. See Dakin and Lutz (1996) for native testimony of how Indians suffered under the excessive demands of servicio ordinario in the 1570s.

5. See Lovell and Lutz (1995) for a discussion of sources related to the operation of the repartimiento de indios.

6. Regarding this point from a Yucatecan Maya perspective, and also from that of the Itzá Maya who lived unconquered in the territories in between, see Farriss (1984) and Jones (1989, 1998). For rich information on one of Guatemala's frontier zones, see Percheron (1990).

7. Casta *regatones*, but not Indians, were often accused by the Spanish authorities of shaking down rural traders and bearers. See Lutz (1982:338, 341) and Lutz (1994a).

8. The first official published Guatemalan census (1880) shows a total population of 1,224,602. Indians constituted 844,744 or 69 percent and ladinos 379,828 or 31 percent of Guatemala's total population. A look at department totals suggests that approximately 84 percent of the country's Indians lived in the highlands in 1880 (Guatemala 1880).

Catherine L. Nolin Hanlon and W. George Lovell

3   Flight, Exile, Repatriation, and Return: Guatemalan Refugee Scenarios, 1981–1998

Central America in the 1980s was one of the most violent, politically unstable regions in the world. During the period that United Nations rhetoric calls the "lost decade," more than 2 million of the region's then 20 million inhabitants were displaced, most of them within Central America itself but with sizable displacements also into neighboring Mexico and beyond into the United States and Canada (CIREFCA 1992b; Jonas 1995). Official and unofficial reckoning for the 1990s indicates that problems associated with refugees were still a notable feature of Central American life, although the situation attracted little international attention (Tables 3.1 and 3.2).

Within Central America, one country in particular has furnished seemingly endless statistics of horror and despair: Guatemala (Falla 1994; Manz 1988a). Other periods besides the 1980s and early 1990s certainly witnessed political upheaval and civil strife in Guatemala. No previous period, however, triggered such widespread slaughter, displacement, and destruction of long-established ways of life as the past two decades (Morrison and May 1994). Historically, ten years of socioeconomic reform (1944–54) ended with a military coup from which Guatemala, as a modern nation, has yet to recover (Gleijeses 1991; Handy 1994). Armed confrontation between government security forces and guerrilla insurgents was sporadic in the 1960s, abated somewhat in the 1970s, and reached unprecedented levels in the 1980s (Lovell 1995). Numerical indicators for the period from 1954 on are chilling: some 200,000 persons killed, 35,000 to 40,000 disappeared (the highest in any country in Latin America), 150,000 to 200,000 refugees in Mexico alone, and an estimated 1 million people displaced internally, roughly half the entire Central American total. Guatemala's national population when the violence was at its peak is estimated to have been between 8 and 9 million people (USCR 1993; CEH 1999).

TABLE 3.1: REFUGEES AND DISPLACED PERSONS IN CENTRAL AMERICA (MARCH 1990)

COUNTRY OF REFUGE	NICARAGUANS	SALVADORANS	GUATEMALANS	ESTIMATED NUMBER OF UNDOCU- MENTED CENTRAL AMERICANS
Belize	N/A	N/A	N/A	25,000–35,000
Costa Rica	46,000	N/A	N/A	150,000–175,000
El Salvador	600	—	N/A	3,000–5,000
Guatemala	3,200	2,800	—	200,000
Honduras	23,000	2,800	450	200,000
Mexico	N/A	N/A	40,500	300,000
Nicaragua	—	7,000	500	N/A
Documented Returnees	30,000 to 35,000	30,000	5,600	—
Internally Displaced	350,000	134,000 to 400,000	100,000 to 250,000	

Source: AVANCSO 1992: 214

TABLE 3.2: REFUGEES AND DISPLACED PERSONS IN CENTRAL AMERICA (MARCH 1992)

COUNTRY OF REFUGE	NICARAGUANS	SALVADORANS	GUATEMALANS	ESTIMATED NUMBER OF UNDOCU- MENTED CENTRAL AMERICANS
Belize	500	8,400	3,000	25,000–30,000
Costa Rica	25,000	N/A	N/A	80,000
El Salvador	250	—	N/A	N/A
Guatemala	4,900	3,400	—	200,000
Honduras	0	0	0	50,000
Mexico	N/A	4,000	43,500	300,000
Nicaragua	—	3,000	N/A	N/A
Documented Returnees	62,000	26,650	7,000	—
Internally Displaced	350,000	150,000 to 450,000	150,000 to 200,000	—

Source: AVANCSO 1992: 215

Coming to terms with the refugee crisis in Guatemala involves sorting through the available documentation with patience and persistence. We seek four goals: (1) to identify operational categories, especially ones that may be time and place specific and that take into account events and circumstances peculiar to Guatemala; (2) to sketch the rudiments of refugee flight; (3) to outline the salient features of refugee life in exile; and (4) to document the vicissitudes of refugee repatriation and return. Given that precise numbers can never be known, the exercise that follows must be viewed as more indicative than definitive of the scenarios we discuss.

Categories

Of major importance is the fact that the vast majority of Guatemalan refugees are Maya Indians, rural indigenous people who fled their homes in towns, villages, and hamlets in the highlands north and west of Guatemala City in order to safeguard their lives from violent attack from forces for the most part originating outside their communities (Carmack 1988). Maya Indians, according to the report of the Truth Commission, constitute 83.33 percent of recorded civil war casualties, a grim statistic by any standard (CEH 1999:85–86). A comprehensive survey by the Asociación para el Avance de las Ciencias Sociales (AVANCSO 1992:15) identified two categories of internally displaced persons: (1) people displaced within Guatemala some distance from their communities, who preferred an attenuated post-flight existence, often in Guatemala City, in plantations along Guatemala's Pacific coast, or in one of the country's smaller provincial capitals; and (2) people displaced within Guatemala only a relatively short distance from their communities, to mountain hideouts or lowland retreats where the safety of isolation allowed them to live in nucleated groups, often for years on end. The latter's strategy of nucleation stood in marked contrast to the dispersed, scattered existence of the former. Until 1997, nucleated groups endured under considerable duress in the departments of Huehuetenango, El Quiché, and Alta Verapaz, most notably in Ixcán and Ixil country (Falla 1994; Manz 1994; Stoll 1993; Taylor 1998; Wilson 1995).[1]

AVANCSO (1992:16) also identified two categories of externally displaced persons, both primarily applied to Guatemalans living in exile in Mexico: (1) officially documented refugees whose displaced status was recognized by the United Nations High Commissioner for Refugees (UNHCR) and who found refuge in a UN-supervised camp or settlement; and (2) unofficial refugees whose status was not recognized by UNHCR and who did not enjoy any legal rights or special provisions under Mexican law.

Returnees are likewise seen to constitute two distinct groups (AVANCSO 1992:17–18): (1) internally displaced refugees, who were often reintegrated into their communities of origin as part of an institutional plan or framework; and (2) externally displaced refugees, who were either repatriated under the watchful eye of government agencies and the international community or who decided simply to go back without any official involvement or persuasion. A distinction is made in the literature between "repatriation" and "return" (Stepputat 1994; Nolin Hanlon 1995). "Repatriation" is seen as something done *to* refugees by government agencies and international organizations, with minimal input from refugees themselves. "Return," by contrast, connotes an active, politicized involvement on the part of refugees, who organized, negotiated, and influenced the conditions under which their usually collective journeys back to Guatemala took place.

REFUGEE FLIGHT

Refugee flight began in response to deteriorating conditions within Guatemala in 1981. That year witnessed the first significant displacements inside Guatemala and across the border into the Mexican state of Chiapas. Refugees from Guatemala also appeared in Belize, Honduras, Nicaragua, and Costa Rica (Map 3.1). From Mexico the refugee exodus spilled north into the United States and eventually into Canada. At the same time that Guatemalans were fleeing from, or being displaced within, their own country, other Central American nationals sought refuge there, especially Salvadorans and Nicaraguans.

Estimates of the number of internally displaced vary enormously. A figure attributed to the Catholic Church estimates that approximately 1 million persons were uprooted from their homes during the counterinsurgency sweeps of 1981–83 (Lovell 1988). The Guatemalan government, in February 1992, estimated that some 150,000 of its citizens were

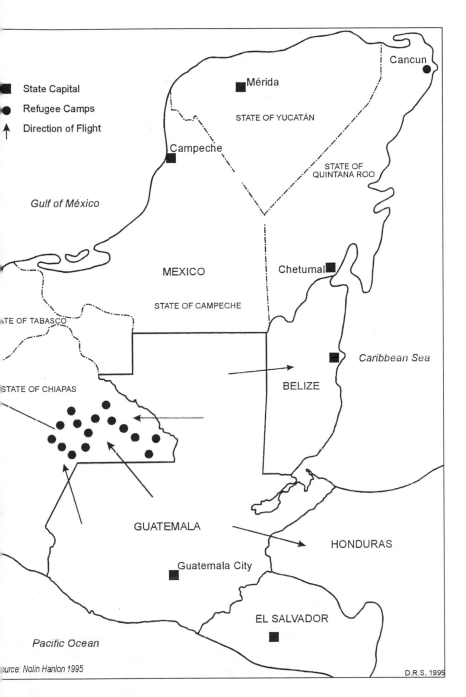

Map 3.1. Refugee Flight from Guatemala. (Courtesy of Darren L. Strange)

still internally displaced, but other sources place the figure as high as 700,000 (USCR 1993).

Of the statistics available, those of Guatemalan refugees in Mexico permit a better understanding of refugee movement and change over time. Some two thousand cases were registered in Mexico in 1981. One year later, that figure had risen to over thirty thousand, with unofficial (non-UN-registered) cases estimated at much higher levels. Mexican authorities at that time were not sensitive to the plight of the displaced, and, in some instances, deported refugees back to Guatemala. International condemnation of these deportations led to more responsible action on the part of the Comisión Mexicana de Ayuda a Refugiados (COMAR), the Mexican government agency charged with furnishing minimal assistance to Guatemalan and other Central American refugees. Since most Guatemalan cases were then confined to camps in Chiapas, humanitarian aid in the form of food, clothing, medicine, and shelter was coordinated by the Catholic diocese of San Cristóbal, many of whose spiritual charges (like the Guatemalan refugees themselves), are Maya Indians (USCR 1993).

REFUGEE EXILE

By 1984 at least 150,000 Guatemalans had fled to Mexico, some 46,000 of them registered with UNHCR. Responding to growing international concern following incursions by the Guatemalan army into refugee camps in Mexico, COMAR developed a plan to move refugees from Chiapas and relocate them some distance away in the states of Campeche and Quintana Roo in the Yucatán peninsula (Map 3.2).

The transfer of Guatemalan refugees from camps in Chiapas to camps in Campeche and Quintana Roo began in May 1984, amid fierce opposition to the move on the part of many refugee families. Fearful of being relocated so far from their native land, some families actually crossed back from Chiapas into Guatemala, primarily to rural areas in the Department of Huehuetenango. Promises of land and food aid lured others away from the border. By the end of 1985, some 18,500 Guatemalan refugees were relocated in the Yucatán region. Final relocation to "settlements" from "transit centres" resulted in 12,500 Guatemalans being officially registered as refugees in four camps in Campeche, with another 6,000 recorded in four

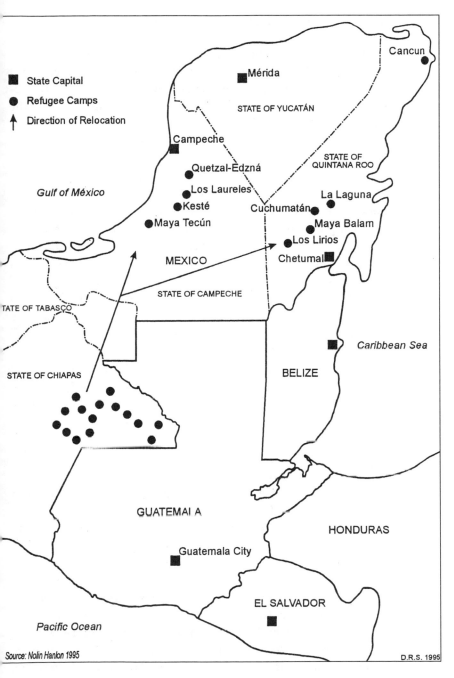

Map 3.2. Refugee Relocation to Campeche and Quintana Roo.
(Courtesy of Darren L. Strange)

camps in Quintana Roo. The plight of these people, and others like them who endured a scattered existence in Mexico, received scant attention until they organized the Permanent Commissions of Representatives of Guatemalan Refugees in Mexico (CCPP) in 1987, and the Association of Dispersed Guatemalan Refugees (ARDIGUA) in 1992.[2] The majority of documented Guatemalan exiles, however, remained in Chiapas, where refugee population figures declined over time. Between 1984 and 1994, official counts indicate a fall in numbers from roughly 40,000 to 23,000 refugees but also show a rise in the number of camps offering protection from 57 to 128. By placing a declining number of people in an increasing number of locations, the Mexican government sought to solve a thorny political problem—the gulf between Guatemalan refugees receiving some kind of assistance and poor (and angry) indigenous Mexicans who received nothing, a gulf that the Zapatista uprising in Chiapas only exacerbated. Estimates of unregistered Guatemalans resident in Mexico range from 50,000 to 150,000, 30,000 to 50,000 of whom live in Mexico City (AVANCSO 1992; USCR 1993). Hundreds of thousands of Guatemalans—Jonas (1996a:121) suggests a figure of 800,000 to 1 million—now live and work in the United States (Vlach 1992; Burns 1993a; Hagan 1994; Wellmeier 1998), with sizable numbers also resident in Canada (Wright 1993; Nolin Hanlon 1998).[3]

REFUGEE REPATRIATION AND RETURN

The risky process of refugee return to Guatemala began in 1984 under the aegis of COMAR and UNHCR. In September 1986, under the civilian presidency of Vinicio Cerezo, the Comisión Especial para la Atención de Repatriados (CEAR) was created and charged by the Guatemalan government to "oversee the return of Guatemalan refugees from abroad" (AVANCSO 1992:229). The creation of CEAR saw the number of official returnees double in size between 1986 and 1987, then double again between 1987 and 1988. CEAR's activities, however, clearly had a limited impact. As of December 1990, some 6,000 persons are recorded as having been repatriated to Guatemala, most of them from Mexico but some also from Honduras, Nicaragua, and Costa Rica (Figure 3.1). The repatriation of only 6,000 people from an officially recognized total of 43,000 over a period of seven years

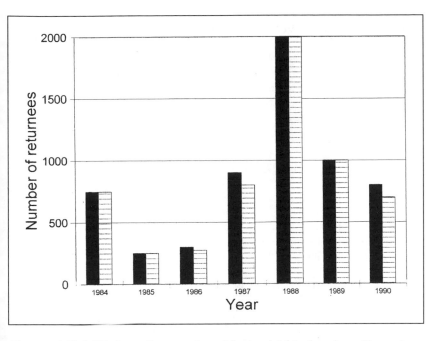

Fig. 3.1. Official Refugee Returns from Mexico *(right column)* **as a Percentage of All Returns to Guatemala** *(left column)*, **1984–1990**

indicates the majority view that Guatemala was not seen as a safe place to be (AVANCSO 1992:56).[4]

Despite this, refugee organizations worked hard in 1991 and 1992 to negotiate certain conditions for self-directed, collective, organized, and voluntary "returns," in addition to the government-directed "repatriations." Their efforts resulted in the Basic Accord of 8 October 1992, an agreement made between refugee representatives and the Guatemalan government that laid the groundwork for the much-publicized return to Guatemala, in January 1993, of 2,480 refugees from Mexico. Additional plans called for another 1,600 families, over 8,000 people, to return between May and August from camps in Chiapas, Campeche, and Quintana Roo. A constitutional coup d'etat on 25 May of that year, however, which saw Cerezo's successor, Jorge Serrano, removed from the presidency and replaced by Ramiro de León Carpio, stalled these plans and reinforced the reluctance of those refugees who refused to participate in the returns.

The pace of refugee repatriations and returns was decidedly slow.

TABLE 3.3: INDIVIDUAL VOLUNTARY REPATRIATION (1984–1998)

YEAR	INDIVIDUALS
1984[a]	700
1985	199
1986	377
1987	1,022
1988	1,933
1989	993
1990	820
1991	1,765
1992	1,719
1993	1,346
1994	1,895
1995	2,501
1996[b]	1,099
1997/98[c]	2,602
Total	18,971

Sources: Nolin Hanlon 1995; UNHCR/Guatemala in GRICAR 1996; Project Accompaniment 1998a
[a]Before 1984 there were virtually no repatriations, as Guatemalans were still fleeing into Mexico. The few returnees were wealthy, well-connected individuals or families who did not experience violence directly but fled to avoid trouble in their home communities.
[b]Include 32 individuals from countries other than Mexico.
[c]Combined total for 1997 and 1998.

Individual voluntary repatriations accounted for only 18,971 individuals between 1984 and 1998 (Table 3.3) (PA 1998a; see "A Note on Sources" in the notes to this chapter). Collective returns were not steady and consistent, though the number of participants was relatively high. The first collective return in January 1993 was followed sporadically by approximately fifty others, large and small (Table 3.4). Total numbers in these collective returns reached approximately 23,000 individuals by January 1999 (Table 3.5). Roughly two-thirds of these refugees have returned to lands they fled in areas such as the Ixcán, Alta Verapaz, and the Petén, with others negotiating for new lands in the Petén and along the south coast (Map 3.3, p. 52). The fatal shooting of eleven returnees in the community of Xamán, Alta Verapaz, in October 1995 again made clear the distrustful, often violent climate of resettlement in Guatemala. Successive administrations, fearful of some kind of military backlash and mindful of the ideological views of a resistant economic elite, have moved cautiously on key refugee and resettlement

TABLE 3.4: COLLECTIVE RETURNS TO GUATEMALA (1993–1998)

DATE	# RETURNEES		DEPARTURE SITE	RETURN SITE
	INDIV.	*FAMILIES*	*(i = individual, f = family)*	
20 Jan 1993	2,480	575	Chiapas (1,280i) Quintana Roo (1,002i) Campeche (198i)	Victoria 20 de enero, Ixcán, El Quiché[1]
9 Dec 1993	1,293	274	Chiapas (120f) Quintana Roo (139f) Campeche (15f)	Veracruz, Ixcán, El Quiché
10–12 Jan 1994	1,000	183	Most from around Comalapa, Chiapas, some from Quintana Roo and Campeche	Chaculá, Nentón, Huehuetenango
25 Jan 1994	25		n/a	n/a
13–27 May 1994	1,970	403	Quintana Roo and Campeche (393f) Chiapas (10f)	Ixcán, El Quiché
8 and 15 Oct 1994	445	94	Quintana Roo	Aurora 8 de octubre (Xamán), Chisec, Alta Verapaz
13–19 Nov 1994	595	135	Chiapas—Part of 2 returns: Nov 1994 and March 1995	Nueva Libertad, Fray Bartolomé de Las Casas, Alta Verapaz
29 Nov 1994	191	37	Quintana Roo (169i/32f) Chiapas (22i/5f)	Veracruz and Pueblo Nuevo, Ixcán, El Quiché
29 Jan 1995	282	68	Campeche (218i/56f) Quintana Roo (19i/3f) Chiapas (45i/9f)	Ixcán, El Quiché
7 Mar 1995	180	30	Chiapas (Las Margaritas region)	Montebello Momonlac, Huehuetenango
25 Mar 1995	385	85	Majority from Quintana Roo, some from Campeche (30f)	Fray Bartolomé de Las Casas, Alta Verapaz

(Continued)

TABLE 3.4 (CONTINUED)

DATE	# RETURNEES		DEPARTURE SITE	RETURN SITE
	INDIV.	*FAMILIES*	*(i = individual, f = family)*	
6 Apr and 15 May 1995	1,121	233	Majority from Quintana Roo, some families from Campeche (Unión Maya Iztá)	La Quetzal, La Libertad, Petén
7 Apr 1995	400	80	Quintana Roo (40f) Campeche (34f) (Nuevo México)	Finca La Providencia, San Vicente Pacaya, Escuintla
19 Apr 1995	1,441		Campeche (574i/145f) Quintana Roo (614i/147f) Chiapas (253i)	Various Ixcán coops, El Quiché
7 Apr 1995 5 May 1995	400 55	80 15	Quintana Roo (40f) n/a	Finca La Providencia, Various Ixcán coops, El Quiché
7 July and 13 Dec 1995	723	170	La Nueva Esperanza— Part of 3 returns: July and Dec 1995, Nov 1996	La Esmeralda, Dolores, El Petén
8 August 1995		131	Chiapas (part of 3 groups: Aug, Sept, Oct 1995)—Nueva Generación Maya	Chancolín, Barillas, Huehuetenango
10 August 1995	185	48	n/a	Various Ixcán coops, El Quiché
28 Sept 1995	58	14	n/a	Various Ixcán coops, El Quiché
4 Oct 1995		181	Chiapas (part of 3 groups: Aug, Sept, Oct 1995)—Nueva Generación Maya	Chancolín, Barillas, Huehuetenango
30 Oct 1995	350		Chiapas Campeche Quintana Roo	Zona Reina, Ixcán, El Quiché

(Continued)

TABLE 3.4 (CONTINUED)

DATE	# RETURNEES		DEPARTURE SITE	RETURN SITE
	INDIV.	*FAMILIES*	*(i = individual, f = family)*	
29 Nov 1995	152	35	Part of 4 groups from Campeche, Quintana Roo, and Chiapas: Nov 1995, Feb, Mar, May 1996	La Lupita, San José El Idolo, Suchitepéquez
14 Dec 1995	249	71	n/a	Various Ixcán communities, El Quiché
29 Feb 1996	52	14	Part of 4 groups from Campeche, Quintana Roo, and Chiapas: Nov 1995, Feb, Mar, May 1996	La Lupita, San José El Idolo, Suchitepéquez
27 March 1996	178	39	Part of 4 groups from Campeche, Quintana Roo, and Chiapas: Nov 1995, Feb, Mar, May 1996	La Lupita, San José El Idolo, Suchitepéquez
18–22 Apr 1996	590	120	El Progreso; Nuevo Porvenir (including Kaibil Balam group), groups from Chiapas (110f), Quintana Roo (19f), and Campeche (19f)	El Triunfo and Valle Río Oxec, Cahabon, Alta Verapaz
27 Apr 1996	420	80	n/a	Ixcán Grande, El Quiché
May 1996		15	Part of 4 groups from Campeche, Quintana Roo, and Chiapas: Nov 1995, Feb, Mar, May 1996	La Lupita, San José El Idolo, Suchitepéquez
13 May 1996	290	70	San Juan Ixcán (Zona Reina) and Campeche	Entre Ríos, Sayaché, El Petén

(Continued)

TABLE 3.4 (CONTINUED)

DATE	# RETURNEES		DEPARTURE SITE	RETURN SITE
	INDIV.	*FAMILIES*	*(i = individual, f = family)*	
May and Oct 1996	290	60	Chiapas, Campeche, and Quintana Roo part of 2 groups: (May and Oct 1996)— Nueva Guatemala	San Francisco El Tumbo, Sayaché, El Petén
28–30 Sept 1996	277	66	Santa María Dolores (Zona Reina) and Campeche	Unión Santa, Santa Amelia, Poptún, Petén
26 Oct 1996	163	50	n/a	Ixcán Grande, El Quiché
20 Nov 1996	337	40	La Nueva Esperanza— Part of 3 returns: July and Dec 1995, Nov 1996	La Esmeralda, Dolores, El Petén
27 Nov 1996	400	80	Chiapas (all in the Las Margaritas region); some from Campeche	Nueva Unión Maya, Xoxlac, Huehuetenango (original lands)
13 Dec 1996	40	10	n/a	Ixcansán, San Mateo Ixtatán, Huehuetenango
Dec 1996	46	12	Back to original lands	Ixcán Grande, El Quiché (3 small returns in December)
26 July 1997	400	100	Quintana Roo and Chiapas	Finca El Carmen, Patulul, Suchitepéquez
Sept 1997	400	100	n/a	El Triunfo and Chaquenalito, San Mateo Ixtatán, Huehuetenango
Sept 1997	635	160	Quintana Roo and Campeche	Huacut, La Libertad, Petén
28 Nov 1997	300	55	ACNP 1 (Nuevo Porvenir) ARDIGUA group	Buenos Aires and El Edén, Nuevo Progreso, San Marcos

(Continued)

TABLE 3.4 (CONTINUED)

DATE	# RETURNEES		DEPARTURE SITE	RETURN SITE
	INDIV.	*FAMILIES*	*(i = individual, f = family)*	
March 1998	90	30	VNO group, Campeche—group originally from Santo Tómas, Ixcán	Laguna Perdida, La Libertad, Petén
June 1998	330	85	VN group (Coop. Nueva Guatemala)	San Martín, San Francisco, Petén
June 1998	1,000	200	CBRR group (El Quetzal)	Quetzal III and IV, Nentón, Huehuetenango
July 1998	250	50	VN group (Coop. Santa Cruz Maya)	Sepamac, Sillab 4 and 9, Senahu, Alta Verapaz
July 1998	300	75	Chacaj, VNO group (States of Morelos, Chiapas, and Quintana Roo)	San Vicente El Baúl, San Vicente Pacaya, Escuintla
August 1998	175	70	VNO group (Santiago Ixcán)	San Rafael Cacahotal, San Vicente Pacaya, Escuintla
August 1998	150	50	n/a	Concepción del Alba, Nuevo Progreso, San Marcos
October 1998	570	145	Unión Candelaría, CBRR	La Trinidad Los Cascos, S.A., Escuintla, Escuintla
18 Nov 1998	230	50	ARDIGUA group (Tercer Bloque)	La Guardiana, San Perdro, Yepocapa, Chimaltenango

1. Those families returning to the cooperatives of the Ixcán Grande, El Quiché in this movement as well as future ones are from the Mexican states of Chiapas, Campeche, and Quintana Roo. The numbers provided for the Ixcán returns, as with most others, are estimates rather than precise figures. Speculation is unavoidable given the obstacles to accurate data collection in return situations. Barriers to accuracy are most pronounced, though, in the Ixcán region, where returnees used some centres (such as Victoria 20 de enero and Veracruz) as temporary sites, others moved between return communities once land became available, and still others joined local community members who remained in Guatemala during the violence of the civil war. The figures cited in this table have been updated from our previous efforts as new data became available.

Victoria 20 de enero and Veracruz were the first settlements for many returnees to Guatemala. People went to many new settlements after spending time in these centers. Victoria 20 de enero and Veracruz both witnessed movement to Río Valle Oxec, Los Angeles, Cuarto Pueblo, Mayalan, San Lorenzo, Saholom Buena Vista, Xamán, and Ixtahuacán Chiquito. Some families left Victoria for Copalaa while others left Veracruz for Fronterizo 10 de mayo, Pueblo Nuevo, Santa María Tzeja, Zunil, San Juan Ixcán, and San Antonio.

TABLE 3.5: COLLECTIVE RETURNEES (1993–1998)

YEAR	INDIVIDUALS
1993	3,773
1994	4,201
1995	7,296
1996	3,158
1997	2,135
1998	3,095
Total	23,658

Sources: Nolin Hanlon 1995; WCC/GRICAR 1999; Project Accompaniment 1998a–e; Cerigua 1998a–c, 1999; UNHCR 1998

issues. Lack of political commitment accounts not only for the slow pace of refugee returns but also for the lack of security extended to returnees upon resettlement.

In October 1996, CEAR announced its "Verification Study of 10 Return Communities," which was carried out between July and September of that same year. The study provides interesting data on current and potential land use, as well as on the population levels and service facilities in each return community. But a critique of the study by the International Council of Voluntary Agencies/Grupo Internacional de Apoyo al Retorno (ICVA/GRICAR) (1996) reveals several problems. ICVA/GRICAR notes that the priority of the Guatemalan government regarding refugee returns is the fulfillment of population quotas established for each returnee community, with little regard for realistic, sustainable development should population be maintained at, or even exceed, the government-established threshold. The CEAR study indicated that space was available in various returnee communities for 680 families, some 3,430 individuals, though the report does not mention the overpopulation of other returnee sites such as Quetzal and Xamán.

In an interview held toward the end of his first year in office, President Alvaro Arzú, who succeeded De León Carpio in January 1996, declared that he opposed the return process and would continue to do so, a pronouncement in clear violation of the accords agreed upon four years earlier (*La Hora* 1996). Due to international pressure, however, a

seven-month hiatus in refugee returns ended with the successful resettlement of two major groups in July 1997, three more collective returns
throughout the rest of 1997, and at least eight in 1998 (*Siglo News* 1997;
PA 1998a).

As of 7 January 1999, the official return process ended with a hand-
shake and a signature between the Arzú government and refugee representatives.[5] Unsure about their future in Guatemala, many returnees
continue to lead a very precarious existence (Taylor 1998; Castañeda
1998). So, too, do the 23,000 "official" refugees still resident in Mexico
(CERIGUA 1999; *Siglo News* 1999). The latter, along with other refugees
represented by ARDIGUA, faced an ultimatum first articulated by the
Mexican government in August 1996 and legislated in September 1997:
Return home before the end of 1998 or integrate into Mexican society.
Amidst talk of closing all remaining refugee camps in their territory, the
Mexican government and COMAR announced a final offer to change
the migration status of the refugees (ICVA/GRICAR 1996; PA 1997).
Though individuals and groups of fewer than fifty people may continue
to return "unofficially" to Guatemala in the years ahead, approximately
11,000 refugees in Campeche and Quintana Roo have been offered permanent resident status there. CEAR indicates that between 2,000 and
3,000 people in four return groups were still waiting to return from
southern Mexico in 1999.

"Voluntary" return, which the UNHCR itself indicates as a *necessary*
component of repatriation, has now given way to "involuntary" return.
After the signing of a "firm and lasting" peace accord on 29 December
1996, Guatemalan refugees were in effect put under pressure to return
home before the end of 1998 or forfeit the opportunity to do so without
future complications. While many Guatemalans in exile continued to
ponder the choices before them, the Arzú government acted in ways that
created obstacles to a just and dignified homecoming. A powerful army
and an intransigent elite still constitute impediments to the peace process
in general and to the land question in particular. A "pluricultural, multilingual nation," which the Unidad Revolucionaria Nacional Guatemalteca (URNG) (1994) envisions as the "Guatemala of the future," a country
ruled "with national unity," seems as elusive as ever. Having fled to a life
in exile years ago, countless thousands of Guatemalans now seem des-
tined never to seek repatriation, never to return home.

Map 3.3. Location of Refugee Camps/Settlements and Returnee Areas.
(Courtesy of Darren L. Strange)

A Note on Sources

Refugee data for research purposes are derived from a variety of sources. Non-governmental organizations (NGOs), volunteers, government agencies, and journalists have been and continue to be generators of most of the available information on the Guatemalan refugee situation. Due to the length of the crisis, it was seldom possible for researchers to be in the field at every critical juncture. Due to the ever-changing realities for the refugees and returnees, however, it is vital to maintain contact with those who work with the refugees on a regular basis. E-mail communication and, more recently, internet sites have facilitated the gathering of material. We indicate below key sources for finding pertinent information and, where possible, provide e-mail and internet addresses.

Two NGOs, Project Accompaniment Canada (PA) and Peace Brigades International (PBI), have been indispensable sources of information throughout the difficult years of refugee flight, exile, and return. Significantly, both organizations ended their accompaniment efforts in Guatemala in 1999, even as they search for new forms of solidarity. Project Accompaniment was transformed into the Guatemala-Canada Solidarity Network (GCSN). Access to PA's archives on the return process is available at accatl@web.net. Regular updates are sent by GCSN's southern coordinator, based in Guatemala, and by regional contacts in Canada to facilitate information exchange. They are available at gcsn@guate.net.

Peace Brigades International is an organization whose self-avowed mission extends "unarmed international protective accompaniment to individuals, organizations, and communities threatened with violence and human rights abuses." Its Guatemala site (http://www.igc.apc.org/pbi/Guatemala.html) furnishes information on the return process and provides links to many Guatemalan organizations with which they maintain regular contact. Its e-mail address is pbi@web.net.

The Institute for Global Communications (IGC) is a base site for five online communities of activists and organizations: PeaceNet, EcoNet, LaborNet, ConflictNet, and WomensNet, (http://www.igc.org/igc/members/index.html#a). The IGC provides computer-networking tools for international communication and information exchange. Researchers must join and pay fees for access. The IGC member conference on Guatemala (reg.guat.news), has consistently supplied up-to-date information on refugees and the return process because many NGOs working in Guatemala and Mexico are members of the IGC. IGC information may also be accessed through e-mail at apc-info@apc.org in English, or apc-espanol-info@igc.org in Spanish.

The United Nations High Commissioner for Refugees (UNHCR) has been directly involved with the refugee crisis since the early 1980s. Its home page (http://www/unhcr.ch/welcome.htm) directs the reader to a myriad of sources. The UNHCR Newswire (http://www.unhcr.ch/news/newswire/newswire.htm) provides links to news wire services that automatically call up current news stories relating to refugees, asylum, or UNHCR. *Refugee Magazine* a UNHCR quarterly dealing exclusively with refugee issues, is now online at http://unhcr.ch/pubs/pubs.htm. To access Guatemalan information in the vast REFWORLD databases, call up http://unhcr.ch/refworld/country/menus/gtm.htm. MINUGUA, the United Nations Verification Team in Guatemala, now provides more current information at http://www.un org.Depts/minugua/.

The Jesuit Refugee Service-Mexico, at http://www.jesuit.org/refugee/jrsmex.html, has been active since the first years of refugee flight and has served the Guatemalan refugee community in Mexico through "active communication for advocacy purposes." Its e-mail contact is jrscamp@laneta.igc.apc.org. The Toronto-based Jesuit Centre distributes "Refugee Updates for Social Faith and Justice." Information on the return process, the situation of refugees in Mexico and returnees in Guatemala has also been accessed from the following sources Network in Solidarity with the People of Guatemala (NISGUA) at nisgua @igc.apc.org; the Ecumenical Program on Central America and the Caribbean (EPICA) at epica@igc.apc.org; the Washington Office on Latin America at wola@wola.org; the Center for Human Rights Legal Action (CHRLA) at chrla@igc.apc.org; the National Coordinating Office on Refugees and Displaced of Guatemala (NCOORD); *CERIGUA Weekly Briefs* at guate@uvalle.edu.gt; and *Noticias de Guatemala Weekly Bulletin* at guatnews@web.apc.org.

News sources often provide information on the refugee return process. The following are accessible on the internet: *Prensa Libre* (http://www.prensalibre.com); *La Hora* (http://www.lahora.com.gt/p1996.htm); *Siglo XXI* and *The Siglo News* (in English) at http://www.sigloxxi.com. The news group CENTAM-L posts Guatemalan information and refugee news daily. To join their mailing list, send the message SIGNON CENTAM-L (first name)_(last name) to listserv@ubvm.cc.buffalo.edu. While by no means exhaustive, the above-listed sites provide interested researchers with sufficient data to develop the scenarios we depict only in rudimentary form.

NOTES

1. Until 1997, some of these "parallel societies," known as *comunidades populares de resistencia* (CPRs) were still in existence, even though the violence that led to their establishment in the first place had diminished (Bayón 1997).

2. ARDIGUA representatives later negotiated with the Guatemalan government for their own collective returns. A fifteen-day hunger strike by ARDIGUA members during a peaceful occupation of CEAR's office in Mexico drew attention to their plight prior to their first return to Guatemala in November 1997.

3. Canadian census figures (1996) indicate that 13,326 Guatemalans are legally resident in Canada, the vast majority living in Toronto, Montreal, and Vancouver. Clearly, this figure does not include those Guatemalans without

documentation or those who overstayed their visas and chose to go underground.

4. The officially recognized total of 43,000 jumps to 60,000 when children born within the refugee camps are included in the count (Taylor 1998:2).

5. Though the official return process ended in December 1998, at least four return groups were still negotiating land deals for their planned returns in 1999 (WCC/GRICAR 1999:26).

Antonella Fabri

4 Space and Identity in Testimonies of Displacement: Maya Migration to Guatemala City in the 1980s

The Problem of Displacement

This chapter is an attempt to understand the phenomenon of displacement in Guatemala during the civil conflicts that occurred over the last three decades (1966–96). Massive displacement originated in the 1980s as a consequence of the military conflicts during the governments of Generals Romeo Lucas García (1978–82) and Efraín Ríos Montt (1982 to August 1983). When the Guatemalan military intensified its war against the revolutionary forces during the 1980s, the state also deployed a policy of *tierras arrasadas,* or scorched earth, which primarily affected the rural population, the majority of which is Maya. Estimates of numbers of Guatemalans displaced either internally or abroad range from 500,000 to a million persons. Of the 150,000 people who fled to Mexico, only a third settled in refugee camps and acquired the status of refugees from the United Nations High Commissioner for Refugees (UNHCR); others went to Honduras, Belize, Canada, and the United States (CEH 1999).

My research focuses on internal refugees who moved to Guatemala City, on the conditions of life they encountered there, and on the strategies they created to work their way out of a dreadful situation. My investigation began in 1989 and followed refugee issues through the steps of the peace accord, which was finalized on 29 December 1996. Working with the refugees was difficult and at times discouraging since the context of war and terror made them suspicious of anyone interested in their history. Some, however, were willing to talk, and thanks to them I was able to acquire some understanding of the complex issue of displacement.

The stories of displaced Mayas excerpted below were gathered during fieldwork in Guatemala City between 1989 and 1999. My interest

56

here is not to provide the reader with an account of recent develop-ments in refugee issues in Guatemala but rather to analyze the rationale that lies behind the creation of internal refugees in the context of Guatemala's civil war and to explore the relationship between dis-placement and the re-creation of cultural identities. In this way I hope to shed some light on the duplicitous process of domination, which serves both to legitimize an ideology of the hegemonic structure and to generate a strategy of resistance on the part of subordinated groups.[1]

Although my project was not originally focused on violence and its effects, the more I talked to displaced people, the more I came to realize that an analysis of migration in Guatemala needed to be put in the con-text of the history of Guatemala of the last two decades, which was char-acterized by repression and ethnocide. In other publications (Fabri 1994, 1999), I link displacement to a form of control that has as its goal the fragmentation, dispossession, and effacement of Maya culture. The forced adaptation of Indians to a new way of life derives from a strat-egy of domination, or what is often called an "institution of terror," that permeated the Guatemalan national security policy in the 1980s (De Certeau 1986; Fabri 1994; Shapiro 1988). This discussion is part of a longer study concerning the relationship between identity, violence, and displacement among the Maya who migrated to Guatemala City in the early 1980s.[2] Both ladinos and Mayas identify themselves as migrant in order to avoid raising suspicions of being displaced, but an initial dis-tinction between the migrant and the displaced can be made. Those who have moved to the city in search of better economic and educational opportunities often use the word *superación*, improvement, to describe their reasons for migration. In apparent contrast are the internal refugees who refer to themselves as *desplazados*, or "displaced," and attribute their migration to the city to the terror raging in their home communities. In short, migrants are primarily motivated by economics, and desplazados by politics.[3] Urban Guatemalans often see migrant identities as more malleable than those of the displaced. While migrants are believed to be easily assimilated to ladino culture, they are hardly ever identified as indigenous because they have supposedly been "ladi-nized" (Adams 1959). The displaced are perceived as *inditos* because they are less easily assimilated to both urban culture and the urban job market. The displaced tend to be viewed as misfits and are less well received by urban Guatemalans than are indigenous migrants.

SOCIOETHNOGRAPHIC CONTEXT OF MIGRATION AND DISPLACEMENT

Beginning in 1977, migration and displacement increased dramatically. Due to the politics involved, however, there are no reliable figures on the number of migrants and displaced for those years. Studies have provided divergent estimates. According to the Association for the Advancement of Social Sciences in Guatemala (AVANCSO), by the late 1980s internal refugees represented 20 percent of the Guatemalan population (AVANCSO 1990:19, 76). One study estimated that by 1987, between 100,000 and 250,000 Maya and ladinos had been internally displaced (Fagen 1988:75). In the same period, the National Council of Guatemalan Displaced (CONDEG) calculated between 100,000 and 150,000 displaced people in the area of Guatemala City alone. A more recent study reports that by May 1997 about 324,000 people, an average of 55,000 families, were internally displaced and returned refugees (Spence et al. 1998). According to more recent data provided by an ongoing AVANCSO study, 250,000 people are displaced within the whole of Guatemala, with only 20,000 in the metropolitan area. The discrepancies in these studies' numbers reflect the lack of consensus on the definition of "displaced," a confusion that has prevailed since before 1990.

By 1991, indigenous migrants lived in three principal districts of the metropolitan area of the capital, in the *municipios* of Guatemala, Mixco, and Villanueva (Bastos and Camus 1991). According to the survey conducted by Bastos and Camus, of the total migrant population of Guatemala City, only 5.8 percent came to the capital between 1975 and 1976, while 17.8 percent arrived before 1960. Further, 28.3 percent arrived in the course of the six years between 1984 and 1990, while only 18.1 percent of the migrants arrived between 1977 and 1983, the most intense period of military repression (Bastos and Camus 1991:28) Although this survey does not indicate the percentage of ladino versus indigenous migrants, the periods of greatest migration for the two groups can be compared. Of the ladino migrants in the city, 33.5 percent arrived before the earthquake (1961–75), while 40.7 percent arrived afterward (1978–90). Apparently, only 20.7 percent of the indigenous migrants moved to the capital in the fourteen years before 1976, while 59.7 percent did so in the thirteen years after 1977. In comparison between the seven-year period of violence (1977–83) and the fourteen-year period before the earthquake (1961–75), the percentage of Indian migrants increased 200 percent to 21.3 percent of the total, while that of ladino migrants remained constant at 16.8 percent. The percentage of indigenous displaced in the city who relocated during the years after the violence reached 38.4 percent in comparison to the percentage of ladino displacement, which only increased to 23.9 percent (Bastos and Camus 1991). The majority of both migrant populations in the capital originated from the rural areas of the central and northwestern highlands. Kaqchikel and K'iche' speakers are among the most prominent groups in the urban center.

These figures highlight two major phases or flows in migration since 1977. The first, following the earthquake of 1976, coincided with the most intense period of government violence and repression in the rural areas. The second wave began in 1983 in the aftermath of the major military operations in the highlands. During this second period not only did migration to the capital increase but migrants tended to identify themselves as politically displaced. Paradoxically, the internal migrants of the earlier period tended to define themselves as economic migrants. The earlier migration of Mayas was indeed initiated by the economic crisis that resulted from the 1976 earthquake. This disaster contributed to an increasing impoverishment of the rural areas as already scarce resources were further limited. However, the military repression of the 1980s became a more critical factor in the massive displacement of the Maya and ladino rural populations. A great majority of the displaced became political refugees. Some fled to Mexico or hid themselves in the mountains, while others chose to migrate to the city.

MIGRANTS AND DISPLACED: A BRIEF CHARACTERIZATION

Of the two types of migrants living in the city, those who came before the violence either to pursue a college education or to improve their economic conditions are the more successful. In contrast to the displaced people, these immigrants have a clear and "clean" status, one underscored by their possession of legal papers and jobs. Although these immigrants did not have to fear military violence, they did experience hostility from the city population, especially from ladinos. In order to overcome ethnic discrimination and improve their socioeconomic status, many indigenous migrants have adopted some typical features of ladino culture, for example, the translation of an indigenous name into Spanish, the exclusive use of the Spanish language, western styles of clothing. Their perceived "apolitical" attitudes and perspectives, which are often criticized by other Maya immigrants, are also part of their effort to mingle and blend into "civilized" Guatemalan society. Among the displaced, two types can be identified: those who are not politically oriented or concerned with ethnic movements, and those who are highly politicized. While the latter tend to become organized in cultural and political groups and forcefully assert their ethnic identity, the former constitute the invisible, silent, and anonymous crowd who often are not even identified as inditos, as most upper- and middle-class ladinos call them, but just as poor, homeless, and, often, as troublemakers.[4]

Mayas from the rural communities who were displaced to the city by violence after 1982 experienced grievously impoverished economic conditions that were aggravated by racial, economic, and political discrimination. They tended to define themselves as migrants who had moved to the city *para superarse*, that is, to improve their economic condition, but such claims derived from a reticence to link their migration to the military repression they suffered in their communities. Their use of the term "migrant" was an attempt to camouflage, for both their own psychological benefit and their reception by the public, the political underpinnings of their migration. The use of this term is thus misleading and inadequate for analytical purposes, since it disguises the fact that Guatemala's politics of control was based on a strategy of violence that formed part of the "institution of terror," which reinforced the system of large land-holding (*latifundios*), scarcity of lands, and the resulting impoverishment of rural communities. All of these factors greatly influenced the decision to migrate to the capital and should be interpreted in the context of the strategy of control and modernization of the state within which the Mayas have had a very limited place. The term "economic migrant" might thus be read as a disguised identity constructed for reasons of safety within the social classification system of contemporary Guatemala.

In the early 1980s, the relation between economics and violence was, furthermore, supported by the military organization of the *patrullas de autodefensa civil*. The civil patrol system incorporated some 600,000

Guatemalans (Spence et al. 1998) and was put into place in 1982 under Ríos Montt's dictatorship as a strategy of counterinsurgency against the guerrillas. But forced enrollment in the civil patrol system of the villages prevented the cultivation of lands and thus limited the ability of families and communities to obtain subsistence. Many of those individuals who were forced to work in the patrols decided to escape from their villages and came to be associated in the public eye with subversive activities and marked as national enemies. Hence, once displaced, these people were generally condemned to silence and anonymity.

It is the displaced who have directly experienced the violence and have lacked the opportunity to flee abroad. Victims of military attacks, they lie in silence and invisibility both enforced and assumed as the only mechanism of defense. These people are suspended between the impossibility of return and the incapacity to survive in the new place. The majority do not qualify for professional jobs due to their low level of education. Given their lack of identification papers, either burned or left behind in their flight, and often also their illiteracy in Spanish, they are condemned to an often hopeless situation. Their homes are typically located in the ravine areas and are made of carton boxes or plastic.[5] The luckier ones are exploited in factories or in ladino households, where many indigenous women work as maids. The high level of malnutrition and the poor hygienic conditions in which they live undermine their chances for improvement. As a result, many displaced live off what charity they are able to collect on the streets.

The emergence and visibility of self-help organizations in the capital since the mid-1980s manifest the cohesiveness and empathy among those who have directly suffered from the violence. GAM (Mutual Support Group) and CONAVIGUA (National Coordinating Committee for Guatemalan Widows) were the groups through which internal refugees initially connected with one another. In 1989, CONDEG (National Council of Guatemalan Displaced) came directly to represent internally displaced people, mostly those who lived in the city, and in 1990 the CPRs (Communities of Population in Resistance), which consisted of displaced groups living in the mountains and the jungle of El Quiché and Petén, went public. The members of both organizations were characterized by a Marxist orientation, here expressed in the testimony of a displaced person and member of CONDEG that appeared in one of the leaflets published by the organization:

For some of us, the condition of displacement began several decades ago, but for the majority it started at the beginning of the 1980s. Most of us left our communities and hid in towns and cities, mostly in the capital, in order to safeguard our lives. Since then, we have been living in fear and with a lot of suffering. On the 5th of March 1989, we were finally able to hold our first meeting. It seemed clearer and clearer to us that we needed to support each other . . . that we needed to form a specific organization for the desplazados in order to confront other people with our reality and make our claims known and become present in the social, economic and political life of our country.

This testimony is acknowledged by the group as representative of the members' experience and as legitimation for the organization of CONDEG. Its goal is to awaken the consciousness of all displaced people in order to acquire a place within civil society. Within the city, however, different forms of communities grant the displaced a wider space for new perspectives on individual and communal conditions.

Secret Network

Before the peace talks, those who defined themselves as desplazados were characterized by their awareness of the conditions of their uprooting. This consciousness was a primary factor or motive for the reformulation of their identity based on a new sense of community, which often took place in an organized group. People who survived the massacres often formed communities in the new places of residence, even though they had to limit their interactions for safety reasons. One group of displaced families, for example, all originated from the same village in the department of El Quiché but lived at a distance from each other in the capital in order to maintain security and elude military control. This group, which in 1989 numbered a hundred people, maintained its unity by a secretive and "displaced" form of communication. Its members entrusted six individuals, the group's coordinators, with the task of communication for all, in order to safeguard their anonymity and prevent the police from identifying them.[6] This network allowed them to share their problems and fears in the new place while avoiding the danger of suspicion that an open organization might trigger.

The assassination or disappearance of a close relative that often causes displacement also makes the displaced reluctant to talk to outsiders or identify themselves. Breaking the silence to discuss one's own experience constituted a great risk, but many were determined to take it nonetheless. Recounting one's story is a form of transgression or rebellion against the code of silence, and it naturally has a cathartic effect.[7]

Many self-help organizations of desplazados (for example, CONAVIGUA and GAM) were started by widows of the violence. Some group strategies of survival and adaptation focused on recounting experiences of violence. Talking openly and sharing memories were a means of defying and perhaps transcending the fear they still experienced. The process of vocalization thus became a method of healing (see Fabri 1999). The shared memories were also part of a process of *concientización*, or awareness, since they became a means of acquiring a political consciousness of the present historical situation. Associations were also formed in churches and medical centers, institutions that have historically provided help to the victims of violence. Again, the goal of these "invisible" communities is to vocalize what the violence has repressed and censored. The recounting of memories always confronts the victims with a present situation that often appears hopeless. The present condition is perceived as one of no return, of an absolute break from the past. Thus people who have lived through a traumatic experience try to devise other strategies of survival than simply "forgetting."

DISPLACEMENT AS CULTURAL ESTRANGEMENT:
MIGRATION VERSUS TRAVEL

Displacement and migration are forms of travel. All travel, whether migration, tourism, or pilgrimage, entails departure and movement to another place. This other, this foreign place, is liminal and marked by anti-structural qualities and activities (Turner 1972; Turner and Turner 1978). Travel involved in a pilgrimage, unlike migration, ends only with the return home. Pilgrims and tourists return to normal life, while migrants are permanently caught in a liminal state and dangerous place. Unable to return, both displaced and migrants are incarcerated in an ineluctable condition of dislocation.[8] Desplazados both feared and desired to return to their communities: Once they left home they became stigmatized. Leaving was in fact perceived by both the military and civilians who remained as a declaration of culpability. Hence, while the displaced always expressed their hope of returning, they knew this dream was unlikely ever to come true. These families, together with their past histories, had been dismembered.

Conditions created by the Guatemalan military forced people to leave their communities and obliged them to seek refuge in enclosing, controllable spaces. The experience of displacement in the city is a form of incarceration similar to the forced relocation into "model villages" or refugee camps (Manz 1988a; Foucault 1979). As one desplazado put it, "We moved from the El Quiché region. The soldiers killed my mother, burned our houses and our belongings, and we moved away. Now [in the capital city] we cannot plant corn, beans, and everything is very expensive. They do not let us go to our villages; they kill people who go back there. We are sad because our families are far away and we cannot communicate with them."

The apparent goal of the government with respect to both migrants and displaced was to produce "domesticated" or controlled bodies that formed a reserve of labor and maintained national security (Black et al. 1984). In the words of another K'iche' person displaced to the capital, "People come to the city because they are threatened. Even in the city they [the military] created forms of control to verify the place of origin of the families. People are quite 'burned,' they are kidnapped. One is not feeling safe in the city. It is not possible to communicate with many people, it is dangerous. Here, everybody is on his own, nonetheless violence is still enraging. People [who are displaced] do not identify themselves with the flag, they are here, marginalized."

The presence and condition of the indigenous population in the capital, then, is a form of punishment. The circumstances and incidents that compel migration preclude the possibility of return as well as of communication.

> In our villages we are forced to participate in the civil patrol. When I was in the civil patrol I realized that I had to leave my work in the field and my family because my shift included two full days of work, for two nights I had to be on the road while my family was inside the house. What might happen? Somebody with bad intentions might come, especially the military, while I am here patrolling the road. At this point I started thinking. I decided that I had to run away from the civil patrol and move to the capital. The village was not safe, one cannot communicate with each other there. Honestly, I would be isolated there. People are told that if they refuse to be in the civil patrol it means that they are with the revolutionaries. Hence, one's own woman and family become threatened.

To leave the place of origin often means a journey with no return. Especially in the capital the displaced are foreigners in a strange place. Everyday life for the displaced becomes what Eliade (1959) identifies as a foundation act: The displaced assumes a new identity in the conditions of estrangement. Identity has been defined as a social place. It expresses one's relation with nature and introduces an order (La Cecla 1988). The passage from the place of origin to the city implies disorientation, expressed here by a displaced K'iché Maya: "We had to abandon our homes, leave behind our belongings and move to the capital. . . . We go there under very unfortunate conditions: I don't know the work here, I don't know the city, I got lost."

Marginalization and social atomization start in native communities and become more apparent and forceful in the urban context (see Bastos and Camus 1991:27), where communication among displaced always entails careful planning in order to avoid identification. Also with migrants, the sense of community and continuity with the past is consciously broken as a means to attain superación, a term used to convey economic improvement. Normal life has been traded for survival, or, in the case of migrants, exchanged for the illusion of money. In this regard an Ixil Maya says, "Some of my relatives refuse to say that they are indigenous and say that they come from the east because they want to be better."

Displacement is a form of mutilation that creates an experience of exclusion and absence. The city lacks reference points and constricts the individual in an ambiguous relation to the environment. The link with the condition of origin is missing. As a displaced Kaqchikel Maya said, "It is very important to have a place and it seems that those people, the indigenous, do not have the right to have one."

Displacement is experienced as misplacement. It entails a "blackout" of the past without a vision of a breakthrough for the future. In this other, hostile place, where foreignness is imposed within one's own homeland, the individual experiences a condition of exile. "Here, we don't know where we are, it is difficult to relate to places outside our communities," said a displaced person from El Quiché. Thus, the more one distances oneself from the village, the more the space around the person gets disorganized and out of control. But there is no return to the place of one's past, or to the normal life and identity that are rooted there.

ERASED IDENTITIES

Displacement is a mechanism of absence and disappearance that has been enforced by the militaries on "undesirable" individuals. As Baudrillard points out, "disappearance is also [a] strategy; it is its way of response to this device for capture, [and] for forced identification" (1988:213). Disappearance as displacement might thus be considered the condition for survival of many displaced people.

In the testimony of the displaced people I interviewed, the city was depicted as an imposing space that threatened to swallow identity. At the same time, it represented the opportunity for anonymity and concealed identity that had been labeled subversive by the military government. As one displaced person remarked, "[If] those who have seen, and those who know too much, are accused of being subversive by the military and thus must dislocate themselves, one is then obliged to disappear." The marginalization of the Maya and the attempt to destroy their culture is, paradoxically, part of an integration policy that aims to create a homogeneous, harmonic, civil body. Once outside their communities many Maya people feel at odds with the urban environment and therefore pressured to change their way of being.

The forced integration into the labor market, poor education, and lack of language skill in Spanish are some of the characteristics that individualize and consequentially undermine the sense of self of many indigenous immigrants who come to the capital. "The traditions in our villages are backward in comparison with those of professional people. I do not disregard my traditions, but, in addition, I can improve my education because it is good. There are no discriminations but we want to be like the ladinos. We 'natural' people, as we call the indigenous, this is it, we need to keep up. Many indigenous people once they are in the capital change even their names and their hair in order to look more like ladinos, but they cannot change their indigenous faces."

Clearly, for some, integration into ladino culture is regarded as necessary to obtain respect and improve one's life. But even if desired, integration is prevented by indelible ethnic markers. This tension reinforces the condition of "in-betweenness," or liminality, in which migrants are suspended, and contributes to a pervading sense of insecurity. In many cases, it undermines their social status and possibilities. Even when some desired traits of superación are assumed by the individual, they nonetheless create profound sadness. Education, for instance, is perceived as a mechanism that disrupts Maya cultural heritage yet is a necessary tool for survival in a foreign environment. "Education devastates our tradition, but now if the indigenous do not speak Spanish they cannot sell their products, they would need somebody else to sell them and they would have to pay a commission to this person. The indigenous would lose a lot due to lack of education. One cannot work without having a scholastic education."

In order to "comply" with the social code of the city, indigenous people often conceal or eliminate the exterior markers of their cultures. The necessity of speaking Spanish is much stronger in the capital than anywhere else. The most visible ethnic marker, the *traje*, or traditional clothing that identifies an individual as part of a specific Maya group, is often abandoned once desplazados arrive in the capital. In fact, the traditional clothing is transformed from a symbol of ethnic identity into a stigma in the context of the dominant ladino society.

The capital has traditionally been a locus of cultural diversity where pluralism can flourish. But it can also be seen as a "cannibal" that eats and erodes cultural identity and ethnic pluralism. In De Certeau's analysis of Montaigne's travel writings, the "cannibal" refers to the uncivilized savage, the man of nature who is forbidden to assume any identity but the "rotten" one. Such an identity seems to apply to the indigenous migrants and displaced in the Guatemalan capital as well. It is a discriminatory label imposed on them because of their supposed threat to the established power structure and cultural order: "The cannibals slip away from the words and discourses that fix their place. . . . They are not to be found where they are sought. They are never there. . . . What is foreign is that which escapes from a place" (De Certeau 1986:70).

My use of the word "cannibal" implies two levels of signification. It refers first to the city as a devouring entity that erodes ethnicity simply by denying the possibility of difference. But in ladino culture, *Indians* are also cannibals. From the perspective of modernization and development, they are regarded as the dark side of the Guatemalan nation. As savage, uncivilized, and subversive, they must be targeted and eliminated by Guatemalan security policy. It seems therefore that the scarcity of resources that creates the conditions for migration also condemns the migrant to comply with new categories, logic, and order. In sum, it forces the migrant to become a misfit, a wanderer in a liminal space, to be "out of place."

Among the middle and upper classes of ladino society, the indigenous in Guatemala are often associated with poverty, sleaziness, ignorance. This view is expressed in the common use of such pejorative terms as *indios, naturales,* or *campesinos,* all of which drift toward the meaning of "savage" and "cannibal." These terms connote those who, like the Guatemalan Indians, fall outside the social conventions of the government and white society. They are cultural categories that fix individuals in their natural origin, without a history or a future, and deprive them of any other form of identity. For example, the name "Maria" is used by many ladinos in a derogatory and depersonalizing way to address the indigenous women working in the city as maids. According to a displaced Kaqchikel Maya woman working as a maid, "In the villages we were respected. In the city, instead we are despised, we are called 'Maria,' but we do not want to give up our traje, it would be just as if we decided to change our parents."

Names impose a truth that must be internalized by the Other. Names that evoke filth, rot, and squalor are imposed on the "Indians." Hence, the cannibal city not only devours the exterior markers of ethnicity but also compels the Indians to swallow their sense of identity and cultural integrity. These tactics of domination may be traced back through five hundred years of government policies toward the Guatemalan Indians. The scarcity of land, the destruction of ecology, and the consequent abrogation of natural economies are not just natural catastrophes, they are part of a specific rationale. Migration creates a trap and imprisonment, because the choice of displacing oneself is actually not a choice. It is coerced. It is a limitation on the control of one's space. In the same way, the displaced's newly acquired or reconfigured identity is a marginal one, like that of the wanderer, the beggar, or the hero, whose place within society is restricted and circumscribed so that society can use and control him. These words from a displaced Ixil Maya speak of this type of coercion:

> Those who are here are compelled not to speak their language but forced to learn Spanish and to associate with the ladinos, that is, they are obliged to change their clothes. These people [the indigenous] do not really have the awareness of the situation in which we are living here, in Guatemala. Rather, these people make themselves available to cooperate with the

army, to collaborate with the government to control the population. There are many indigenous who have studied and detached themselves from the indigenous group, from the same problem of the indigenous, from their own families. These ones [the educated indigenous] want to live a ladino style of life. When they obtain a degree they forget the people and switch to the side of the ladinos.

It would seem that the initial apparent distinction between migrants and displaced is erased by the cultural logic of displacement as a form of violence. Mayas are labeled with categories that confine them—both symbolically and literally—to the lower strata and margins of society. The dominant logic indicates that the subversives are "cannibals," always sought out by the military in their homes, in their "proper" place. But they are not to be found there, since they have already dislocated themselves in the mountains or in the city. In this misplaced context, where they are not supposed to be because they are not fit for that environment, the Mayas, like cannibals, are forced to "eat" their identities. In light of Pratt's concept of transculturation, I suggest that what appears to be a self-imposed negation is nothing more than a mechanism of power relation to which Mayas, as Others, respond by proposing a different presentation of self, one that is located in the interstices of outlined or allowed identities or self-representations (Pratt 1992).[9]

The concealment of indigenous traits and traditions has been a necessary everyday practice for the majority of the Indian population who live displaced. It might be seen as a process of assimilation that many adopt as a strategy of survival. However, while some Mayas set as their goals the achievement of ladino traits and feel honored to be identified as ladinos, others adopt only the minimum number of changes required for personal defense and safety. What might at first glance appear an instance of "ladinization" and loss of one's own culture, or the erasure of an "essential" identity, should instead be interpreted as one of variety of expression of identity. Identity becomes in fact an issue of choice, or practice, for the individual, a "tropos," rather than a "topos," or fixed place. Thus, identity, or rather *identities*, both for the migrants and displaced Maya alike, shift place from a "natural," ahistorical, and uncontested category to a practice of everyday life. From this perspective, then, identity and space are separated from the logic that creates them as paralyzing mechanisms of control. The adoption of new cultural traits, whether as a rejection or as a camouflage of one's traditional values among the displaced, points to a process of reinvention of identity. Migrant and displaced thus seem to share each other's experiences, from the dynamic of creation of their places in history to the strategies of self-representation.

Unfulfilled Returns

Specific historical and ideological formations underlie the processes of migration and displacement in Guatemala. They both arise as mechanisms of repression derived from the complementary policies of national integration and the military strategy of ethnic genocide. Testimonies of both migrants and displaced attest to the cannibalism of the city and show how everyday urban practices "consume" a certain identity, in this case Maya identity. The city represents one of the many stops on the paths that migrants and displaced have chosen. It constitutes a temporary stage, the termination of a liminal condition and the beginning of another impending transformation. The culmination of displaced and migrants' travel might be either an improved economic situation or the return to the home community, but the goal keeps shifting along the way in its pursuit. The several transformations that occurred in the place of displacement have affected individuals' cognitive maps. The newly displaced identities are products of deep historic changes, the result of a mechanism of terror and violence. This is the case for displaced people who have assumed the names imposed, that is, the image of "cannibals," but at the same time have used that image as their own strategy of resistance. Although they have assumed the mask of the "Other," have been transformed into either cannibals or "bad copies" of ladinos, they have nonetheless actively participated in the forging of their identity.

The excerpts of testimony presented here constitute texts of foundation of these representations. But these individuals certainly do not need to recount their stories—or cause anthropologists to recount their stories—to assert their own presence in history. The headquarters of various self-help organizations such as GAM, CONAVIGUA, CONDEG, CPR, and many others that have been more recently formed, become centers in which Mayas, especially the displaced, plan not only their struggle for a better life, but also the re-creation of their abandoned and often lost communities. Within these nascent communities, people are drawn together by the similarity of their life experiences. Within these institutional contexts, individual memories, dreams, and fears are shared. These individual stories are familiar to everyone and constitute the ground for the mobilization of social action.

The everyday life of an immigrant in a new place can be compared to a foundational act. While some are compelled to charter a new life by complying with the values and canons of a different culture, others, out of an imposed identity such as that of the subversive, carve out an autonomous space where the re-creation of a shared identity is undertaken. In this way, the travel seems terminated, and yet a new departure is on its way because the return is never definite. Closure, resolution, and return to the origin always occur in the sphere of desire and exist in the process of becoming. In the cannibal city, the displaced people, after a search for anonymity, create their own spatial order and identity without erasing the longing for return. In the establishment of one's own presence, the interplay between visibility and invisibility constitutes a strategic feature. The displaced, forced by the politics of the nation-state to be invisible, have turned their de-territorialization into a collective experience, creating new spaces and new identities and thereby reversing the initial logic of terror. Thus one objective of Guatemalan policy, to alter and control Maya identity through stripping Mayas of their communities and labeling them terrorists, has failed. The displaced have resisted and have, in their emerging exile communities, displaced the very policies of the nation-state to which they were subjected.

NOTES

Acknowledgments: This article is an expanded and updated version of a paper by the same title presented in 1991 at the Latin American Studies Association meeting in Washington, DC., for the panel "The Maya Diaspora," organized by James Loucky. I would like to acknowledge the valuable help of Marilyn Moors in the latest edition of this paper. My greatest indebtedness goes, however, to the Maya people who have honored me with their trust and their accounts of these experiences.

1. The interviews were conducted with displaced people from different communities in Guatemala (municipios) who have been living as displaced persons in the capital for the last decade. Given the sensitive political situation at the time of my fieldwork, I conducted the interviews mainly with representatives of popular organizations such as GAM (Mutual Support Group), CONAV-

IGUA (National Coordinating Committee for Guatemalan Widows), CONDEG (Campesino Unity Committee), and CPR (Communities of Populations in Resistance).

2. While the term ladino is used to describe Guatemalans of Spanish descent, the term Maya refers to the indigenous population. Although there are twenty-two distinct Maya groups, each with its own language in Guatemala, indigenous intellectuals use it as the general term to designate Mayan-speaking people. In short, the term "Maya" homogenizes the distinct indigenous groups in order to distinguish them from the ladinos, or the Spanish or Spanish-indigenous mixed-descent groups. In the words of a Maya leader, "Guatemala is culturally a nation, but it is politically divided—atomized—in that all the indigenous people in Guatemala are Maya, and so is their collective memory. We are alive, but we need symbols because we do not have a community yet, since the governments divided us as Maya people" (Cojtí 1991).

3. Aguayo (1987a) uses the term "internal refugee" to describe those people who migrated to other places within their country due to armed conflicts, i.e., those of political-military origin. These patterns of migration differ from and stand in opposition to migrations that are strictly determined by economic necessity. Also see O'Docherty Madrazo (1988), who affirms that most of the migration movements, for economic reasons prevailing in Central America in the last decade, have been triggered by political crises. Hamilton and Chinchilla (1991) also consider these issues.

4. Such has been the case of indigenous intellectual groups, particularly those represented by La Academia de las Lenguas Mayas, whose ethnic heritage was re-elaborated and consciously adopted as the fundamental structure of their identity. Therefore, the vindication of ethnic values such as local language, dress, and religion shaped their everyday practices.

5. Gayla Jameson, in her film *Approach of Dawn* (1997), offers a vivid representation of the conditions of immigrants and displaced Maya in the city.

6. Being identified as displaced in the 1980s implied risking one's own life. To survive, many of the displaced people remained anonymous and dispersed, hiding their history and identity from other people, since anyone could be a potential spy.

7. The act of talking, according to Scarry, allows the passage of pain into speech, since one of the dimensions of pain is to destroy language and the ability to extend oneself out of the body. The embodiment that the pain causes "destroys a person's self and world, a destruction experienced spatially as either the contraction of the universe down to the immediate vicinity of the body or as the body swelling to fill the entire universe" (Scarry 1985: 35).

8. The return of displaced people from the Mexican border has constituted a problematic issue for the Guatemalan government (Manz 1988a, 1988b). Even though the preliminary accord on refugees (2 October 1992) bound the government to accept and integrate the refugees, it has not been able to solve the massive problem of the refugee access to lands. (For a more complete history of these refugee issues see Taylor 1998.) The experience of the refugees among the

Communities of Population in Resistance (CPR) was profoundly different. Before the peace accords the army adopted a policy of forced returns, especially among the population that escaped army control to live in the mountains. This strategy was based on the politics of psychological operations and was geared toward "voluntary" return using reconnaissance flights, anti-insurgent propaganda, messages from relatives, and false news about the political situation and the state of democracy in the country (AVANCSO 1990:53). After the accords, both the CPR refugees and those who became organized in the capital felt that the government had not complied with the their needs, but only those of refugees under the protection of international agencies.

9. "Ethnographers have used this term to describe how subordinate or marginal groups select and invent from materials transmitted to them by a dominant or metropolitan culture. While subjugated peoples cannot readily control what emanates from the dominant culture, they do determine to varying extent what they absorb into their own, and what they use it for" (Pratt 1992:6).

Deborah L. Billings

5   Organizing in Exile: The Reconstruction
      of Community in the Guatemalan
      Refugee Camps of Southern Mexico

One day, generations from now, the son of a *Todos Santero* will ask his father,
"Papa, why does your *traje* have such different colors?" "Well, son, about a
hundred years ago my grandfather was a refugee in Chiapas [Mexico],
together with Mames, Jacaltecos, Kanjobales, Huistecos. . . . He lived together
with Chujes and Chiantlecos, with people from San Juan Ixcoy. And thus our
ways of weaving became mixed." It will be seen that our combining things
together leads to many questions that future generations will take into
account—questions whose answers will illuminate the consciousness of many
generations.

                                      —A Mam refugee and weaver from Todos Santos

WEAVING AND traje style have been markers of indigenous
communities for hundreds of years for the Maya of Guatemala. What
began as a tactic used by the Spanish conquerors to identify, divide, and
control indigenous people has been appropriated and reformulated as
a complex mode of expression celebrating identity and recognizing history. The years of armed confrontation and generalized violence against
indigenous communities in Guatemala are reflected in changes in
weaving and traje. In search of anonymity and relative safety, some
men and women stopped wearing their traditional clothing in an effort
to hide their identity. Others incorporated symbols, colors, and styles
from groups different from their own into their weaving as people from
different language and ethnic groups, and from different areas of origin, lived side by side after their own communities had been destroyed.

     This chapter explores the question of how and why the Guatemalan
refugee population living in the camps of southern Mexico organized
effectively to create new forms of community. The multicolored traje
donned by the Todos Santero embodies the core dynamic of such organizing processes created and experienced by the refugee population—
the actual weaving together of distinct communities and identities into

new entities that both include and expand pre-exile definitions of self and group affiliation. Over time, Guatemalan camp-based refugees came to view themselves as a united community; unification gave camp residents a powerful collective voice that they used to articulate their needs and demands at local, national, and international levels. This became particularly important in the process of negotiations regarding their return to Guatemala, in which refugees themselves participated to an unprecedented degree relative to other refugee populations throughout the world.

MASSIVE DISPLACEMENT INTO MEXICO

From late 1981 to 1983, an estimated 1.5 million people, or 80 percent of the population of the Departments of El Quiché, Alta Verapaz, Huehuetenango, and Chimaltenango were displaced internally or forced to seek safety abroad (CEH 1999; GHRSP 1992).[1] This chapter concentrates on the group of forty-six thousand Guatemalans, Maya and ladino, who fled "la violencia" in the early 1980s to settle throughout Chiapas and to build what would later be recognized as "camps" by the United Nations High Commissioner for Refugees (UNHCR) and the Mexican government (AVANCSO 1992; GHRSP 1992; WOLA 1989).[2] From 1982 to 1984 the Guatemalan military made numerous incursions into the camps, killing several refugees and terrorizing the population in general. This, combined with the view of many Mexican officials that the refugees intensified existing political problems in Chiapas (see Aguayo 1987b), prompted the Mexican government to attempt to relocate all refugees from Chiapas to the sparsely populated states of Campeche and Quintana Roo. Most refugees resisted forced relocation: approximately twenty-three thousand remained in Chiapas, spread over 127 camps, while over twelve thousand relocated to four settlements in Campeche and over six thousand to four settlements in Quintana Roo.

Overall, more than 90 percent of the recognized refugee population was comprised of impoverished *campesinos* who arrived directly from rural areas in the Departments of Huehuetenango, El Quiché, San Marcos, Alta Verapaz, and El Petén. Eighty to 90 percent of the total recognized refugee population were indigenous Maya and 10 to 20 percent ladino (CIREFCA 1992; García and Gomaríz, 1989, vol. 2). Survey data collected in the camps in 1991 (Mamá Maquín 1994) indicate that the majority of refugees were from the northwest *municipios* of Huehuetenango, in particular Nentón, San Miguel Acatán, Barrillas, San Mateo Ixtatán, and Santa Ana Huista, and that four Mayan languages predominated: Q'anjob'al (51 percent), Mam (16 percent), Chuj (16 percent), and Jakaltek (7 percent). Spanish as a mother tongue was spoken by approximately 10 percent of the population, mainly ladinos (CIRE-FCA 1992). Spanish as a second language was spoken, however, by a substantial part of the indigenous population. Thus while the refugee population shared a similar class position, it was heterogeneous along the axes of ethnicity, language, and community of origin.

THE CREATION OF COMMUNITY IN EXILE

Early writings on Guatemala suggested that indigenous communities were areas of cultural isolation located on the margins of Guatemalan society, largely unincorporated into the country's political and economic life (Redfield 1934; Tax 1937). Since the 1970s, researchers have challenged the static, closed portrayal of indigenous communities and have focused instead on their simultaneous incorporation into national and international systems of production and consumption and resistance to such incorporation (Handy 1990; Smith 1990a; Warren 1978; Watanabe 1990). Since the days of Spanish conquest, indigenous labor has been forcibly incorporated into Guatemala's economic system through various laws and exploitative practices. Community has served as a base for Indian identity as its members have resisted proletarianization by the state (Smith 1987). Manning Nash (1989) adds that community has been used defensively to protect residents from the constant intrusion of the national economy, which, in the highly racially stratified society of Guatemala, has continuously led to Indian impoverishment and subordination. Communities have thus served as places of sanctuary for the formation and maintenance of the multitude of Maya identities, as well as in the reinforcement of an identity opposed to that of the dominant ladino (Manz 1988a). Thus, for example, a Q'anjob'al-speaking Indian woman from San Miguel Acatán would identify herself as an "Acateca," while a resident of Santo Tomás Chichicastenango would describe himself as a Maxeña. Geographic locale or "place" and some "minimal consensus of tradition" or "premise" have

)een key components of defining community in the highlands of west-
:rn Guatemala (Watanabe 1990).

The parameters of community and identity necessarily changed
during the refugees' years of exile and challenged the conceptualiza-
:ion of community as something based on place and common culture.
This definition was essentially negated by the forcible removal of peo-
ɔle from their place of residence in Guatemala, a pattern that has con-
:inued during the years of exile in Mexico, where camps have
:onstantly been relocated due to shortages of land and other resources.
.n addition, refugees had no rights to land ownership in Mexico. Sim-
larly, shared culture (largely based on blood ties and territory) as a
:oundation of community has largely disappeared as campesinos from
different areas of origin, speaking a multitude of languages, live side
ɔy side in the camps.

In exile, the roots of community are grounded in a set of shared expe-
:iences, stories, and memories, as well as in a process of collective labor
:hat used these resources to create new and meaningful social ties and
.nstitutions (see Falla 1992).[3] This process belies the notion that community and cultural identity are destroyed in exile and instead high-
.ights the ways in which refugees have resisted attempts to destroy their
:ulture and have created meaning out of the atrocities to which they
nave been subjected. In exile, many Guatemalans who experienced the
nardships of racism and poverty at home were able to share their sto-
:ies with one another and start to develop a common sense of history.
The excerpts below are taken from interviews with refugee women liv-
ng in various camps in 1992 and capture some of their experiences during flight.

Maria, a forty-nine-year-old Mam woman and mother of twelve,
grew up in the northern town of Todos Santos, Huehuetenango. For
years, she and her husband traveled with their children to the plantations on the southern coast to earn money, since, in her words, "there
was no work in the north." At age twenty-two, she and her husband
decided to make the trek to the Ixcán cooperatives, a fifteen-day trip by
foot. There they lived and worked until the violence hit their community:

> There were no problems when we began to work [the land in the Ixcán].
> Everything was tranquil. We were working. But the army came to kill us.
> Because of this the people ran. When they [the military] came to Ixcán,
> they burned everything. Everything. Everything up until we did not even

have clothes. They killed a pregnant woman, they cut her and took out the baby and threw it against a rock. They closed the people in the church and then set it on fire and everyone inside died. Everything of mine stayed there, my hens, my oranges. (Maria, personal interview, 1992)

The municipality of Jacaltenango, Huehuetenango, was also hard hit by the violence. Sonia, a forty-seven-year old Jacalteca woman from Limonar, relates what happened in 1982, when the army arrived in her town:

In the year 1982 was the massacre of our village. The army arrived at about 6:30 in the afternoon. They entered our village; and we knew that on the third of January they had massacred many in a village very close by. And we knew what suffering had occurred there. We always feared the army but never thought that they would do the same in our village. But on the sixth of January, only three days later, it happened to us. Many of us lost our families, our parents, our brothers and sisters, our children. . . . We could not even bury any of the dead because we had to flee. This date, January 6, we will never forget. This is why we are still living here in Mexico. (Sonia, personal interview, 1992)

Many, like Maria and Sonia, directly witnessed and experienced the incursion of military forces into their communities. Survivors escaped into the mountains as their villages were destroyed and family members and friends were killed. Often they were pursued by the army as they fled. Others lived near areas in which massacres took place. When news reached them, many abandoned their homes before the army arrived to destroy their villages.[4]

Flight to Mexico was filled with danger. The length of the trip depended on the community's distance from the Mexican border and the persistence of the army. Refugees without exception arrived on foot hauling their children and few possessions on their backs. Maria recalls "We did not bring anything, just one traje to wear and another to change into. The army burned many of our trajes. Burning and killing. It really took a lot to come here. No one was at peace. We slept in the mountains and it was raining. We did not have anything, only some plastic that we used to cover ourselves a bit, or at least cover the little ones, the children. We did not eat anything, nothing all day long."

Many refugees recounted that Mexican campesinos came to their aid during the initial stages of exile, offering them food, water, and small pieces of land on which to grow subsistence food (see Earle 1988). While this relationship was maintained to some degree, it was also strained over the years as refugees competed with impoverished Mexicans for scarce resources in the region.

Community formation in exile was a process that evolved over time to meet the needs of the refugees. It was also a multilevel process (Falla 1992). The first level involved the integration of different ethnic and linguistic groups into a cohesive body. Maria Guadalupe García, a Mam woman from San Ildefonso Ixtahuacán and a member of the group Mamá Maquín (described below), illustrates the power of that cohesiveness (Mamá Maquín 1993a):

> Something that is very important is that we have learned to live as brothers and sisters. When we left Guatemala we all came from different villages and we had all lived in different ways, that is, our traditions and place of origin were different. As refugees, we started to live in communities. We formed many camps. In each of them we were from various places. Between us we are from nine different ethnic groups, including the ladina. We have learned to care for each other as sisters and brothers, between men and women. We respect each other, especially since we left our country for the same reason.

Ricardo Falla defines the second level as the coalescing of all the camps in each Mexican state, a process that created a "Chiapas community," a "Campeche community," and a "Quintana Roo community," in which everyday living conditions were relatively different. The third level he identifies is the community of all Guatemalan refugees in Mexico, although I would argue that an intermediary community of camp refugees exists as well. Each of these levels, but particularly the latter two, can be seen as types of "imagined communities" (Anderson 1991) where, regardless of direct personal contact among members, each feels or "imagines" that the others are joined in the same communion.

New, interlocking, sometimes overlapping identities have emerged from this process. While refugees retained and often harkened back to their place-specific and culturally specific identities in Guatemala, they also now referred to themselves as Maya or Indigena, recognizing the historical linkages between different language/ethnic groups, and also as refugiado Guatemalteco, or Guatemalan refugees, thereby bridging the indigenous-ladino divide so pervasive in Guatemalan society. The two components of this new identity were important. "Refugee" emphasized a common status in exile, while "Guatemalan" highlighted a newfound consciousness that they are an integral part of the Guatemalan nation.

SHARED EXPERIENCES IN EXILE

In this section I focus on the experience of refugees who stayed in Chiapas throughout the 1980s. An estimated twenty-three to twenty-four thousand refugees lived in 127 camps (AVANCSO 1992; CIREFCA 1992) scattered along the Mexico-Guatemala border region of Chiapas in the municipalities of Amatenango de la Frontera, Bellavista del Norte, Frontera Comalapa, La Independencia, La Trinitaria, Las Margaritas, and Chicomuselo. All were officially recognized by the Mexican government through the Mexican Commission for Aid to Refugees (COMAR) and the UNHCR, and received varying levels of subsistence support and infrastructural aid beginning in 1984. The camps varied in size, ethnic composition, infrastructure, accessibility, access to resources, religion, and land tenure. Despite these differences, common experiences were identified across all camps.

Overall, Guatemalan refugees did not become "Mexicanized" but rather have developed a strong national identity and consciousness in exile. This sense of being Guatemalan rarely prevailed among indigenous campesinos while living in Guatemala. Los refugiados Guatemaltecos recognized that indigenous identity was an important component of national identity. As such, many parents worked to teach their children the mother tongue (Mamá Maquín 1994). Bilingual schooling in the camps was conducted by Guatemalan refugee education promoters who taught children Guatemalan history, emphasizing the sequence of political events that had forced them into exile. These were a few of the ways in which camp life played "a generative role in the elaboration of national and historical consciousness" (Malkki 1990:37).

Another important shared experience was the mobility of the Guatemalan population since its arrival in the early 1980s. In the Comalapa region of Chiapas, for example, the amount of rentable land contracted throughout the 1980s as Mexican owners dedicated larger tracts to cattle grazing each year. Refugees were left no choice but to move their families and homes to areas of greater land availability. Work was also scarce, and since Guatemalans depended on wage labor to supplement the small amount of food aid they received, they often had to follow the supply of jobs. Many with whom I spoke also noted problems they experienced with their Mexican neighbors in the competition for scarce resources. One man whose family had moved five times since their arrival in 1982 noted, "When we first entered one of the camps, the Mexican people were content with us. But after a while we noticed that they tired of us. They did not want us there and would not let us gather branches, firewood, or water."

Others noted exploitative labor practices to which Guatemalan workers were subjected, most notably the below-minimum wage they were paid for long hours of arduous work. Unfortunately, the barriers placed on refugee self-sufficiency during exile often pitted impoverished Mexicans against impoverished Guatemalans in the search for land and jobs in a region lacking in both. Refugees used this constant uprootedness as yet another basis for unification and alliance.

El Porvenir (The Future)

The following is a more detailed description of one camp, El Porvenir, situated directly on the border in the municipality of Las Margaritas. I will provide a brief overview of the characteristics of the camp and will focus specifically on the camp's modes of internal organization. These structures will then be related to their significance in the construction of community. I then provide a brief discussion of how this camp is an essential component of a much larger refugee community that has been formed in exile.

Approximately 150 families resided in El Porvenir, a large camp relative to others in Chiapas. In 1987, the Catholic Church was instrumental in facilitating refugee access to two large tracts of land, one on which the camp was located and another, approximately ten miles from this site, on which numerous camp communities farm cooperatively. Like all refugees, the inhabitants of El Porvenir had lived in numerous camps prior to this most recent settlement. The relative security of this camp made it unique and provided the residents with some semblance of stability after so many years in exile.

Basic homes, made of wooden boards lashed together by twine or vines and topped by an aluminum or cardboard-like material, were spaced throughout the camp. Most had an adjoining small plot of corn. Floors were made of pounded dirt and, until July 1992 when most families received gas-burning stoves, women cooked all of the family's meals over an open fire. Many women continued to use the fire to make tortillas and coffee in the morning since gas cylinders were expensive (costing in 1992 about twenty-nine new pesos), and refilling the tanks was a burdensome and time-consuming task.

One of the most interesting features of this camp was its ethnic and linguistic diversity; Q'anjob'ales from Ixcansán and Yolanhuits and Chujes from El Quetzal, Yuxquén, Aguacate, La Trinidad, Yalcastán, and Gracias á Díos lived side by side. While all inhabited the same area, five subcommunities formed, each with its own specific place within the camp. At one level, divisions were defined linguistically, as Q'anjob'ales lived in a central area between Chuj groups, while the Chuj, comprising about 95 percent of the camp population, divided themselves into four smaller subcommunities. Inhabitants of these subcommunities were most often from the villages to which their names referred.

Q'anjob'ales organized among themselves to begin their own community-run store, the earnings of which were used for medical emergencies. They were also able to obtain a corn mill that was managed by both men and women on a rotating basis. Two of the four Chuj subcommunities also had their own stores and mills which were managed in a similar fashion. Consequently, refugees maintained an identification with their communities of origin and often spoke nostalgically of their homes.

El Porvenir residents often crossed the invisible camp boundaries to come together as refugees, as Mayas, and as Guatemalans to create social institutions that served the camp as a whole. When asked why they organized together rather than by subcommunity, many noted that they had to join forces since, as one midwife stated, "We are all in the same place. There is injustice, and we need to defend our lives. For those reasons we are organized."

Representatives, health promoters, education promoters, and midwives were appointed by the Porvenir community to receive training from outside organizations and institutions and serve the needs of people in the camp. Often, though not always, individuals with some prior leadership experience were named to these posts. However, roles such as health promoter or teacher were new to many in El Porvenir, as they had little or no access to health and education services in their own villages in Guatemala. In El Porvenir, as in all camps, men dominated most leadership positions (except that of midwife), a trend that was challenged during the latter years of exile by a number of refugee women's organizations.

As Falla (1992) has noted in his research, tension remained between local and national refugee identities, yet local identities presented few obstacles to the creation of a larger-level group consciousness. Contrary to the experience of Guatemala's internally displaced living under army control in "model villages," where ethnic divisions were manipulated by the military to divide people and prevent them from "constituting themselves as authentic communities" (IGE 1989), refugees in Mexican camps successfully and creatively used their diversity as well as their common experiences to unite with one another.

THE PERMANENT COMMISSIONS AND MAMÁ MAQUÍN: TWO ORGANIZATIONS LINKING CAMPS, COMMUNITY, AND IDENTITY

The constant movement, displacement, and intermingling that Guatemalans experienced in exile enabled them to connect with one another on the basis of their shared experiences. In Guatemala, unless one migrated to the southern coastal plantations to work, a Chuj might never meet a Jakalteko or ladino peasant, whereas in Mexico they together attended training workshops aimed at education promoters or catechists, or they participated together in celebrations such as "International Women's Day."

The creation of a "Guatemalan Refugee" community was perhaps the most important development in prompting large-scale refugee organization, especially in their demands for direct participation in the negotiations for the conditions of their return to Guatemala. José Carlos Nolasco (1989:13) states, "the idea of the return is a point of union, of social cohesion within the camps." The refugees' demands to be included in a critical process affecting their lives was seen as an extension of the more general struggle for basic human rights in which they had been engaged since their arrival in Mexico. Falla (1992:213) notes that "demands that their rights be respected has been the force which has most significantly united the refugee community." The existence of such a strong community, combined with their constant struggle to have their human rights respected, necessitated the creation of organizational structures through which the community's demands and concerns could be voiced, represented, and addressed.

Two of these were the Permanent Commissions of Representatives of Guatemalan Refugees in Mexico (CCPP), comprised almost completely of indigenous refugee men, and Mamá Maquín, comprised solely of indigenous and ladina refugee women.

The Permanent Commissions

In 1986, Vinicio Cerezo was sworn in as the first civilian president Guatemala had had in twenty years. With this change in governmental leadership, many hoped that the time of La Violencia was over and that the Guatemalan people could at last begin to rebuild their lives and their country. Various popular movements, many of which arose directly out of the violence of the early 1980s, capitalized on newly opened, albeit small spaces within Guatemalan society. Shortly after his inauguration, refugees were informed by Cerezo, via his wife Raquel, who was sent to the camps, that secure and necessary conditions would shortly exist for their safe return. From 1986 through 1989 some three thousand Guatemalans acted on this hope and repatriated as individuals or small groups. Most, however, did not trust these good tidings and began to meet to devise a way in which to take more control over their own destiny. As one document states, the CCPPs were "born in response to the demands and worries of the refugees" (Noticias de Guatemala 1991).

At the same time, the military—which ultimately defined the boundaries of any opened spaces—began to close them once again. In the context of ongoing counterinsurgency warfare, human rights abuses continued and actually increased by 1990, Cerezo's last year in office. Repatriation slowed as refugees responded to the unending violence as well as to accusations made by high-level officials that they were subversives, guerrillas, and communists.[5]

Negotiations for an "organized, collective, and voluntary return," however, continued. This distinction between return and repatriation was clear in the language used by Guatemalan refugees and returnees and is crucial to understanding the emergence and development of the Permanent Commissions and Mamá Maquín. The term "return" rather than "repatriate" highlighted the importance of going back to Guatemala as an organized community rather than as a collection of individuals or families. It thereby recognized the strength, protection, and resilience that community cohesion offered.

From late 1987 to early 1988, in the context of rising hopes for peace and change in Guatemala, general assemblies were held in camps across Chiapas, Campeche, and Quintana Roo in which representatives from each camp were elected. Officials from the UNHCR, COMAR, and Mexican immigration service were on hand to witness the proceedings. The refugees elected a seventy-two-member body they named the Permanent Commissions of Representatives of Guatemalan Refugees in Mexico (CCPP), the basic initial goals of which were: (1) to initiate a direct dialogue with the Guatemalan government compelling it to comply with the terms of Esquipulas II; (2) to find available lands where returning groups could settle; and (3) to make the Guatemalan refugee situation known internationally.[6] Members were also responsible for traveling to Guatemala, always with international accompaniment, to locate and present to the government possible available lands where returning groups could settle. In El Porvenir, as in most camps, CCPP representatives were men who held leadership positions in Guatemala, sometimes as representatives, catechists, or health and education promoters.

New people were named sporadically to the CCPPs, though there was no established cycle of elections. The work was risky and difficult and carried with it no formal salary. Representatives traveled frequently and subsequently spent much time away from their families and income-generating activities, which made their work even more difficult. In general, CCPP representatives held community *asembleas* in the camps after their attendance at important meetings or visits to Guatemala. Through this type of gathering, people were able to ask questions, express doubts and support, and in general garner information about the most current events affecting their lives. The CCPPs also produced an informational bulletin, *Noticias del Retorno*, which was distributed throughout all of the Mexican camps.

The work of the CCPPs was known to all the refugees I interviewed, and most of them viewed their work with favor and solidarity. "We have to be supportive of the work of the Permanent Commissions," said one woman. "They talk of the return, the struggle, and how we are going to reach these goals." Overall, I found great support for the work of the CCPPs because refugees viewed them as their key to realizing their dream of returning to Guatemala.

MAMÁ MAQUÍN

During the initial stages of CCPP negotiations with the Guatemalan government regarding the refugees' return, the particular needs and demands of women (who comprised 52 percent of the population) were given little if any attention. Mamá Maquín, the mass Guatemalan refugee women's organization, emerged directly out of that void when a small group of women gathered in May 1990 to discuss how women in the camps could be incorporated into and mobilized for the return. Subsequently, the organization grew to a membership of approximately eight thousand women (Mamá Maquín 1993b; Billings 1995). Named for a Kekchí leader who was killed in the 1978 Panzós massacre, Mamá Maquín carried on in the martyr's spirit by providing a major public forum in which women across camp and state boundaries were able to voice concerns, define needs, and take action. By recognizing overlapping identities along gender, ethnic, class, and national lines, Mamá Maquín prompted the creation of yet another imagined community—that of *la Mujer Refugiada Guatemalteca.*

Mamá Maquín differed from the many projects that were created by and for women in exile, because from its inception it focused on raising the consciousness of women regarding their rights as women and as human beings. Objectives of the organization included defending women's rights to equality with men in education, health, work, and mobility; defending their right to organize; defending their right to conserve their language, dress, and identity as Guatemalans; and providing literacy programs so that these goals could be reached by women.[7] As one coordinator stated, "Through the Organization women realize that they have rights. Now no one says: we cannot speak because we are women. Now they all know that women are equal to men" (Mamá Maquín 1994:65).

While Mamá Maquín sponsored a number of projects, including a literacy campaign for women, members purposefully expanded the organization's focus since, as one Junta General member stated, "We have seen that if we organize by project, that the day the project ends, the organization ends. The objectives of Mamá Maquín have to do with women's rights. There is no end to this because we are always thinking about our rights." As the organization's newsletter put it, "Our demands should not be reduced to small-scale economic projects, but rather to return ourselves as active subjects, women with a gender, ethnic, and class consciousness in order to participate in social and national projects, where women play active roles that correspond to us, side by side with the men" (Mamá Maquín 1994:69).

In exile, the boundaries of community were broadened and with them some of the ways in which women organized were included. Through the work of Mamá Maquín many women came to new levels of consciousness about themselves and their importance to the maintenance and continuance of their communities. With this newfound recognition, many women challenged long held gender-based power structures and worked to create new kinds of communities from within.

THE RETURN TO GUATEMALA: IMPLICATIONS FOR ORGANIZING AND COMMUNITY

Until the Peace Accords were signed in December 1996, Guatemala was the only Central American country with an enduring, large-scale refugee population living outside national borders in camp communities. This proved to be problematic for the Guatemalan government since, as one NGO representative in Mexico City noted, "It's proof that there aren't conditions of security there. . . . Guatemala began to act on the idea of a return to show that its human rights record has improved" (USCR 1993:10). Stipulations outlined by the 1987 Esquipulas II Accords and the first of a series of UN-sponsored meetings of CIREFCA in 1989, combined with international pressures such as the possible naming of a UN-appointed human rights rapporteur and the threatened suspension of U.S. military aid, compelled the Guatemalan government finally to engage in negotiations with the Permanent Commissions.[8] The CCPPs were well prepared and in 1989 were able to publicly present a list of six demands—minimal conditions necessary for the refugees' return—through their participation in Guatemala's National Dialogue.

On 8 October 1992, after more than three years of negotiations, the CCPPs and the Guatemalan government signed an accord guaranteeing the six original conditions of return as well as one additional stipulation. The final accord stated that: (1) the return of the refugees must be a voluntary decision, under secure conditions and with dignity; (2) the right to free association and organization by the returnees must be recognized; (3) there must be international accompaniment of the returnees; (4) freedom of movement within Guatemala, along with free entry to and departure from the country for the returnees and members of the CCPPs, must be guaranteed; (5) the returnees must have the right to personal and communal life and security; (6) the returnees must have access to land; and (7) there must be continuing mediation of issues of dispute during the return and the establishment of a verification agency to oversee compliance with the accords.

The pressures on the refugee community to return to Guatemala were numerous and stemmed from both internal and external sources. While recognizing that theirs was a country still at war, many refugees wanted to return to recover their heritage. Others emphasized their identity as Guatemalans and the rights that accompanied their citizenship: "We are Guatemaltecos and we have rights in Guatemala," said one. In their own country, among their compatriots, many wanted to continue their struggle for better living conditions, human rights, and justice. It should be noted, however, that not all refugees wanted to return—either immediately or ever.

Push factors emanating from outside the refugee community included the continued unavailability land on which to plant and build more permanent housing, low wages, and decreasing assistance from COMAR and the UNHCR. In Chiapas, impoverished refugees competed with equally impoverished Mexicans for land, water, firewood, and jobs; in Campeche and Quintana Roo, unpredictable weather destroyed crops, and water and firewood were in short supply. Those who decided to return to Guatemala saw few prospects for their families in Mexico and wanted to reclaim their rights in Guatemala, as a community of campesino civilians and, for the most part, as indigenous Guatemalans. "We want to return together, everyone, to make a new community of those of us who sought refuge in Mexico."

On 20 January 1993, the first of numerous planned "collective and organized" returns began as approximately 2,480 refugees and some 240 international accompaniers crossed the Chiapas-Huehuetenango border at La Mesilla. The caravan of more than seventy-five buses snaked its way along the Pan American Highway and was greeted by cheering crowds at virtually every village and town intersection. Many of those returning had not seen their homeland in ten years; others, those born in exile, were experiencing this land for the first time—a place they had known previously only through the stories told by family and friends. The convoy's final destination, which would be reached many days later, was Polígono 14 of the northern Ixcán region. Here this first group of returnees began its resettlement process.

The term "return" rather than "repatriate" was emphasized by those participating in the collective *retornos* as it highlighted the importance of returning to Guatemala as a community rather than as an individual, single family, or small group of families. But the term "repatriate" has been encouraged by the Guatemalan government's representative organization, the National Commission to Aid Repatriates, Refugees and Displaced Persons (CEAR). Approximately 7,041 refugees were repatriated to Guatemala between 1984 and 1991 (CIREFCA 1992). Repatriates were never included within the guarantees negotiated by the CCPPs and did not have any concerted base of organizing power. In fact, no systematic follow-up of repatriates has been undertaken and scant information exists concerning their circumstances. The greater number of refugees in Mexico resisted individual repatriation, recognizing the strength, protection, and resilience that community cohesion provided.

From 1992 to 1999 over thirty thousand refugees participated in organized returns to Guatemala. Following a series of returns in 1993, the CCPP divided into three sectors, corresponding to the three guerrilla movements within the Unidad Revolucionaria Nacional Guatemalteca (URNG) and its areas of operation. In later years, some sectors broke completely with the URNG and by 1998 six different refugee organizations were arranging returns to Guatemala. Dispersed refugees throughout southern Mexico joined the return movement through the creation of ARDIGUA, the Dispersed Refugee Association of Guatemala.

After the signing of the Peace Accords in December 1996, the returns lost some of their political character and focused more on the social and economic needs of returnees (Gilbreth 1999). The last official return under the terms of the October 1992 Accord took place in April 1999, involving fifty-seven families (297 individuals) who had been in exile for seventeen years. These families were not part of the camp population but were members of ARDIGUA, demonstrating the changing nature of the composition of the returnee movement over the years. Approximately twenty thousand refugees decided to stay in Mexico, where the government has agreed to a process of naturalization. International accompaniment, organized in large part through the Guatemala Accompaniment Project (G.A.P.) has been key to ensuring the safety of return communities and has played an important role in their reconstruction within Guatemala. By 1999 the G.A.P. had established links between thirteen resettled communities in Guatemala and sponsoring communities in the United States.

With the formal end of the collective return process, the first phase of the October 1992 Accords, known as "transfer," was concluded. The Guatemalan government has reiterated its commitment to support any future repatriations under the terms of the Uprooted/Displaced Agreement of the Peace Accords, signed in June 1994 and put into effect with the signing of the Peace Accords.

CHALLENGES

Numerous challenges face all of the return communities. As Manz (1989) has noted in her work on repatriation and return, an important distinction must be made between relocation/return and the longer process of reintegration. The latter requires material assistance, human rights protection, and cooperation from governmental agencies and surrounding communities. In addition, the returnees themselves must be actively engaged in all projects and decisions that have an impact on their lives. Outside institutions and organizations must be willing to work in an open and cooperative manner with the community. The refugees, through the work of the CCPPs, successfully negotiated the terms of their return. What remains a serious obstacle is the government's and military's unwillingness to participate in a more protracted reintegration process, one that recognizes the demands and identity of the returnees' communities and organizations.

As Carol Smith (1990a:21) has observed, "How Guatemalans define their communities has been and will be the most significant determinant of Guatemala's political future." This chapter has outlined some of the major ways in which war, exile, and return have profoundly affected many Guatemalans' view of community. Perhaps most significant is the refugees' recognition that they are part of the Guatemalan nation. With this self-identification they demand a role in defining what the future of that nation will look like.

NOTES

Acknowledgments: Please note that all personal names included in this chapter have been changed to ensure anonymity. I want to thank Sasha Khokha for her extraordinary work in conducting interviews with women throughout Chiapas, pieces of which are included in this chapter. I want especially to thank all of the women and men who were willing to speak with me during my work in Mexico. This article is dedicated to all in the Guatemalan refugee community to whom I made a commitment to return to my own community and share their words of strength and inspiration.

Epigraph: This quotation comes from an interview conducted by one of the authors with a participant in a weaving project in Chiapas, Mexico, in 1987. See Anderson and Garlock 1988:22.

1. Five categories of displaced people were developed by the Association for the Advancement of the Social Sciences in Guatemala (AVANCSO 1992). These categories illustrate the complexity of the impact of military operations on civil society: (1) internally displaced-dispersed; (2) internally displaced—in the mountains; (3) recognized refugees; (4) unrecognized refugees; and (5) externally displaced (sometimes referred to as undocumented, but distinct from economic migrants). Unrecognized refugees are often included in the category of the externally displaced.

2. Mexico is not a signatory to either the 1951 U.N. Convention Relating to the Status of Refugees or its 1967 Protocol, and thus the category of "refugee" did not exist prior to reforms made in Mexico's General Population Law, Article 42 VI, in July 1990. Only Guatemalans living in camps were legally recognized as refugees, i.e., those "who have been threatened by general violence, foreign aggression, internal conflicts, massive human rights violations, or other circumstances that have greatly upset public order in their nation of origin" (USCR 1991:7).

3. Community was redefined in similar ways for those who populated and constructed the cooperatives of the Ixcán region, but Ricardo Falla (1992:213) notes that in exile the "experience [of community life is] more vast and deep rooted." The Communities of Population in Resistance (CPRs) underwent a similar process in internal exile.

4. For example, the San Francisco *finca* massacre (see Cultural Survival 1983) was one that spurred the flight of people from many surrounding villages.

5. See Manz (1988) and WOLA (1989). For example, then Minister of Defense Hector Gramajo stated in 1987 that the refugees' return "would create a series of complex problems for the Guatemalan government, problems which would range from family matters to guerrilla infiltration" (WOLA 1989:24).

6. There were more than seventy-two camps in the three states. In some cases smaller camps united with larger settlements to be represented as a whole.

7. Only 34 percent of all camp refugee women in Chiapas can read and write in Spanish. By age group, the breakdown is as follows: 12–19 years, 67 percent; 20–34 years, 26 percent; 35 and older, 9 percent (Mamá Maquín 1994).

8. The CCPPs first presented the refugees' demands to the Cerezo administration on 20 March 1988, after refugees who owned parcels in the Ixcán were notified that if they did not return to Guatemala in ninety days to reclaim their land, they would lose all property rights.

CLARK TAYLOR

6 Challenges of Return and Reintegration

WHILE THE previous chapter focused on the experiences of Guatemalan refugees in Mexico, this one looks at the issues those refugees faced when they returned to their homeland, to the villages they fled in terror twelve years earlier. I want to address the origins of the contrasting subcultures, developed under quite different conditions, of those who fled to Mexico and those who stayed in Guatemala.

This chapter chronicles and analyzes the experience of the mostly Maya population of one village, Santa María Tzejá, located in the Ixcán region of the northwestern Guatemalan Department of El Quiché, near the Mexican border. Roughly half the Santa María population fled to refuge in Mexico, first to the state of Chiapas, from which they were later relocated to the states of Campeche and Quintana Roo. The other half of the residents were either captured or gave themselves up and were, after a time, allowed to form the core of the re-population of the village. At that time village lands vacated by the refugees were given over to others who would be friendly to the army. These people were told that the refugees had "abandoned" the land for subversive reasons. New occupants were thus given to understand that the land would be theirs forever. The refugees did return, however—in May of 1994—and the occupants were induced to leave to make way for them.

First settled in 1970 as a rain forest colonization project, the village of Santa María Tzejá was destroyed in February 1982, when the rampaging Guatemalan army stormed through. In the months that followed, people made decisions to seek refuge in Mexico or to take their chances with the army and stay. Those in Mexico then adapted to their new circumstances and were closely controlled but free from the humiliating domination of the Guatemalan army. Those who stayed in Guatemala had to deal with that humiliation. In the years that followed, the two groups formed contrasting cultural patterns, patterns that would have to be reconciled when the refugees returned. That reintegration was just the first of the challenges they would face. Other issues had to do with development, human rights, the ongoing effects of trauma, and defining space outside the army's control.[1]

Santa María Tzejá is important because it is one of the few Guatemalan villages where those who fled and those who stayed behind were reunited following the refugee return accords reached on 8 October 1992. It thus represented a kind of ideal "laboratory" of reintegration in which to examine the challenges returnees faced. Santa María returnees had to confront many problems on their return, but at least they were surrounded by relatives and friends of the same Maya language group, K'iche' (both groups also had a small proportion of ladinos). If the challenges could not be met in Santa María, the chances were even worse in places where the variables were even more complex. If the people of Santa María could resolve their difficulties, they could perhaps provide a model for others.

SANTA MARÍA TZEJÁ: MICROCOSM OF STATE TERROR

The full force of the army's savage campaign fell on Santa María on the afternoon of Saturday, 13 February 1982. Word had already knifed through the population that nearly the entire population of nearby La Trinitaria had been slaughtered only three days earlier; just two inhabitants survived to spread the news. On the morning of the 13th, men from Santa María whose *parcelas* were close to neighboring San José la Veinte saw smoke billowing up from that direction and guessed the burning had started there. They hurried to warn the people of Santa María that they would be next.[2]

Given two hours' warning—the time it would take the army to arrive—people fled in terror. On any given day family members would be scattered throughout the village, and this day was no exception. People frantically searched for their families, but in many cases it was impossible to find them all in time. Most precious possessions, including corn-grinding stones, were buried. The destination of most of the villagers was the parcelas, located from thirty to ninety minutes from the center by foot. Once in their parcelas, families found hiding places where they spent months in isolated terror. Normal rainfall in a rain forest area, unimaginable for those who have not experienced it, lashed at them as they braced for its fury without shelter.

One man's search for his wife and two daughters ended in grief with the discovery of their bodies. Two days later, another man was with his mother, his wife, and their six children. Slowed in their flight by the fragile health of his mother, he left the group in a ravine and took his eldest soon with him to look for a more secure hiding place. Before they had gone very far, they heard gunfire coming from the direction of the ravine. The man's five-year-old son survived by hiding behind a bush, from which he saw the rest of his family killed by machine gun fire from an army patrol. The boy's little sister survived the initial gunfire, only to be thrown into the air and bayoneted before his eyes. The man lost his mother, wife, and four of their children, along with other members of their extended family. Nine in all were murdered in that massacre.

From their parcelas families made contact with people on neighboring land and began to sort options. A few left within a couple of weeks and found their way to Mexico, ten to fifteen miles away, through heavily forested terrain. Others were captured or gave themselves up in response to a government-sponsored "amnesty" assuring them that they would not be harmed if they came out. Roughly half the population held out on their land, expecting the army to leave eventually, at which time they could return to rebuild their lives. These people quickly devised ways of communicating with each other, including writing on the backs of banana leaves, to develop and maintain a form of resistance. Gradually the army lured defectors who gave away the group's secrets, at which time all food was burned and survivors were reduced to living like savages, as one put it. After staying on their land for seven months on average, they left, small group by small group, to take refuge in Mexico.

Refuge in Mexico: Survival and Learning

The traumatized population that crossed the border into the Mexican state of Chiapas found itself in the company of tens of thousands who had fled the devastation in other villages. Together they told their story to the outside world and looked for ways to rebuild their shattered lives.

An initial warm welcome from Mexican Maya campesinos soon gave way to vexation and resentment on the part of the receiving population toward this overwhelming flood of refugees. The United Nations High Commissioner for Refugees (UNHCR) was called in to help. Its efforts were channeled through the Mexican refugee agency COMAR, which had originally been created to respond to refugees from El Salvador's civil war. But the most effective and compassionate assistance came from the Roman Catholic diocese of Chiapas, under the progressive leadership of Bishop

Samuel Ruíz. His commitment to the refugees was the same as that to the other people of his diocese, and he sought to empower them to shape their own lives and future. With his help the refugees began to offer a progressive form of education to their children (Manz 1988a).

After just two years, a majority of the Guatemalan refugees in Chiapas were taken, largely against their will, from Chiapas to the Mexican states of Campeche and Quintana Roo. This move included nearly all those who had fled from Santa María Tzejá, the majority of whom went to camps in Campeche. Padre Luis Gurriarán, organizing pastor of Santa María in the late 1960s, said that one of the underlying reasons for the relocation was to remove the refugees from the influence of Bishop Ruíz. It was true, he said, that another reason was to prevent military conflict on the border, but the third official reason—to make the refugees more secure—was merely a pretext.

Over the course of the decade the refugees spent in Campeche (1984–94), control of their movement and activities was relaxed somewhat. The experience there became more and more what one woman described as "a school for us. We learned many things in Mexico. We had freedom of expression and we learned about rights, rights in general, as well as women's rights. . . . Back in Guatemala we would never have been able to gain that learning. [Before the violence] women couldn't participate or perhaps we could participate, but because our culture didn't support it, we ourselves devalued ourselves in our activities. By contrast, in Mexico we received help from non-governmental organizations, so we began to receive courses, many things."

During the year before their return, the pace of learning among the adults picked up. Many were enrolled in human rights workshops and, in the last months, in daily afternoon meetings to prepare for the return. Among other things, they studied the constitution of Guatemala and international human rights documents. The adaptive culture of the refugees in Mexico had increasingly become a culture of learning.

THOSE WHO STAYED: A CULTURE OF FEAR

The experience of Santa Maríans who stayed in Guatemala contrasted sharply with that of their friends and relatives who made it across the Mexican border. Their life involved a constant interaction with threat and fear. Psychologists, including Elizabeth Lira in Chile, have studied the life-distorting effects of chronic fear. "Daily life changes. There is the constant fear of pain, loss, even of loss of life itself" (Lira and Castillo 1991). Informants spoke of the fear of organizing, of doing anything that would raise the suspicions of the army. Those who raised questions about the mandatory service in civil patrols were accused of being guerrillas, which made them potential targets of persecution. Any talk of human rights was associated with guerrilla activity. One man who courageously refused to take his turn in the civil patrols was given three choices: rejoin the patrol, leave the village, or be killed. He left for three years, only to return with the refugees in 1994.

These profoundly different experiences of the two halves of Santa María Tzejá created broadly contrasting subcultures: a culture of learning and a culture of fear. Anticipating the return, the army did all it could to ensure that the two groups would not find common ground. The army's framing point was that the refugees were allied with the guerrillas, and in army propaganda the guerrillas had been demonized as enemies of the people of Guatemala. Human rights, a central theme in the education of the refugees, was wrapped in the same demonic clothing as the guerrillas—"human rights are of the guerrillas," several informants said they had been told. Families who had stayed in Guatemala were threatened with the message that if they involved themselves with the returnees, the violence of 1982 was likely to happen again.

In spite of all that, the original settlers who had stayed in Santa María looked forward to the return of the refugees, many of whom were their close relatives and friends, after a twelve-year separation. The occupants, who had been invited by the army to take over lands vacated by the refugees, agreed after contentious negotiations to vacate them, once they were paid for the improvements they had made. On the Mexican side of the border, refugee representatives from all the camps had negotiated a set of accords with the government, signed 8 October 1992, enabling them to return in a dignified, organized, and secure way. These accords provided freedom of movement, freedom from service in civil patrols and the army, the right to land, and the right to be accompanied by international observers. Most of the Santa María refugees returned in May 1994 to an enthusiastic welcome from their fellow villagers.[3]

Refugee Return: Challenges of Reintegration

Problems of adjusting to the dramatically different experiences of the two groups began almost immediately. The refugees were organized and generally confident—once they got past their initial anxiety of stepping back onto land they had fled, as they said, like animals. Those who stayed, by contrast, had not been allowed to do anything of their own choosing in an organized way, and had had to hunker down under military domination in order to survive. People who had endured the rule of the army now found themselves overwhelmed by the energy and organization of the returnees, whom they found themselves resenting. Every detail of life about which there were differences became a source of division between the two groups.

The impact of army propaganda was evident two months after the return, when I spent a month in the village. Women who had stayed in the country said, in various settings but as with one voice, "We don't know those people; we don't know what they stand for." The returnee women had organized themselves into a group called Mamá Maquín, a group the army had tagged as subversive. In this as in other matters, the two factions of villagers based their actions on contrasting views of how to relate to the army. Those who had stayed in Guatemala wanted to express willingness to cooperate with the army, possibly through formation of an unarmed civil patrol, whereas returnees wanted nothing to do with the army. They would not deliberately provoke the army, they said, but they would go to any lengths not to let it influence how they lived their lives. Both sides desperately wanted to avoid any "return to 1982," but each feared the other's way of dealing with the military.

Another issue involved attitudes toward guerrillas. For those who had stayed, armed resistance was the devil the army had painted it as. Returnees had a more nuanced view, often supporting the guerrillas' goals but opposing their violent tactics. Yet another contested area was the question of who should be teaching the children. Accustomed to deferring to authority figures, those who stayed believed that their children would get a real education only if they were taught by state-certified teachers. Returnees, by contrast, were convinced that the uncertified "education promoters," young people who had learned to teach in Mexico, would provide students with a far more relevant and effective education. And so it was, issue by issue; those who stayed and those who returned came down on opposite sides in debates over common concerns.

Yet as the months passed and the first anniversary of the return approached, the disagreements became less pronounced. One division that took longer to heal concerned, as one might expect, religion, where values and practices are associated with the nature of God. Lay religious leaders, called catechists, commissioned by priests to manage local religious affairs and distribute the pre-consecrated host in the mass, found themselves accustomed to fundamentally different ways of interpreting the faith. Catechists with the returnees linked their Christian beliefs with social change and justice, while catechists who stayed were conditioned to avoid any challenge to the social order. But even there, differences did not lead to hostility. Patience prevailed on all sides, and for that credit goes to the returnees, who were determined not to provoke division. One general meeting, for example, called to elect a health committee was attended only by returnees. Rather than elect only returnees to the group, those in attendance decided to postpone the decision until other villagers could participate.

The schools became a major healing force in the community. Several factors contributed to this: the enthusiasm and effective work of the education promoters, uncertified in Guatemala but experienced in teaching in Mexico; the eagerness of returnee parents to have their children educated; and the support of the Needham (Massachusetts) Congregational Church, which entered into a partnership with the village, agreeing to pay the promoters so they could teach full-time. But the key factor in the village's becoming a site for a much-sought-after middle school was the decision by Randall Shea, a North American, to accompany the Santa María returnees back to the village. He had worked with them in the Campeche camp as part of his work with the North American solidarity group Witness for Peace. In January 1995 he brought his vision of progressive education to fruition with the enrollment of more than forty students in the new middle school. By October 1997 the first thirty-one students graduated, all but one of whom went on to attend high school on scholarships Shea secured. The middle school soon became a magnet for surrounding towns, and within two years of its inception students from outside Santa María were attending classes there.

Within the first four years of the return, then, the focus shifted from mutual suspicion, manifested at every turn, to a focus on the schools and the general development of the community. By August 1998 this remote village had some thirty-three students in high school (three of whom had completed middle school in Mexico), and nine students in the university (all of whom had completed high school in Mexico). One year later those figures had grown to forty-three in high school and eleven at the university. Some of these students' parents had spent their youths working as little more than slaves on the plantations; now their children were studying at levels they could not have imagined even a few years earlier.

REFUGEE RETURN: THE CHALLENGE OF DEVELOPMENT

Social reintegration of the community was the first challenge for the community of Santa María, but it was not the only one. A second task was to distinguish the sound from the spurious in developing the economic life of the community, an arena framed by the larger context of the world economy. With the Cold War at an end, industrialized nations shifted emphasis from containing and rolling back communism—the stimulus for U.S. support of counterinsurgency forces against guerrilla movements like the one in Guatemala—to creating a stable environment for capitalist business interests. To that end, money was made available for "development projects" with the underlying purpose of dismantling guerrilla forces and pacifying the areas in which they had fought.

Development issues in Santa María Tzejá unfolded in the context of the ongoing Guatemalan peace process described in the introduction to this book. Outside nations made substantial sums of money available for the economic development of Ixcán, the area in which the village is located. At the heart of the matter, however, was whether "development" would be something essentially "done to" the area, or whether it would be in some real sense under the control of the people affected by it, and responsive to their vision. Therein lay the challenge.

With all the preparation the refugees had received in the area of human rights, they were little prepared to sort through the seductive issues involved in economic development. As refugees, no matter how hard they worked, they never had enough land or resources to become independent of external agencies, and they had become used to receiving what they needed from external sources. So they were not prepared for what lay ahead after they crossed back over the border. Before they left Mexico, they had been promised, as one man said, "a great deal of help on the part of various agencies that would be giving money, especially the European Economic Community—which had designated various millions of dollars for the development of the Ixcán. Also, UNHCR, before we came here, had told us they would have programs, as they called them, of 'rapid impact,' in which there would be, for example, one head of cattle for each family. There would be twenty-five chickens for every family as well."

He went on to speak of his disillusionment that many of the promises had gone unfulfilled. The ones that had been kept—a cardamom drier, corn-grinding mills, and so on—all had one thing in common: their dependence on external funding. This is unremarkable in one sense, as the refugees returned with nothing and could not create resources out of thin air. But the underlying question is whether the community was in control of the agenda, and whether the outcome of the process would result in their sustained economic well-being and relative independence. Would they become "historical social subjects," in Paulo Freire's sense—people with the power and vision to manage their own destiny (Freire 1970)?

Padre Beto Ghiglia, a priest at the local parish that serves Santa María along with a hundred other villages, noted three kinds of development. The first was the people-centered type imagined by Freire, "a type of development that doesn't violate nature, that respects the rights of all the communities, that is available to everyone, and, above all, to the poorest and those most affected by the violence." This is the most difficult type to promote with the funding sources, he said, which want quick, photographable results.

The second type of development in Padre Beto's model was promoted by non-governmental agencies and was more about building things and offering services. Agencies have budgets and must disburse funds by a given deadline in order to receive new funding. Officials of these agencies spoke of their commitment to involving the people, who in turn felt they had been heard by the funders. As important as these projects might have been, they did not address the issues of political empowerment, nor did they get at underlying structural issues like the distribution of land and wealth.

The third type of development, Padre Beto noted, was linked to the global economy and involved big infrastructural projects that promise roads, potable water, electricity—all undeniable benefits to local communities. But, as he pointed out, they were tied in with the oil and big timber interests. This kind of development was also supported by the army, which saw its interests tied to the globalization strategies of the national government.

All of this is very complex, but it comes back finally to the people-centered perspective. If local people control the planning and the vision, they can fit agency projects into their long-term interests. And if there is enough "people power," there may be enough political force to bend global economic interests to the needs of the community and allow it to thrive in a holistic way.

In Santa María Tzejá the jury is still out on the development challenge. But there are some very hopeful signs. In interviews conducted in June 1997 there was still not much evidence of systematic long-range planning regarding economic production. One respondent, when asked about planning mechanisms, could only point to the committee of the cooperative that laid out projects and tasks for the current year. But by August 1998 the picture had changed. An agronomist had been employed by the cooperative to assist the community in moving in the direction of organic farming, including the production of organic cardamom and rice crops for sale on the world market through strategies that avoid many of the profit-diluting middlemen in the commercial process. One of the agronomist's proposals was the use of irrigation pumps to make possible the growing of crops in the dry season as a means of increasing income.

These hopeful signs may still be overwhelmed by the oil and timber interests, who appear to be hell-bent on turning the rain forest into a desert, with catastrophic consequences for Guatemalans and the rest of the world. What is clear is that the people of this one village, at least, are making a valiant effort to wrest economic progress from very difficult conditions. The added hope is that as the young people return from high school and college, they will generate additional ideas that can anchor economic development in the initiative and vision of the people.

REFUGEE RETURN: THE CHALLENGE OF HUMAN RIGHTS

Beyond reintegration and development, the third challenge returnees face is the incorporation of human rights into the reality of everyday life. Here the task is enormous. The Guatemalan constitutional provisions guaranteeing human rights were largely unknown in the area before the return of the refugees. The army had been the unquestionable law in the Ixcán region for twelve years, and the very notion of human rights was demonized by being linked with the guerrillas. One rural organization south of the village used the constitution to argue that men were not obligated to serve in the civil patrols. Its leaders were threatened and many were killed.

In Santa María the process of reintegration of returnees and those who stayed, while contentious and difficult, did move to resolution without violence. And the army, which so effectively sowed division in many other communities, found no major opening to foment conflict here. In the absence of open conflict, human rights did not become a pivotal issue. Yet the active observance of human rights in the community was dependent on a growing level of consciousness and commitment to them strong enough to prevent their being swept away in some emergency or social breakdown.

Shortly after the return, the people of Santa María, under the active prodding of the returnees, elected a group of five "human rights promoters," people charged with educating the community on human rights issues. In November 1995 the group was functioning but in a very limited way, in part due to a serious accident that befell its leader. But the members were attending workshops outside the community sponsored by the United Nations and other groups and were making an effort to replicate the workshops in the community, albeit with meager results. Some were still afraid of the whole concept. Others told the promoters that, given the lack of human rights violations at the local level, more pressing matters required their attention. By February 1998 the leader of the human rights group had announced that the group's work henceforth would be to infuse human rights principles into all ongoing activities and decision making in the community, as this was a more viable way of increasing human rights awareness than was offering workshops.

But other factors worked to enlarge the consciousness of human rights in the village. The schools, primary and middle, have been at the center of the effort. Here the progressive vision of the education promoters and of Randall Shea have had real impact. As of August 1999, all of the teachers in the school were from the community. They had been trained to use "popular education" techniques, which draw on the experience of the students themselves in the context of community life to build the curriculum. In this framework, the rights of girls and women receive particular attention. Another important theme has been the role of the environment in human rights, with emphasis on environmental protection as vital to human well-being. Students read the most progressive works on local and regional human rights history. Ricardo Falla's book, *Massacres in the Jungle,* which describes the violence in the Ixcán in the early eighties in vivid detail, is studied by middle school students, as is the Spanish-language version of Eduardo Galeano's massive work, *The Open Veins of Latin America.*

Perhaps the most moving and powerful expression of commitment to human rights in the village came with the writing and production of a play called *The Past Is with Us.* Based on the testimony of adults about the violence that destroyed the village, the play was written by Randall Shea. Its actors were middle school students who in effect played their parents. *The Past Is with Us* features the human rights articles of the Guatemalan constitution and shows how they were violated by the massacres and indiscriminate killing perpetrated on the people of Santa María. It won a regional award and has been taken on tour throughout the country. It was filmed on tour by the BBC when it was performed in another village, where people were profoundly moved when they realized that the same horror they had experienced had happened repeatedly elsewhere in the country. This play was performed many times in Santa María, each time deepening the consciousness of the central role of human rights for the people.

In an August 1998 interview, one of the human rights leaders described workshops he had attended that were keyed to developing mechanisms at the local level for the handling of minor to moderate crimes. The idea was to develop a group of trained mediators who would work to resolve disputes and respond to crimes with sanctions decided by, and limited to, the local communities. By the summer of 1999, three "judicial promoters" from Santa María had been selected to join with representatives from other villages to receive training in national law and options available for enforcing rights. Since the national criminal justice system continues to be ineffective, this program could become a building block in a stronger program of law enforcement. In a country where crime is rampant and lynchings are carried out by communities desperate to control criminals, the development of an effective mediation system would be an important step for human rights.

REFUGEE RETURN: THE CHALLENGE OF TRAUMATIZED MEMORY

The fourth challenge returnees face—in addition to reintegration, development, and human rights—is to find ways to heal the terrible trauma of memories of violence, torture, flight, survival under unimaginable conditions, and the brutal deaths of loved ones. The mother whose thirteen-year-old daughter was machine-gunned by the army cannot talk about her tragedy without becoming distraught, and suffers from clinical depression, as do other members of the community. A health promoter spoke of nightmares, stomach disorders, and chronic headaches that stem from the violence, of hurt that cannot be healed with medicines.

A team of psychologists working in four countries—Chile, Guatemala, El Salvador, and Argentina—developed a theoretical framework for thinking about the trauma to memory resulting from state-sponsored violence by repressive regimes. They started with the notion of "chronic fear" and added the concept of "sequential traumatization," which includes experience with political repression, and then added the image of "frozen grief," in which the usual healing process is blocked and the pain of loss is carried forward without relief. Finally the group added the contribution of the Salvadoran psychologist priest, Martín Baró, who wrote about "psychosocial trauma," which includes the social aspects of trauma when whole communities are attacked or destroyed (Becker 1994). This discussion points to the profound nature of the damage created by state terrorism and violence, to the unhealed psychological wounds that last for years when not dealt with. The people of Guatemala generally, except for the elites, carry this ongoing trauma of memory, and Santa María is no exception. When they returned in May 1994, the refugees themselves were only dimly aware of the nature of the damage they carried in their psyches. According to the health promoter quoted above, they had been told in Mexican clinics that some of their physical ailments were caused by the violence, but they had no strategy for dealing with them.

After the return to Santa María, a turning point came when Randall Shea invited a psychologist friend of his to spend three months in the village. The man was able to provide a safe environment in which many people felt comfortable enough to tell their stories. They would feel better, and begin to heal, he said, as they unburdened themselves. The individual testimonies led to group meetings where further sharing took place in a supportive atmosphere.

These testimonies, with the permission and encouragement of the adults who gave them, became the basis for the play *The Past Is with Us*. That play, of course, not only had human rights themes, but also served as a catharsis for those who chose to experience it. For some, the play was too controversial because of the political danger it posed. But for an increasing number, including most of the returnees, it had great emotional impact as they saw their own lives affirmed and their pain externalized beyond their own bodies.

Another trauma of memory is rooted in the fact that the remains of those massacred in February 1982 still lie in the unmarked graves where they were hastily buried by their loved ones. The families determined to exhume the remains and have them transferred to the village cemetery where they will be properly laid to rest. This effort is currently underway and is being carried out publicly to remind the community what happened. A monument will be erected to ensure that the dead are not forgotten. The exhumation has been preceded by some months of education and preparation for the community, so that it can achieve maximum healing with minimal political fear. Fully dealing with the trauma of memory may take generations, but at least in Santa María the returnees have found a way, along with those who stayed, to initiate the process.

REFUGEE RETURN: THE CHALLENGE OF CREATING SPACE FREE OF ARMY CONTROL

The final challenge the returnees face is to enlarge the political space in which they can move free of military domination and harassment. This is a perilous undertaking, and false steps could lead to disaster. Prior to the return, the army was the state power in the Ixcán, despite the presence of a civilian in the presidential chair. People were regularly summoned to the military base to answer for one suspicion or another. Allies of the army reported on other members of the population, creating threats from unknown sources.

After the return, even when the community made clear that it would not stand for military interference, the army made its presence known in a threatening way. In October and November of 1995, for example, the army entered the community on three occasions. The first intrusion took place when some ambassadors were supposed to visit the village but failed to arrive when all helicopters were commandeered to respond to a massacre in another village. The army came that day even though there were no ambassadors to protect, and its presence sent a chill through the community, made deeper by knowledge that the army had perpetrated the massacre the day before. Then a company of 500 soldiers passed through in early November. Two weeks later, when I was present, a group of 150 soldiers in full battle gear, faces blackened, appeared uninvited and stayed overnight in the center, yet another living nightmare for people whose existence had been terrorized by this same army.

The returnees in Santa María, working closely now with those who stayed, have taken important steps to enlarge the sphere of their influence in the area, which means less room for army dominance. The chief agent in this effort has again been the schools. Randall Shea has traveled to neighboring villages to invite parents in those communities to send their children to the middle school. At first the parents were reluctant, precisely because they had been told not to get involved in any way with the supposedly subversive returnees. But when the parents saw the advantages children in Santa María were gaining, they changed course and sent some of their children to school there. These young people are treated exactly like those from Santa María, and are just as likely to get scholarships for further study in high school. This outreach of the schools has gone a long way to break down the barriers of suspicion in the area and to reduce army control. In fact, Padre Beto once said that the army saw Santa María as "lost territory," and that it was determined that there should be "no more Santa Marías."

Since the signing of the peace accords, the army's presence has been more muted. The accords call for the army to limit itself to defending national borders except in stated emergencies. That provision of the accords, however—along with many others—required amendments to the Guatemalan constitution. In a May 1999 national public referendum, after a right-wing and racist campaign, all the proposed amendments were defeated, leaving the implementation of the accords in limbo. Rising crime rates and social volatility have led some to long for the army to take a stronger role in maintaining order. Others believe that the army is in fact behind some of the disruption so as to create conditions where its heavier hand will be needed and welcomed. A few communities have gone so far as to offer to form a new version of the civil patrols on a voluntary basis. In another maneuver, the army's civilian affairs section has made resources available to local communities to support their festivals, an insidious interference in civilian life.

Santa María Tzejá is determined to take care of its own local policing needs. In response to a recent robbery in the community, leaders made a civilian arrest and transported the alleged violators to the nearest holding facility and judge, which required plane fare for the three suspects and five other adults to the far-off city of Cobán. But that was a very expensive undertaking, for which the village had to borrow money. Should there be an increase of such problems the village would be sorely pressed.

In the whole of the Ixcán, with more than one hundred villages, there are only five police, with a maximum of three on duty at a time. They have one car, no radio, and very little capacity to respond to anything. The military, meanwhile, has 984 soldiers at its base. Santa María is exceptional in its determination to keep its own house in order. In a time of increasing crime and disorder in the region the army has a massive opening to reassert its power in the area. When Padre Luis Gurriarán recently was asked for his response to a list of problems in the Ixcán, he voiced the view that the army is in fact working to regain its power in the region. An astute observer, Padre Luis spends a considerable part of his time in the Ixcán and his observation is ominous.

DREAMS, REALITIES, AND REALISTIC PROSPECTS

These five challenges have been formidable for the returnees to Santa María Tzejá, though the village has been remarkably successful in addressing them. But the community is surrounded by others that refused to let returnees recover their original lands. And there are nearby communities made up exclusively of returnees, where deep divisions have so torn them apart—some say with infiltrated army provocateurs—that they are unable to function effectively.

The people of Santa María have lively dreams for themselves, their children, and their children's children. They long, at a minimum, to recapture the momentum they had before the violence, when they had been making impressive gains in economic prosperity and social cohesion. At that time cardamom was "green gold," a cash crop that brought enough to move beyond the necessities of survival. Most families had had a small herd of cattle that served as another measure of wealth and well-being. Life had been difficult then, as well, living as they did between the call of the guerrillas to resist and the determination of the army to defeat the guerrillas. But the future seemed hopeful at that time.

Now these dreams, nurtured by positive images of the past, are enriched by the reintegration of the community, the formal end of the civil war that tore at the region, and the vitality of the schools in the community and the opportunity some young people have to study outside the community. One older man who began life as a plantation hand spoke of his dream that his children or grandchildren would become national legislators and ambassadors. The leap in the content of dreams from one generation to the next is enormous.

Even in the face of such vibrant dreams and relatively high morale, current realities are sobering. Though less an isolated island of progressive reintegration than it was in the past, in large measure because it provides educational and other services to neighboring villages, Santa María still exists as something of an anomaly in present-day Guatemala. It has gifted internal leadership and external support from Padre Luis, Randall Shea with the schools, and the Needham church partnership. But the fact that surrounding communities lack these advantages can give rise to resentment. And the possibility cannot be ignored that, if this one village becomes too successful and the army regains former levels of control, Santa María could be seen as a threat.

Beyond these speculative cautions, current reality presents very substantial obstacles to the economic improvement of the community. While external resources have resulted in major infrastructural projects—a new cooperative store, a new large community building, a new health clinic, a house for visitors, a new school—these changes have not brought appreciable improvement to the long-term economic viability of the community. People say again and again that there is no market for their products. In the summer of 1999 there was a lot of talk about shifting to niche markets with organic cardamom and organic rice, but the hoped-for gains were speculative at best. What can be said for Santa María is that it is probing every marginal frontier possible to find ways to expand income. The hiring of a skilled agronomist is one clear indi cation of this.

While future prospects are difficult to anticipate, several potentia threats can be named. One is the possible exhaustion of the land. On way of defining the issue is summed up in the saying that "the voca tion of this land is forest, not agriculture." The top soil is fragile, anc with increasingly intensive use it becomes less productive. And as the rain forest is reduced year by year, the amount of rain is reduced, fur ther limiting the yields. A second threat is the likely extraction of oi from the area, with resulting ecological damage and distortion of the social fabric of the area. A third is the need for employment as popu lation growth exceeds the availability of land. With the expansion o roads, the Ixcán may well become viable for the finishing *maquila* fac tories that would provide exploitative employment to the area. Peo ple would be desperate enough for work to jump at the jobs, whicl would take them from their families for long periods with minimum compensation. The fourth threat was noted by Padre Luis: the move by the army to reassert something like the level of control it had dur ing the war.

These potential threats are formidable, but they are not inevitable The hope is that a village like Santa María will find enough ways tc improve economic production that the community will be viable withir an acceptable level of its traditional culture. Hope lies, as well, in the possible return of its young people as graduates from high school anc college with ideas for sustainable alternative development. In Augus 1999, several of the Santa María university students detailed specifi proposals for development in the Ixcán, based on their studies in agron omy and law. The analysis that introduced their document and the pro posals themselves were very impressive.

One important factor in this mix is that, out of its commitment born of years of violence, the external solidarity organizations will maintair a focus on the rural areas of Guatemala, to provide support anc resources in ways that promote sustainable development. At a mini mum such hope serves notice to the military that it cannot act withou scrutiny and promises the likely intervention of the outside worlc should the army turn abusive. But such outside support can also pro vide important links to ideas and resources that can serve to empowe the people to build a future they can be proud of.

Notes

1. I learned the history of Santa María Tzejá through many visits to the village beginning in December 1985. In 1987 my local church, the Needham (Massachusetts) Congregational Church, began a partner relationship with the village that involves twice-yearly delegations. I have made additional trips to the village, many of them for research purposes, since 1994. A more formal source of the history was given in an interview by Padre Luis Gurriarán, the organizing pastor who brought the original population of the village together in the late 1960s. The transcribed interview, "History of Santa María Tzejá," was translated by Kay Taylor in 1993.

2. This information and what follows came from many conversations I had over the years, most notably in July 1994 just after the refugees returned home, when their memories of the violence were freshly stimulated. In house after house, individuals described the exact time of day on that Saturday, 13 February, when the army came to their part of town.

3. The refugee accords, signed between the Guatemalan government and representatives of the refugees, called Permanent Commissions, were a unique accomplishment by which a refugee population negotiated the conditions for its own return.

DOMINGO HERNÁNDEZ IXCOY

7   A Maya Voice: The Maya of Mexico City

TO START out, I would like to clarify that this is the first time I have given a talk on the refugees living in Mexico City.[1] At other meetings we focused more on the conditions the Guatemalan people have had to endure—the situation in the interior of the country, the situation of the refugees in the camps in southern Mexico—but the Maya refugees in Mexico City are little known and their situation is somewhat different from that of those in other places. Here in the United States, as in Canada, refugees are more concentrated in defined locations. That makes for better communication and perhaps better understanding.

The large number of Indian refugees in Mexico City are greatly dispersed. Current estimates [as of 1991] indicate that there are roughly 45,000 Maya refugees in Mexico City. Of these, only 2,200 are acknowledged by the United Nations High Commissioner for Refugees (UNHCR/ACNUR), which means that roughly 42,000 are scattered throughout the city and live in very difficult circumstances. One of the refugees' problems in Mexico City is that the least-known people are the ones who receive the least help and are also the least organized.

On one occasion my *compañeros* and I were discussing our situation as refugees in Mexico City. One person in our group said, "Our situation as refugees in Mexico City is like being on a hanging bridge which carries us but is not solid and is always moving; always on the defensive, trying to hide our identity, having to speak Mexican, having to accustom ourselves to a number of things." We found three areas in particular where the refugees have trouble: their economic situation; their lack of unity and organizational structures; and the cultural issue, principally that of maintaining an identity as Maya.

Regarding the economic situation, for a variety of reasons, most of the refugees work in the lowest-paid jobs in Mexico City. Many of them are illiterate, and the great majority lack papers or legal documents. They have to pass themselves off as people from Oaxaca or Chiapas to avoid discovery and deportation. Some make even less than minimum wage, and the minimum wage in Mexico is truly pitiful and miserable.

It doesn't buy more than one or two meals. Poverty is the typical economic condition of Guatemalan refugees in Mexico City. Many children who have completed elementary school at home in Guatemala cannot continue their schooling in Mexico because they lack the necessary papers. Then there are children who were born in Mexico City and are now five or six years old. They cannot be registered as Mexicans and receive Mexican schooling because, again, the parents have no legal documents. And so, as in Guatemala and other places, very young children must go to work in order to help their parents survive.

Another big problem in Mexico City is drug addiction. In the Netzahualcóyotl area, drug use is rampant. Young Maya who grow up on the streets join up with other Mexican youths to become drug users and ultimately addicts. We have no precise numbers but the problem is a serious one. Drug addiction is also a problem for Maya women, especially those who take up with Mexican men. Often when these women become pregnant they are abandoned; as refugees without papers, they have no rights and cannot defend themselves. These conditions cause great suffering for the refugees living in Mexico City. The lack of legal status, the very precarious economic conditions, and the temptations of street life make it very difficult for Maya refugees to have much hope for the future.

I believe that the refugees' identity as Maya is in danger of eroding, possibly even disappearing. For one thing, the language is being lost among Maya children born in Mexico City who do not speak Mayan anymore. And it is very difficult for them to learn it because they must hide their true identity, pretending they are from Chiapas or Veracruz in order not to be deported. Maya in Mexico are also losing their national identity, which is compounded of the history, symbols, anthem, and feelings associated with a particular place. The Mexican national anthem and much of the state propaganda are unfavorable to Maya culture, and this is what Maya children are taught in Mexican schools. These children learn Mexican history, geography, and language, not Guatemalan. This, I believe, contributes to the identity problem.

For us Indians, I feel, there is great danger. Our whole worldview, our way of thinking, is related to nature; it is related to the land. When we leave and forsake this land, when we are forced to go to other countries, a great number of our traditions can no longer be practiced. We have a vision, we have certain rites connected to the land. We celebrate during harvest time, but in Mexico we have no harvest and we have no land. We must live an urban life which introduces us to new products new work and living patterns, and produces changes in the way we think, in what we say and how we behave. Guatemaltecos have certain characteristics, and Maya from Guatemala are different from other Indians living in other countries. One cannot say that one is good and the other bad, but they are different, and this is the reality of each country. For instance, a Guatemalan who wants to ask for something will first give an explanation: "Excuse me," he will say apologetically. "Could you do me a favor?" Then he will explain at length. In other places, especially in Mexico, a person might say: "Give me this." And so, as the Maya man learns to respond in ways suitable to his circumstances in Mexico, he will slowly lose his Guatemalan identity, his Indian identity, his *chapina* identity.

Another important aspect of our problem as refugees in Mexico City is organization. Part of the problem has to do with the large size of Mexico City. It is extremely difficult for refugees living in many areas of this vast city to develop a sense of community or commonality. Visiting friends and relatives living elsewhere in the city takes almost all day. Therefore it has been difficult to form organizations, to have a feeling for each other's problems, and to look out for one another as we would have done in our home villages.

I think that we have little communication. There are organized groups in Mexico City but these seem to be more connected to work undertaken in Chiapas and Guatemala for the benefit of the refugees there than for any benefit to the refugees in Mexico City. It is true that in many ways we identify with the refugees on the border: the problems of exile, voluntary return, conditions for return, and many others we share with them. But we are not organized to defend these claims for them or for ourselves. I think that very difficult times lie ahead for all Maya refugees in Mexico. The High Commissioner for Refugees of the United Nations in Mexico City has made statements about withdrawing support. Maybe about a year and a half, two at most remain. What are we refugees going to do? There is no clear or easy answer to this question, and no major initiative as to how we should organize everyone.

Refugee projects do exist, but their work does not come close to what needs to be done. We have initiated and worked on several projects in

Mexico City for the last three years. Before that, almost all of us thought we would be returning to our country soon and thought only about how to get home as quickly as possible. But with the passing of time we also began to appreciate the level of dispersion and disorganization in Mexico City, and the need to organize ourselves.

We began by organizing a children's camp, and for several years now we have held this camp, where Indian and ladino children from ages seven to fourteen can spend a week. The camp has been held in different places in Mexico City, but most often in Tlaxcala. At the camp the children learn about Guatemala. They draw maps, learn about their homelands; and they all know Belize, all of them. This camp initiative helps the children grow up without being totally cut off from their country. It may also help to defuse tensions between Indians and ladinos by promoting exposure to each other at an early age, and perhaps even create a new culture for the future. The Indian-ladino conflict in Guatemala cannot be resolved in a day, but progress will come from coexistence between Indians and ladinos. The camp is popular with the children and has achieved promising results.

There is also in Mexico City a group, mainly of Maya women, that has formed to organize a course on mental health. This mental health group exists primarily to support women and to provide a space where they can speak about the events of the war in Guatemala—the losses of family members, separation from parents, problems with children, and other issues that have affected all of us. Often these emotional burdens fall disproportionately on women, and they pay the price. Women also carry many of the financial burdens of refugee life; they must go to the market, feed their families, find work without legal papers, and face other problems. This mental health program was established to train people to work with women and help them find outlets for their anxieties. By participating in this group, they have come to see that they are not alone but that others share their problems.

Another interesting project involves an annual seminar that began in 1988 in Mexico City on the ethnic-national question in Guatemala. The first two seminars addressed the issues of learning, questioning, and understanding the underlying concepts: What is identity? What is nation? We are now in the third seminar and are covering more ground each time. We have both ladino and Indian participants and spend time questioning how one group or the other behaves or discussing how we might get beyond the situation and overcome this Indian-ladino conflict in Guatemala. Each year we come closer to seeing that it is not enough to denounce bigotry and discrimination; we must seek solutions. If we can never move beyond lamenting and complaining, then this means we are not really interested in finding a solution. We all hope for a Guatemala where we can coexist with each other. The Guatemala for which we fight today is a Guatemala of both Indians and ladinos; it is a Guatemala where we want to build something better, a different country, open to all.

Yet another project is run by a group of young people between four-teen and eighteen years of age, who have come together in Mexico to educate themselves about the struggle in Guatemala and the part they can play in it. These youths are learning not only Guatemalan history but the history of the popular movement, the revolutionary move-ment in Guatemala. They have begun to have contact with the refugee camps at the border to further their understanding of this history and this movement. Last year they went to Campeche, and they and the Campeche refugees lived together for a week.

All of this gives us opportunities to make and continue ties with our country, so that we ourselves, despite living in Mexico City, the largest city in the world, can still maintain links with our country. This will allow us greater connectedness and knowledge of Guatemalan history. The young people who participate in these events almost all hope to return to Guatemala, if not to live, at least to visit and get to know it, for many of them left when they were only five or six years old. They feel they can now identify with their homeland but do not yet know it. They are beginning to talk about returning.

As for myself and my work, we have four projects. In one, we make crafts that we sell in the United States through solidarity groups and sympathetic people. In another we denounce human rights violations, providing information for people concerned about human rights who live outside the area. In the third we support a better understanding of the Indian-ladino problem in Guatemala. And the fourth supports the defense of women. At the beginning we did not understand much about women's issues, but people later sought us out and asked why the majority of the group were women. They said, "And you, what do you think? Are Indian women oppressed or not?" We did not know how to answer. We all started to talk and discuss this a little and to give our point of view, and out of these discussions the group was formed.

Maya Indian refugees in Mexico City are considerably disadvantaged relative to their counterparts in the camps in Chiapas or in North America. They must survive in a tough, dangerous urban environment; they have no legal standing for decent employment and lack assistance from international agencies; they are losing their culture because they must hide their identity; and they live scattered throughout an enormous city, which makes community and communication very difficult. We look forward to the time when we can return home.[2]

NOTES

1. This is a transcript of an oral presentation given at a panel entitled "The Maya Diaspora" at the Latin American Studies Association Congress, March 1991. Translation by Elisabeth Sirucek, edited by Marilyn Moors.

2. Following the signing of the Peace Accords in 1996, some of the Mexico City refugees returned to Guatemala, while others took advantage of the Mexican government's program to become Mexican residents.

MICHAEL C. STONE

8 Becoming Belizean: Maya Identity and the Politics of Nation

PEOPLES OF Maya and Maya-Spanish, or mestizo, heritage, natives and refugees alike, assume a common subordinate status in Belize, the former colony of British Honduras. The historical struggle on Central America's Atlantic coast between Anglo-identified Belize and the region's so-called "Spanish republics" has schooled Belizeans in a heroic idiom of defending their beleaguered haven of English civility against the hereditary assaults of *panya* (Spanish, and by extension Maya) violence and incivility.[1] Since at least the mid-nineteenth century, that antagonistic narrative has ascribed subordinate status to native Maya and mestizo Belizeans, ideologically merging their condition with that of incoming Maya and Spanish-speaking Central Americans, whom Belizeans have been educated to vilify as "aliens."

Today, development discourse and practice condition the ideological arena within which Maya and mestizo Belizeans and their refugee counterparts struggle to alter the cultural contours of—and their place within—national life. This essay, based on ethnographic observations in three rural villages of distinct cultural and social configuration, offers a provisional exploration of how members of a historically transient identity formation comprehend and reframe reductive views of their cultural, racial, and territorial identity within the dynamic and contradictory ideological framework of Belizean nationalism.

HISTORICAL BACKGROUND

The nominally English-speaking Caribbean nation of Belize (Map 8.1) is striking in its actual cultural, racial, and linguistic diversity, although the national ideology proclaims a dominant Anglo-African or Creole pedigree. Yet prevailing ethnic categories are quite fluid, and a long history of cross-cultural influence and interracial union makes it difficult for most Belizeans to define these categories precisely, let alone

118

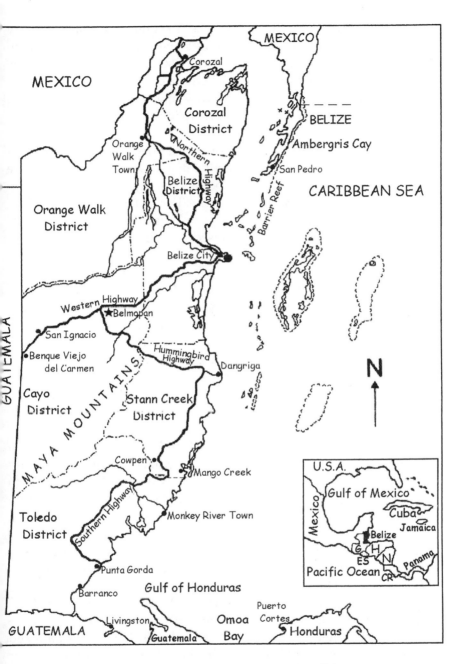

Map 8.1. Belize. (Courtesy of Shanna Castillo)

claim exclusive membership in any one. The dominant ethnic category is the Creole, popularly understood as being of mixed African, Anglo-European, Hispanic, and Amerindian descent. In popular discourse, Creoles represent the Protestant inheritors of an English cultural heritage. Notably, many so identified have emigrated in growing numbers following World War II in an attempt to improve their socioeconomic lot in the United States.[2]

Garifuna, of primarily African-Amerindian descent, remained largely endogamous until recently. Formerly known as Black Caribs, they are ordinarily Catholic, but they have been popularly portrayed as sustaining pagan, that is, African, spiritual practices and beliefs. And like Creoles, they have emigrated in growing numbers to the United States since the latter 1940s. Mestizos are of mixed Hispanic, Amerindian, Anglo-European, and (less acknowledged) African descent, nominally Spanish-speaking and Catholic. Mestizos also have joined the emigrant stream, but in relatively fewer numbers. Kekchi, Mopan, and Yucatec Maya are also largely endogamous, generally Catholic, and commonly stereotyped as "bushy," or primitive rural subsistence farmers. Urban Belizeans consider them marginal to national politics. Generally, Maya groups also have been the least inclined to emigrate.

While prevailing national ideology assumes Creole ascendancy, Table 8.1 illustrates the relative decline of every ethnic category compared with mestizos, whose growing numbers Creole Belizeans often rue in ominous tones.

The human diversity of Central America's Atlantic coast zone reflects a characteristically Caribbean settlement pattern that has brought together peoples of disparate pasts, while subjecting them to a singular present, one conditioned by the territory's articulation with the labor demands of an incipient global capitalist economy (see Mintz 1989) and identity constructions linked. In the mid-seventeenth century, English buccaneers settled on the Bay of Honduras at the site of present-day Belize City. Uninhabited at the time, the location is shielded by the barrier reef and offshore islands on a stretch of coast notorious for its navigational hazards. Thus protected, the English allied with the indigenous inhabitants of Nicaragua's Mosquito Coast, archenemies of the Spanish. Together these partners harassed Spanish settlements and hijacked cargoes from Yucatán bound for Europe.

TABLE 8.1: ETHNIC COMPOSITION OF BELIZE (1946, 1980, 1991)

	1946 #	1946 %	1980 #	1980 %	1991 #	1991 %
Creole	22,693	38.3	57,099	40.0	55,051	29.8
Mestizo	8,360	31.0	47,689	33.4	80,477	43.6
Maya	10,030	16.9	13,642	9.6	20,410	11.1
Garifuna	4,112	6.9	10,816	7.6	12,274	6.7
White	2,329	3.9	5,998	4.2	7,257	3.9
East Indian	1,366	2.3	2,997	2.1	6,455	3.5
Chinese	50	0.1	214	0.1	747	0.4
Other/no resp.	280	0.5	4,392	3.1	1,884	1.0
Totals	59,220	100	142,847	100	184,555	100

Sources: Barker (1985), Central Statistical Office (1991), Hopkins (1948)

However, late-seventeenth-century treaties between Great Britain and Spain forced the English adventurers to cease their depredations. Thereafter, the Baymen (as they were known) began to extract logwood and mahogany in Belize (Craig 1969; Joseph 1987; Wilson 1936). By the 1720s, growing world demand for tropical timbers stimulated the introduction of enslaved Africans to Belize. At its height, the English enclave stretched from Belize to present-day Nicaragua. In a pattern typical of the Caribbean, the English presence brought European manufactured goods to the Atlantic coast zone, while fostering the encounter of a variety of African, Amerindian, and European peoples, furthering a process of cultural and racial hybridization whose social consequences remain manifest today. Belizean economic history also exhibits a familiar boom-and-bust cycle, with the sporadic employment patterns and transitory, ethnically diverse migrant work forces characteristic of tropical extractive ventures.

MAYA AND HISPANIC IMMIGRATION

African emancipation in 1838 created a demand for new labor sources. English and Creole entrepreneurs recruited Maya and Spanish-speaking mestizo immigrants, who (unlike the freedmen) were seen as a cheap, tractable labor supply. As the following data indicate, Maya and mestizo immigration has continued into the present, constituting the major portion of all immigrants since the mid-nineteenth century, beginning with the Caste War of Yucatán. Since the 1960s, Central

American immigration has steadily increased, while native Belizeans have left in growing numbers to seek economic opportunity in the urban United States (Figures 8.1 and 8.2; data from Barker 1985; Dunk 1921; Francis 1964; GOB 1991; Hopkins 1948; Phillips 1912).

Indeed, combined Maya and mestizo immigration from Mexico and Central America has averaged a steady 75 percent of all immigration since at least 1861, the date of the first official census. Yet Belizeans little recognize the ongoing contributions this has represented for national life, despite the eclectic ethnic, cultural, and linguistic mix that has prevailed throughout Belizean history.

Census figures also indicate the growing prevalence of Spanish for the period from 1911 to 1991. English (actually, Belize English Creole) as the primary language of Belize peaked at 59.7 percent in 1946 (Table 8.2). Linguistic trends reflect combined Creole emigration and Spanish-speaking immigration.

Belizeans of all ethnic backgrounds overlook the sustained role of Hispanic and Maya immigration as a defining feature of the national experience. Citizens see farming and manual labor as the stereotypical occupations of Maya and mestizo peoples. Even today, Belizeans persist in designating this portion of the population as aliens, that is, anyone who appears to be Spanish or Indian, especially those who speak Belize Creole poorly or not at all. Since emancipation, leading Creoles have sought to erase the stigma of slavery by promoting an ideology of Belize as a color-blind society. This constitutes a firmly held popular belief, but it poses a fundamental social contradiction. The racial other becomes the Maya-mestizo alien as native Belizeans flatten their own history and deny their mixed ethnic and racial heritage, seeking to assert their legitimacy as the inheritors of the English cultural mantle.

In sum, the ethnic equation presents Creole identity as the defining national cultural ideal. One manifests Creole identity by speaking Belize Creole, by subsuming one's ethnic and linguistic background, and by embracing an ideology of Belizean cultural superiority vis-à-vis the rest of Central America and southern Mexico. English-speaking, Protestant, Creole Belize promotes an Anglo-identified cultural heritage that stands in moral and ideological opposition to Spanish-speaking, Catholic, Maya-mestizo Central America, whose character traits, cultural features, racial markers, and political institutions signify the

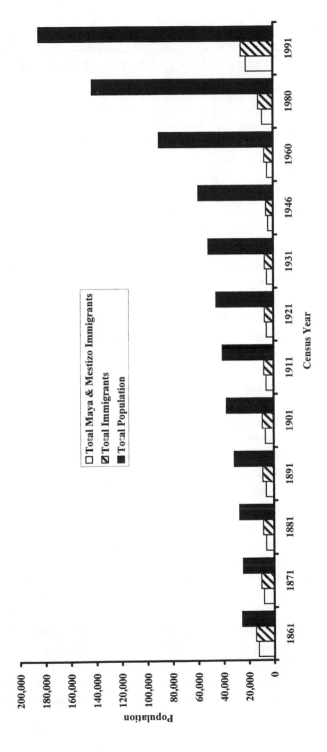

Fig. 8.1. Maya and Mestizo ("Hispanic") Immigrants, Total Immigrants, and Total Belize Population (1861–1991)

TABLE 8.2: PRIMARY LANGUAGES SPOKEN IN BELIZE BY PERCENTAGE (1911–1991)

CENSUS	ENGLISH	SPANISH	MAYA	GARIFUNA	OTHER/NS
1911	52.8	22.9	15.2	9.2	0.0
1921	52.5	25.4	13.9	8.1	0.1
1946	59.7	22.2	10.0	8.0	0.1
1960	50.8	30.7	10.3	8.3	0.0
1980	50.6	31.6	6.4	6.0	5.3
1991a	54.3	43.8	n/a	n/a	n/a

Sources: Barker (1985), Francis (1964), Government of Belize, Central Statistical Office (1991), Hopkins (1948)
aSpeak language very well.

imputed political violence and cultural degeneracy of the Spanish Central American republics.

Historically, neighboring Guatemala has aggravated the issue by pressing a claim to the whole of Belizean territory, citing Great Britain's failure to meet the terms of an 1859 boundary treaty intended to resolve the issue. Guatemala's military governments have a history of episodic threats of military takeover, a fact Belizeans remain keenly aware of, whatever their ethnic heritage. The past decade has seen some tentative advances toward permanent diplomatic resolution, but the issue remains one that in a pinch politicians in both nations occasionally reference in seeking to enhance their domestic political standing (Payne 1990; Thorndike 1978; Young and Young 1988).

At a time when changes in the global political economy send growing numbers of Creole and Garifuna Belizeans to U.S. inner cities (where they once again encounter the despised Spanish other, albeit in a very different guise), Belizeans imagine an alien takeover from within. In fact, demographic growth, economic stagnation, political upheaval, and civil war elsewhere in the region have displaced massive numbers of rural people from Guatemala and El Salvador, making Belize the destination of upwards of twenty-five thousand refugees, about one-seventh of the official national population (USCR 1990). This presence is palpable to Belizeans, providing anecdotal evidence to confirm their fears and support their jaundiced view of immigrants.

In Belize, destitute newcomers inhabit provisional dwellings on marginal land, plant subsistence crops, and find low-wage seasonal work in sugar, citrus, and banana plantations. Others hire out informally in

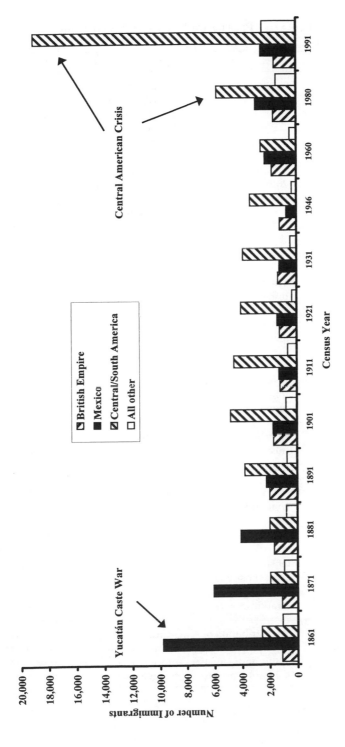

Fig. 8.2. Major Sources of Immigration to Belize (1861–1991)

TABLE 8.3: COMPARATIVE PROFILE OF THREE IMMIGRATION-IMPACTED
BELIZEAN VILLAGES

	SANTIAGO, TOLEDO	RIO INDIO, TOLEDO	CANTON CAYO
Ethnic Composition	Belizean Kekchi Maya	Guatemalan Kekchi; Belizean Maya, Creole, and Garifuna; foreign overseers	"Spanish" foreign Guatemalan and Salvadoran; Belizean Maya; foreign and Creole overseers
Immigration and Settlement History	late 19th and early 20th century (from Guatemala)	recent, economic and political (from Toldeo interior and Guatemala)	recent and extensive from Guatemala, El Salvador, and Belize; economic rural and political mix
Land Tenure	Maya Reserve (now under state legal assault), nominal rent paid to state, alcaldes control local land access	recent colonization, open access, nominal rent paid to state or private landlord	recent colonization, open access, squatting or small rent to private landlord
Geographical and Environmental Status	remote southern Belize; tropical rain forest under threat of foreign logging	emergent agro-export area	adjacent to national capital; established agro-export area
Economy	subsistence and semi-proletarian mix	recent influx of foreign agro-export capital	market farming and local service economy; foreign agro-export capital
Local Labor Profile	traditional communal labor; some migrant plantation labor	semi-proletarian; local and migrant plantation labor	semi-proletarian, service sector, migrant plantation and construction labor
Drug Trade	intensive, part of the local subsistence mix; incipient class-stratification	collateral impact	extensive production; international links; nationality-stratified
Political Configuration	local distribution of episodic political spoils; indigenous solidarity group	disenfranchised from political process; Kekchi refugee coop;	citizenship-based political participation; party patronage; multi-

(Continued)

TABLE 8.3 (CONTINUED)

	SANTIAGO, TOLEDO	RIO INDIO, TOLEDO	CANTON CAYO
	with international links; NGO aid	NGO and multi-lateral aid	lateral and NGO aid; clandestine drug-trade politics
Local Leadership	age-based hereditary hierarchy (alcalde system); insurgent charismatic	charismatic, open	charismatic, citizenship-based
Role of Women	contribution undervalued; prevalent machismo	some women involved in community orga-nization; prevalent machismo	contribution undervalued; prevalent machismo
Religion	predominantly Catholic; insurgent evangelical Protestantism; vestiges of constumbrismo	predominantly Catholic; insurgent evangelical Protestantism; vestiges of costumbrismo	Catholic and evangelical Protestant mix; vestiges of costumbrismo

low-paid jobs as construction workers, gardeners, ranch hands, and domestic servants; still others are self-employed market vendors and petty entrepreneurs. Popular opinion scapegoats recent arrivals as abusing social services, importing drugs and epidemic disease, taking work from Belizeans, and perpetrating all manner of crime and social disorder. While it may personify the problems that plague any developing nation, as with every refugee flow the influx represents a material asset, as Belizean employers freely admit.

Overall, for Maya and mestizo in Belize (whether native or immigrant), life entails daily accommodation to a lowly status conditioned by 350 years of conflictive regional history. But taking a page from that history, many Maya and mestizo actors actively contest their status in the unstable public arena of a country still forging a unique post-independence identity.[3] Ethnographic research in three rural villages where Maya and mestizo groups of national and immigrant origin reside reveals the partial and contradictory character of their uneasy accommodation to the ideological and material order (Table 8.3).

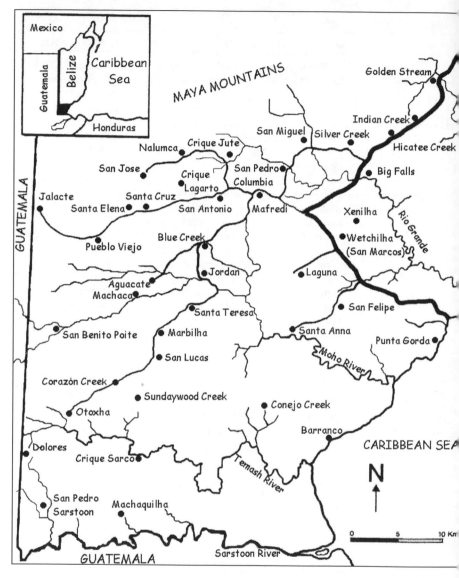

Map 8.2. Toledo District, Belize. (Courtesy of Shanna Castillo)

A BELIZEAN KEKCHI VILLAGE: SANTIAGO, TOLEDO DISTRICT

Santiago is a predominantly Kekchi village founded in southern Belize after Kekchi and Mopan Guatemalans fled the economic and political repression of Liberal Guatemala in the mid-1880s.[4] The newcomers learned to submerge their national origins, internalizing the British attitude of disdain for Guatemala. Their presence also served Britain as a convenient buffer against Guatemalan territorial designs on the English colony. Britain protected new arrivals from occasional Guatemalan harassment across an ill-defined border, but a general policy of benign neglect allowed indigenous peoples to govern their domestic affairs at the local level. Toledo District (Map 8.2) has remained an isolated, predominantly Maya dominion into the present, as the census data of the past century confirm. Even today, Santiago and other predominantly Kekchi villages of the Toledo interior maintain cultural links with neighboring villages in Guatemala, where young men trek overland to seek spouses, engage in soccer rivalries, and rent the masks and costumes necessary to perform the dances (for example, Deer, Jaguar, Moros y Cristianos), associated with traditional village fiesta cycles. Concurrently, Maya experience with the outside world is considerable, reflecting the long influence of Jesuit missionaries and their English-language schools, church-sponsored cooperative ventures, wage-labor out-migration and a boom-and-bust cycle imposed by extractive forestry and plantation operations, as well as more recent forays into Pan American indigenous identity politics and Toledo ecotourism development (Ch'oc 1996; ILRC 1998; Medina 1997, 1998; Stone 1995; Wilk 1987, 1991).

During and after the transition to independence in 1981, politicians have finessed the status quo, dispensing the limited spoils of development on the basis of village political loyalties and the expediencies of electoral politics. This has fostered interpersonal, factional, and intervillage competition, as well as a pervasive cynicism toward national politics when the promises of development go unfulfilled, as they ordinarily do once votes are cast.

Consider an anecdote from the 1989 national election campaign in Toledo. The national assembly representative, a Mopan Maya, drew criticism for having become a "belly-full" man during his tenure (that is, for having violated norms of communal redistribution and enriching himself through his office). Having built a modern concrete-block house and acquired a four-wheel-drive vehicle through party largesse, he personified the government's failure to address basic socioeconomic problems endemic to rural Toledo. As voting day approached, the prime minister swung through Toledo, dispensing promises on all sides. Santiago villagers greeted his entourage with a ceremonial feast. After obligatory invocations and patronizing words about the patient, hard-working villagers, the government ministers sat down to eat.

Along with the feast, villagers had prepared a litany of complaints. As their distinguished guests finished eating, a series of leaders rose and prodded the prime minister to send more school teachers, fix district roads and bridges, improve water supplies and health care, and provide farm-market support, all of which the ruling party had promised to do five years earlier. They also faulted government for doing little to control the influx of Guatemalan Kekchi refugees, viewed with suspicion by both Kekchi and Maya Belizeans in Toledo. The last speaker wondered where the politicians had been since Toledo Mayas helped vote them into power and why they only came around at election time. In closing, he chided them, "Enjoy your meal and suck the bones dry, because this is the last time you will fatten yourselves as ministers of government at the expense of the people of Santiago."

Stung by this bitter breach of the patron-client relationship, the prime minister and company piled into their vehicles and left Santiago in the dust. Newspaper coverage of the ruling party's southern campaign tour did not register the incident, but Toledo villagers took considerable glee in recounting and embellishing the tale, especially after the UDP failed to win re-election. Their moral rebuke sidestepped the saliency of their Maya identity; indeed, they attacked government for failing to act in the Kekchi refugee matter. Instead, Kekchi Belizeans offered a blunt assertion of Belizean citizenship in laying claim to development benefits they felt had been denied them, even as they conceded limits to their ability to alter their dependent relationship with government. But their dramatic repudiation has weighed heavily. The UDP regained power in 1994, making it payback time in Toledo. Without local consultation, the Ministry of Natural Resources negotiated logging concessions with a Malaysian corporation on rain forest lands long administered under the Maya land reservation system. A party-based reprisal cloaked in the guise of rational development policy thus unleashed an all-out attack on the long-sacrosanct reserve of Maya swidden farming, the very basis of village cohesion in southern Toledo.[5] In a recent manifesto, Toledo Maya Belizeans framed their plight in terms of their primordial belonging, while invoking the specter of genocide and national sacrifice: "The Mayas are endangered by the resource exploitation of their land. Can the Mayan People survive this attack or will they become part of the statistics as another victim of ethnocide in the world today? The government . . . is indicating that the Mayan People are too poor to contribute anything worthwhile to the Belizean economy and are a worthless ethnic burden" (Ch'oc 1996).

With help from the U.S.-based Indian Law Resource Center and a variety of international conservation groups, Toledo Mopan and Kekchi Maya initiated a lawsuit before the Supreme Court of Belize to defend their traditional land rights, challenging the unilateral granting of logging licenses on lands where government has long recognized their ancestral rights. They also forwarded their case to the Inter-American Commission on Human Rights, a division of the Organization of American States (OAS). Well-established principles of international law stand in Maya favor, and supportive legal precedents exist in other British Commonwealth countries, including Australia and Canada (ILRC 1996). As of this writing, however, the conflict remains unresolved, and logging has already severely affected traditional subsistence patterns. Toledo Mayas' internal divisions, and their relative isolation from the pan-Maya movement of Guatemala and Mexico, have limited their ability to respond in concerted and efficacious fashion.

GUATEMALAN KEKCHI REFUGEES IN RIO INDIO, TOLEDO

Kekchi Maya refugees fleeing economic displacement and political repression in northeastern Guatemala were most numerous among the settlers of Rio Indio during the 1980s. Finding no welcome in the Belize Maya villages of the interior, due to native hostility and the fact that all arable land has long been allocated under the indigenous village tenure system, Kekchi refugees carved out an economic niche nearer the southern coast as wage laborers in foreign-owned ranches and banana and citrus plantations (see Moberg 1997), living in depressed socioeconomic conditions on or near the plantations.

Lacking official political franchise but sensitive to the importance of cultivating local and regional patronage relationships, they found allies among non-governmental organizations (NGOs) working in development. Politicized Kekchi refugees built a cooperative organization, occupied unused government land, and sought legal title in order to pursue commercial farming. With NGO support they also managed to obtain a vehicle and government assistance in building and staffing a local school and health post. Living close to the main highway to protect themselves from theft and extortion at the hands of Belizean natives, refugee Mayas formed watch groups to deter Belizeans from victimizing their community. But their modest organizing success aroused envy among Belizeans, including Toledo Mayas, who read refugee achievement as perverse evidence of the stereotyped "aggression" of Guatemalans, a readiness to exploit Belizean largesse, and a conspiracy of NGOs to "sell out" Belize to aliens and refugees.

Maya Belizean farmers objected that Guatemalan Kekchi squatted illegally on government land, stealing crops, growing marijuana, and abusing the forest ecosystem. Toledo Mayas echo generalized Belizean attitudes toward the Central American influx, regarding it as one more "alien" encroachment. As one Belizean Kekchi farmer complained, "The Guatemalan Kekchi? It's not fair—they're against the Belizeans. They just want to grab a piece of land here. The Guatemalan Indians are rough—they have it in their blood. They come and plant their marijuana, do their nonsense in our country, and jump back over the border. Then we Belizeans get the blame."

Toledo Mayas thus emphasize their Belizean citizenship rather than their Maya identity in seeking to better their own depressed socioeconomic situation. But their response also reflects the conditioning of the prevailing model of patronage politics and clientelism, in a moral discourse that chides a government derelict in its obligations to a respectable citizenry. Their educated consent to the prevailing order leads them to consider their own situation as a mere aberration, even as their acquiescence to the framing discourse endorses the prevailing structure of their own subordination. As a Guatemalan Maya refugee—schooled in his country's deadly labor struggles—observed of Maya Belizeans' inability to mobilize their own communities, "The politics of paternalism in Belize has created the mental illness of dependency among the Toledo Maya. This will be tough to uproot. It is very difficult to organize people for their own benefit. They always worry that their neighbor will get ahead. That is the challenge we confront here in our community."

Parallel issues arise elsewhere in Belize, including the provisional settlement of Canton Cayo, populated in part by Belizean Mayas who emigrated from Toledo to the country's agro-export heartland, only to find themselves confined once again to the margins, living among despised Maya and Spanish-speaking refugees of Guatemala and El Salvador.

REFUGEES AND NATIONAL IDENTITY IN CANTON CAYO

Throughout the 1980s, a disparate group of native Maya and refugee workers and their families settled Canton Cayo, situated in the jungle outside Belmopan, the nation's capital. Most rent plots for their palm-thatch houses, as tenants and employees of expanding foreign-owned citrus plantations and cattle ranches being established in the Belize River Valley and along the Hummingbird Highway connecting the capital with Dangriga to the south. These landless tenants and squatters are in effect semi-proletarian milpa farmers, settling close to a variety of convenient alternative job prospects when local plantation work slows.

Contrary to Belizean popular wisdom, Belize Mayas and refugees from El Salvador and Guatemala do not see themselves as natural ethnic allies. Indeed, Maya subordination within the national ethnic hierarchy encourages them to assert their Belizean identity whenever benefits and rights are at stake. The government, multilateral agencies like the United Nations, and NGOs seek to downplay this distinction when working in these mixed rural communities. There is ample potential for discord in settlements that maintain distinctions between Belizean and alien. So the disruption of local social, economic, and political networks gives villagers some incentive to band together, despite potentially divisive ethnic and national differences, in hopes of maximizing the anticipated distribution of resources while stabilizing the local status quo.

One source of conflict is tenants' tendency to clandestinely cultivate more swidden land than allocated in their lease, thus encroaching on land from which expanding cattle and plantation operations will find it difficult to dislodge interlopers once they have established squatter's rights. Such is the case in Canton Cayo. An additional factor is rampant marijuana cultivation, part of a highly organized production and export network with reputed ties to Guatemalan military officers managing their operations from across the border in the department of El Petén. This fact of daily life has given villagers a nefarious explanation for a variety of local conflicts, including several disappearances and unsolved murders that occurred during my residency there.

Intervening against the village status quo, the foreign plantation owner asked a local NGO to prepare a plan to relocate villagers in a concentrated settlement on land the corporation would deed to them, in order to clear the way for a major expansion of the citrus and cattle operation. Squatting, rent-dodging, and unauthorized milpa cultivation had long posed a problem for the company, whose sixty-thousand-acre holding also was peppered with clandestine marijuana plots protected by elusive, heavily armed interlopers. This presence conditioned a violent undercurrent in labor and community relations.

A key local figure was Carlos Chan, a Toledo Mopan Maya who left home as an adolescent to enter the Creole-dominated world of wage labor in central Belize.[6] His blunt, gregarious manner and lifetime experience as a milpa farmer, chicle collector, lumberjack, plantation laborer, and petty entrepreneur made Chan a good choice for village chairman, especially given his multilingual facility in Belize Creole, Spanish, Mopan, and Kekchi. Spanish-speaking refugee support was important to build a political constituency because multilateral agencies insisted that development aid must extend to the entire village population, Belizean and refugee alike. Chan seemed to be riding a fortuitous political wave.

An initial burst of enthusiasm followed a socioeconomic survey of the village, but this soon waned as villagers clashed over choice plots, while rumors circulated that Central American refugees would be denied land titles. The ability to claim Belizean citizenship was critical. Politicians catered to refugees and citizens alike but assured their franchised constituencies that contrary to multilateral agency preconditions, citizens would be allowed to stay even if the refugees were forced to relocate to a designated refugee settlement.

Numerous false starts, unfulfilled promises, local political backbiting, public denunciations of malfeasance with village funds, and two mysterious, apparently drug-related deaths ensued. Then, early on Good Friday morning, an effigy appeared inexplicably on the roadside. Villagers immediately recognized the figure as Judas, or San Simón, the accusatory folk figure who appears in Guatemalan villages on the day of crucifixion, carrying dire warnings for all and sundry (see Mendelson 1965; Nash 1994). Judas had a hand-sewn, pencil-scrawled booklet in his pocket, full of scandalous sexual revelations and darker threats against those supposedly trying to undermine equal participation in the project, including the plantation owner and prominent Belizean Maya and mestizo villagers.

An animated discussion ensued. Most agreed that Judas was the work of disaffected refugees, or perhaps of the drug lords who viewed the project's institutionalization as a threat to their clandestine penetration of the community (speculation was that some refugees were drug operatives, although it seems more likely that Belizeans controlled the trade). The project's future seemed in jeopardy. Multilateral funders had grown weary, both of government attempts to re-channel aid to voting Belizeans and of the general atmosphere of antagonism. The Judas visitation crystallized a core political conflict of the settlement, in a pointed commentary on the exclusionary politics that would separate Belizeans and refugees and deny the latter what had been promised under the banner of development.

A local Belizean political casualty was Mr. Chan. He took offense at the insinuating threats of Judas and the whispering campaign of a Belizean Maya rival who would ultimately succeed to the village chairmanship. Voicing his disgust with the entire process, he vowed not to move regardless of what happened. He went beyond asserting his Belizean citizenship, advancing his Maya identity in a primordial invocation to trump competing national claims to the promises of development:

> This land is our inheritance from the Maya, our ancestors. I can show you all the relics they left behind on this land right here. They won't run me off. I'll stay here to the death. They can come with their machines to knock down my house, but when the first corner post goes down, the first man will go down with it. I haven't long to live, but they'll leave a young widow and four little ones with nothing. I planted all these fruit trees, and I tell you, if I have to leave, within a year someone else will come in here to squat and harvest the fruits of my labor. . . . I'm hard-headed, and here I'll stay. I'm a Belizean, and I'm not moving.[7]

Judas's appearance, presumably the work of disaffected Guatemalan refugees who saw their own fortunes deteriorating in the local deal-making process, resonates with the reaction of the Belizean Maya villagers of Santiago and confirms the remarks of the Guatemalan refugee organizer of Rio Indio. In each case the response repudiated a political process in which the respondents experienced their own marginalization, while it simultaneously affirmed a resilient sense of identity and belonging that would not easily surrender to a process that threatened individual and group survival. Yet the unwelcome visage of Judas, the betrayer, also served notice of the sustained influence of Central American folk idioms, providing a metaphor whose critical edge cuts to the paradoxically plural core of the Belizean cultural experience as Caribbean nation and Central American state.

BELIZE DA FU WI: DECLAIMING AND DELIMITING THE CREOLE NATION

Belizeans cite a Creole phrase to sum up the country's populist, color-blind ideology of equality. Colloquially, *Belize da fu wi* means "Belize is ours, Belize is for us." Yet as one young Belize mestizo ironically commented to me, "*Belize da fu wi* is written in Creole." He and other Maya and mestizo Belizeans know what it means to fight to assert their status as Belizean citizens. Consider the words of a Belize mestizo woman who spoke before a national forum on refugees and development:

> I am mestizo, but I am Belizean. It hurts me when the Belizean treat me like an alien in my own land. Well, I can defend myself, because I was born here, and I know the Belize people. We say we are a democracy, not like Guatemala, but sometimes I have to think . . . *todos somos beliceños* [we are all Belizeans]. *Pero esos pobrecitos* [those poor (refugees)], they also are my neighbors, and when the Belizean treat me like a refugee, I know how the refugees feel. When we Belizeans say, *Belize da fu wi*, it means, *all a wi*. Belize people, *all a wi da fu wi* [we are all for each other, we are all one].

Belize da fu wi is an expression of Creole ascendancy in an actually hybrid, culturally plural society that has accommodated a sustained Maya and mestizo influx since the mid-nineteenth century. It encapsulates a problematic ideological formulation, a popular coding of who belongs and who does not, and why this should be so. But, re-situated, it also constitutes a social critique of the ideological and material marginalization that is part of the everyday experience of Maya and mes-tizo Belizeans. In post-colonial Belize, politicians have downplayed racial difference in order to forge a more inclusive sense of national identity. That ideology reframes the society's actual diversity in a plu-ralist proposition that ethnic groups should assimilate to an explicit Anglo-Creole national ideal, one whose cultural and racial scope remains deliberately ambiguous. Leaving aside the unspoken matter of class differentiation, one becomes Belizean by denying or casting off one's racial, ethnic, and cultural identity. But to do so is to engage in an act of educated consent that helps to reproduce the prevailing features of a commonsense ideology of national belonging, one whose structural features sustain the subordination of people identified as Maya and mestizo.

Asked to characterize Creole culture, self-identified Creoles typically reply, "There is no Creole culture, just Belizean culture." But the social order is never so unproblematic, even though, as Renato Rosaldo observes: "In 'our' own eyes, 'we' appear to be 'people without culture.' . . . Indeed, full citizenship and cultural visibility appear to be inversely related. When one increases, the other decreases. Full citizens lack cul-ture, and those most culturally endowed lack full citizenship" (Rosaldo 1993:198).

The imposition of a cultural standard stripped of the colonial history from which contending identities emerge perpetuates into the present a profound antagonism, expressed in the nested complex of pejorative cultural, ethnic, and racial ideologies and practices. Belizeans are edu-cated in myriad ways to see the nation as besieged by a putatively vio-lent, culturally degenerate, and politically destabilizing Maya-mestizo threat to the national body politic. The pursuit of national hegemony, a fractured, contradictory, never-completed undertaking, seeks to essen-tialize Maya and mestizo actors, regardless of citizenship, so as to ratio-nalize their exclusion from the national project. But the actual tensions engendered in their simultaneous resistance and conditioned consent to the hegemonic cultural order emerge clearly in an ethnographic scrutiny of ordinary social practice.

The regional conflict that created refugees in El Salvador and Guatemala and drove them abroad has propelled them into centrifugal status under the distinct cultural and historical conditions of Belize. And despite their own discrete cultural genesis, native Maya and mestizo Belizeans gravitate to the same ideological and material margins, according to commonsense understandings that reduce the diverse expressions of human history to a unitary subaltern category of singular national construction.

But the varying responses of native and immigrant Maya residents in three villages of differing social composition highlight the mundane local contradictions of national identity politics. To understand the responses sketched here requires appreciating how people bring to bear their distinctive cultural understandings and repertoires in the context of everyday political struggle—as documentary evidence confirms Maya and mestizo newcomers have done for the past 150 years. Just how deeply those insurgent cultural influences have conditioned the contemporary social formation is something that Belizeans and others habitually misperceive, even when the tangled narratives of their own disparate family histories speak differently.

Indeed, from its inception Belize has been what we now characterize as a multicultural society, one whose notably modern social character entails profound socioeconomic and political displacement and cultural disaffection. The elaboration of cultural significance and the forging of social consensus in Belize remains an uneven and contradictory undertaking. A residual ideology imbued with the dominant Creole or Anglo-African heritage offers ready-made justification to exclude the Maya and Spanish-speaking populations whose insertion into national life has in fact been ongoing for the past 150 years. The Belizean quandary thus offers a useful comparative frame for analyzing the complex historical dynamics of cultural encounters throughout Central America's Caribbean littoral.

The popular view of Belize as an egalitarian social democracy, embattled in a troubled isthmus, constitutes an exclusionary national ideal that denies the breadth of its own diverse cultural heritage. It reproduces the exploitation of new Maya and mestizo arrivals, and perpetuates the very inequities against which Belizeans of all backgrounds define their own founding democratic traditions. This fuels continued low-level enmity framed in terms of familiar ethnic oppositions, even as the nation takes in those whose simultaneous resistance and consent help to replicate the general features of a hegemonic cultural order. In this the ideological tensions and structural constraints upon Maya accommodation in Belize—ironically an area of Maya occupation for millennia—offer a trenchant comparison with the Maya diaspora elsewhere in the hemisphere. Of fundamental concern is how Mayas and mestizos simultaneously mobilize around and reconstruct their own understandings of what is vital in terms of their own sense of identity and history, even as their strategies help to perpetuate insistent contradictions in the ideological and material order. But theirs is not an exercise in false consciousness. The preceding account outlines how diverse constituencies in three rural settlements deliberately contest dominant views, seek to transform their ascribed Maya and mestizo subalternity, spin alternative claims of belonging from the tangled warp of a commonsense popular history of nation and identity in Belize. But even in disputing dominant national narratives to assert their belonging within a shifting ideological and material terrain, they confront a paradox. In an ever-tentative articulation of the dominant and subordinate themes in which diverse Maya and mestizo peoples find themselves reflected, their incomplete and conditioned consent (a la Gramsci) has helped to reproduce the general hegemonic framework of a relentless if historically mutable rationale for the continued marginalization of people so identified.[8]

NOTES

Acknowledgments: Research for this chapter was supported by grants from Fulbright-IIE, the Wenner-Gren Foundation for Anthropological Research, the Institute for Latin American Studies of the University of Texas at Austin, and the trustees of Hartwick College My thanks especially to Richard N. Adams, Milton Jamail, and Joseph O. Palacio for support and encouragement. Staff at the following institutions were immensely helpful: Government Refugee Office in Belmopan; Belize Archives in Belmopan; Belize Enterprise for Sustained Technology (BEST) in Belmopan; Society for the Promotion of Education and Research (SPEAR) in Belize City; Toledo Maya Cultural Council; the Vatican Microfilm Archives at St. Louis University; the Midwest Jesuit Archives in St. Louis; and the Benson Latin American Collection at the University of Texas at Austin. The research assistance of David Bruno and Shanna Castillo, who also prepared the maps, has been invaluable. Thanks are also due to the many people who, though here anonymous, offered their patient collaboration in a spirit of great and instructive goodwill. Errors of transcription and interpretation are entirely my own.

1. This popular rendition of national history constitutes a paradoxical local adaptation of themes drawn from the notorious Black Legend, a product of Fray

Bartolomé de las Casas's 1552 polemic against Spanish mistreatment of Amerindian people.

2. This and succeeding ethnic characterizations represent, of course, salient reductive understandings widespread in Belize. Popular emphasis on reified essential features should not obscure an analytical necessity to shift the theoretical focus instead to the actual variety of local processes through which racialized, culturally and territorially associated individuals and communities identify with and distinguish themselves in mundane daily practice from other individuals and identity formations (see Gordon and Anderson 1999).

3. Belize gained its independence from Great Britain only in 1981, and the Belize Defense Force continues to rely on a Royal Air Force and Army contingent to discourage Guatemalan designs.

4. At the request of informants, the Toledo villages profiled here are pseudonymous.

5. See Anaya 1998; Aslam 1996; *Belize Times* 1994; Chapin 1995; Ch'oc 1996; Collymore 1996; ILRC 1996, 1998; InterPress 1996; Loftis 1996a, 1996b; and RAN 1996.

6. Carlos Chan is a pseudonym.

7. Chan actually spoke in a bilingual, code-switching harangue tailored to my own facility in Spanish and English

Chan added, "Mr. Joe [the owner's representative] me dijo, 'As long as the company doesn't need the land, Mr. Chan, you can stay here.' I say to him now, 'Mr. Joe, I'm not against you, but I'm not moving from this place. I don't want to go into your project. Why should I go among these aliens when I don't know who they are.' *Yo soy caprichudo pero ya me quedo aquí.* I'm a Belizean. *No me muevo otra vez ya.*"

8. My consideration of the ethnographic and ethnohistorical evidence summarized here reflects the trenchant insights of James Brow 1988 and Michael Woost 1993.

Nancy J. Wellmeier

9   La Huerta: Transportation Hub
     in the Arizona Desert

THE RAIN had been steady for the three days that Mario and his friends had been living under the orange trees.[1] The grey Arizona December sky darkened as they sloshed through the mud toward the place where they had learned a meal was served every evening. The six young men, all from Barillas, Huehuetenango, in the remote mountains of northwestern Guatemala, spoke softly to each other in Q'anjob'al, their Mayan language, and wondered how long the rainy season lasted in Los Estados, the United States. They hoped that the church people who brought the food would have blankets or shoes tonight. Grateful for the hot food and the dark green garbage bag he was given to use as a raincoat, Mario hoped desperately that tonight he and his companions would find a ride to Florida, where he had heard he could earn $30 a day picking tomatoes.

From sometime in the early 1980s until July of 1997, the citrus groves around the periphery of Phoenix, Arizona, were a distribution point for groups of Mayas coming into the United States from Guatemala.[2] In one particular grove, known from the Maya homeland to Florida as La Huerta, or the orchard, from twenty to a hundred Mexican and Guatemalan indigenous people, mostly young men, arrived every week on their way to find work and to connect with relatives and friends. Women and children at times accompanied the men. During their stay in the groves, they lived and slept hidden under the thick foliage of the orange and grapefruit trees, venturing out only for the daily meal provided by local church volunteers and perhaps to use the telephone and mail services at a nearby general store. To go farther without the protection of the night or of a vehicle would be foolhardy; it would risk losing all the investment of time, money, and physical effort required to reach this point. The *migra,* the Border Patrol, would escort them to the border and the whole difficult crossing would have to start over.[3]

In La Huerta, shelter was a piece of plastic draped over the branches of a tree and a bundle of rags and blankets spread on the ground. Con-

141

trary to popular belief, it both rains and gets cold in the Arizona desert, and people caught in bad weather could not build fires, for they would attract the attention of the Border Patrol. Occasionally the church workers who brought the food, clothing, and blankets would take women and small children home for a night, but not often. In the summer, the problem was to find sufficient clean drinking water to avoid dehydration; all the irrigation canals carry pesticide-laced water.

Every day at about 4:00 P.M., several trucks and cars pulled up beside La Huerta. Quickly, volunteers hauled out huge pots and tubs of steaming beans or stew, sandwiches, sweet rolls, coffee, juice, and clean water. The hungry travelers were lined up and led in prayer; then, one after another, women and children first, they received a plate piled high with food. Distribution of leftovers for tomorrow's breakfast, clothing, blankets, and shoes followed. On days when more than fifty migrants appeared, some went away empty-handed. On some days there were toilet kits; other days a volunteer doctor was available for examinations and to dispense medicine. The county health department occasionally sent nurses to vaccinate against measles, typhoid, and diphtheria. Often the newly arrived were given a short talk about their legal rights in the United States and a list of phone numbers of legal services agencies around the country where help could be found for political asylum applications.

This scene was repeated daily without fail for at least ten years.[4] Although statistical information on the number of migrants is nonexistent, the church volunteers from several Christian denominations agree with the estimate made by a supervisor of the citrus ranch itself: five thousand immigrant workers per year over a period of fifteen years. There were probably larger numbers in 1987 and 1988. The great majority were young men between the ages of fourteen and thirty-five; about half were single and the others had left wives and children behind. They spent from two days to two weeks in La Huerta, dependent on the availability of the "coyotes," or clandestine transportation providers, to take them to their destinations. The most often mentioned places of origin were the departments of Huehuetenango and San Marcos in northwestern Guatemala, the homeland of Q'anjob'al, Mam, Chuj, and Jakaltek Mayan speakers. K'iche' Mayas from Quetzaltenango or Totonicapán, Mixteca people from Oaxaca, Mexico, and some Maya from Chiapas were also in the stream after 1990. The destination for the

Guatemalans was almost always another state where work was wait-ing—in the early years, Florida, and later North Carolina, Colorado, and even Ohio.

Four-fifths of those questioned said that this was their first time in the United States, although most groups from the same point of origin had at least one member who was an "old hand" and guide. The reasons for coming were often given in a prudently vague and ambiguous manner, since there was no reason to trust an interviewer just met and no reason to tell the truth to someone they never expected to see again. "I came to see if I can find work; there is no work where I live." Upon closer ques-tioning, one learned that most of them owned some property in the form of *milpa*, or corn fields, and had left the fields planted and under the care of a wife or a brother. Even though they are landowners, 89 per-cent of Guatemalans are unable to meet basic food needs (Scott 1994:23). Those who came before 1995 reported forced participation in the oblig-atory civilian patrols, which required a twenty-four-hour turn at guard-ing the town or *aldea* every week or ten days (Carmack 1988:63; Anderson and Simon 1987:15, 16, 30, 32; Smith 1988:227–29; IGE 1989).[5] Those from Huehuetenango usually claimed that in the area from which they came things were *tranquilo*, calm and quiet; others spoke of clashes between guerrillas and the army, or of communities of resis-tance in the jungle, or of the bombing of their villages. All agreed that it was not convenient to be an unemployed young man in Guatemala. One would be suspected of collaboration with the "subversives" or hauled off to army service. Ironically, by leaving, they placed them-selves under even greater suspicion; they were suspected of having "gone with the guerrilla" and could be in danger if they returned.

A typical journey was that experienced by Juan, a corn farmer from Tacaná, San Marcos, in 1994. In Tapachula, Mexico, he caught one bus to Mexico City and another to a Sonoran town a little south of the U.S. border. It cost the peso equivalent of about $27 to travel the whole length of Mexico, and Juan felt lucky he had not had to pay any bribes to officials at various checkpoints. He avoided this by getting off the bus, before getting to Mexico City, for example, and walking on back roads to catch another bus farther on. He knew what to do because he had consulted with returnees in his town. At the Sonoran pickup point, he contracted a car and driver to take him to an Arizona drop-off site about twenty-five or thirty miles from La Huerta. This ride cost $55.

Juan still had a little money left, but he didn't want to expose himself to the Border Patrol by going out of the orchard to a store. He was traveling with four male companions, all from Tacaná. There were other groups in La Huerta that day from El Tumbador in San Marcos, from San Juan Ixcoy, San Rafael la Independencia, and Aguacatán in Huehuetenango, all in Guatemala, and a large group of Maya from Chamula, Chiapas, in Mexico, including four women and eight small children. Juan was not sure how much it would cost to get to Florida, where he had heard there was work and where one could get papers. Others in the group had already called their relatives in Florida and were waiting for them to arrive to take them there.[6]

Domingo, from Santa Eulalia, Huehuetenango, came through on another day; he had already been arrested and had spent several days in the federal detention center in Florence, Arizona, in the desert between Tucson and Phoenix.[7] Fortunately for him, a nonprofit legal aid agency interviews all Central Americans held at this INS facility and arranges releases for those who have political asylum claims. Released on his own recognizance (OR'd in legal-services speak), and told to report to the immigration office in Miami, Domingo was headed for Immokalee, Florida. His journey had already taken fifteen days.

Rain and cold weather prolonged the journey north for Pedro and Tomás, uncle and nephew from Cuilco, Huehuetenango. They, like many others, crossed into Mexico at La Mesilla near their hometown and caught a bus to Villahermosa, Tabasco, and on to Mexico City and the border. There they waited in a small Sonoran town until the weather cleared and the guides who do business there told them it was safe to cross and how to find their way. They made the crossing themselves, to save money, and walked toward a mountain peak they were told was in the United States. They crossed the Tohono O'odham reservation in southern Arizona, gratefully receiving gifts of food and water, until they arrived at La Huerta and found some forty other Guatemalans, all waiting for a "ratero" or "coyote" to make a deal to get to West Palm Beach or Indiantown, Florida. They knew the going rate was $500 per person, on credit, to be paid in installments after securing a job. This seemed fair, since travel by bus or plane was unsafe for undocumented people and could not be done on credit. They also knew that the coyote would know the most secure route to Florida, certainly not the direct and obvious Interstate 10, filled with INS checkpoints. The trip would be made without stops except for refueling, the two coyotes taking turns sleeping, and they would be in Florida in two days.

Why are Pedro and Tomás here? "La situación allá es imposible, no hay trabajo y no tenemos dinero para vivir." (The situation there is impossible; there is no work and we have no money to live.) Pedro had taken out a loan from a store owner in his town; if he didn't pay off the $300 or Q1800 within six months, his land would be forfeited. Before 1997, the urgency to find work was doubly pressing: all men of military service age had to send a monthly payment to the persons who took their places in the civil patrol. Both men hoped to earn enough to pay these debts quickly, then begin sending money home to support their families. To this end they were willing to live in crowded quarters, eat simply, and avoid buying big consumer items until it became possible to visit home (see Wellmeier 1998 on living conditions).

The future looked cloudy. Would Pedro and Tomás return to Guatemala? Only when things improve there, they said. Had they wanted to come? They confessed they were a little curious to find out what the United States was like; people returning to their hometowns had brought stories, information, advice, and, especially, good clothes, gold chains, televisions, stereo tape players, video cameras, and more. But they missed their families, especially the sixteen-year-old Tomás.

It is well known that the longer people stay in their new situation, the more likely it becomes that they will make the transition from sojourner to immigrant, a distinction neatly discussed by Leo Chavez in *Shadowed Lives* (1992) and a process widely documented in the literature on immigration. In some areas, particularly in Arizona, Colorado, and Los Angeles, where the Maya have found work other than agricultural labor, the rate of home ownership has mushroomed since 1995.

Church volunteers involved in serving the immigrants during the period from 1986 through 1994 varied in their understanding of the political situation in Guatemala but were invariably sympathetic to the physical hardships the migrants underwent and never questioned their own duty to extend help and a welcome. Many of the volunteers were "hooked" by the situation in La Huerta because the recipients of their kindness were so unfailingly grateful, so polite, and so obviously in need only temporarily. It always seemed the stream of migrants would never end, but individuals would be gone tomorrow or next week, off to a better life somewhere else. Pushing and shoving only occurred when blankets or shoes were in short supply. The communication between most of the volunteers and the immigrants was carried out with smiles and pantomime; rough language, unkempt appearance, and rude behavior were rarely encountered, as they often are in other centers that offer aid to the homeless.

Although the configurations changed over the years, most of the volunteers served in La Huerta at least once a week for three or four years, and some came regularly three times a week. Some of the church groups had members who spoke Spanish. Each of the main denominational groups had some Spanish-speaking members, and each group recruited its own new volunteers. An informal organization sprang up among them and coordinators of each group communicated by telephone when special needs appeared—newborns, pregnant women, severe illnesses such as a case of leprosy in 1990 and one of epilepsy in 1991, the frequent cases of dehydration. Most of them talked about their motivation in terms of biblical injunctions to welcome the foreigner, to share food and clothing with the needy, and to treat the stranger as a brother or sister. Most volunteers testify to having experienced personal growth as a result of their involvement.[8] They were grateful for donations of clothing and blankets from other groups who wanted to help but lamented the seasonal fluctuation in outpourings of generosity. One of the regular volunteers explained, "For the last two weeks I have been flooded with clothes and blankets since there are many people who have a generous heart at Christmas. This week [in January] the new boys are just as cold and hungry as those that were here before Christmas."

The county health department personnel explained their policy that it is easier and cheaper to prevent than to contain outbreaks of disease, and that they found duty in La Huerta a welcome change from their usual crowded clinics. The doctors and nurses who volunteered their time enjoyed the opportunity to practice under field conditions and to see some diseases, such as parasitic infections, they would not ordinarily encounter. The legal workers were often sponsored by groups of activists driven by a desire for peace and justice in Central America; they wanted to ensure that each Guatemalan had the opportunity to present a case to stay in the United States as a person seeking political asylum. They often expressed anger at official policy, which supported the Guatemalan government, the author of so much repression, and refused to consider the victims of the repression as refugees.

The owners of the citrus groves, speaking through their crew leaders, saw no problem in allowing the migrants in transit to sleep and eat in their orchards, since this allowed them access to a constant labor supply during citrus season. They were also able to keep their workers, Mexican migrants, happy by bringing them to the daily meal-and-clothing distribution. Alfredo, a crew boss, reported that most of those who lived under the trees moved on quickly, although the company hired three hundred men with work permits during the picking season, November through March. He claimed that no "gringos" would want the job. He understood that the Guatemalans came from a much more depressed economy than the Mexicans did, and he liked to work with them because they enjoyed outdoor work. He would frequently bring his crew in for the soup line and allowed the church volunteers to take away some citrus fruit in exchange for used shoes for his men. Because of the number of years that this arrangement prevailed, there was speculation among the volunteers that the owners of the property, as well as the managers of the citrus operation, must have been profiting in other ways as well, perhaps with kickbacks from the coyotes.

The transportation providers ranged (and still do) from outright frauds who take a person's money and documents and dump him in the desert far from any settlement, to semi-legitimate coyotes who charge a fair price considering their risk. Many of these coyotes are Guatemalans now living in the United States who have managed to buy vehicles for this enterprise. Their vans, with Florida or North Carolina plates, often came into view just as the church workers were leaving. By mutual agreement, communication between the two groups was minimal. Church volunteers did not want to be connected to the coyotes since they risked being accused by the INS of collaborating with the system (see Golden and McConnell 1986). In some instances, interventions were necessary when coyotes held people prisoner until they could pay, or kidnapped children from parents who did not come up with the full fare.

The coyotes have a network that lets them know when there are "pollos" or customers waiting in La Huerta, although for many years it was safe to assume that there always were. Reports and arrests at the present time indicate that the coyotes hold hostages in "safe houses" in Phoenix or nearby cities until ransom is paid by relatives or friends. By late 1994, the coyotes had started to use U-Haul-type trucks with Midwestern license plates to avoid the obvious profile of their vans.

The residents of the area surrounding the grove were occasionally roused to complain when there was a burglary they could blame on the migrants. The Border Patrol would oblige them by making a raid or two and taking away six to eight prisoners, which would pacify the neighbors until the next incident. The migrants were afraid to leave La Huerta because of their undocumented status; even those who had legitimate work permits often left them with relatives in other states while they visited in Guatemala. The Border Patrol also evidently felt obliged to make a show of force when the news media, particularly the local television channels, presented stories about the "soup line in the fields" around Thanksgiving and Christmas. This was also probably in response to public demand that the Border Patrol "do something," a demand that escalated when the situation was made more visible. Short on both funds and personnel, the Patrol for years made early-morning runs past the corner where migrants waited for day labor, but limited efforts, for the most part, to cruising the outside perimeter of La Huerta, for two obvious reasons. First, they knew they would fail to arrest many migrants where the thick orange trees offered instant cover and one row looks like every other row. Second, an outright raid on the church-sponsored food service would have brought down on the Border Patrol more bad publicity and public outrage than they cared to face. In one incident in 1988, a Border Patrol helicopter did land in a central clearing and officers ran after the fleeing migrants, but they may have realized that this was a lot of force for a minimal result, though the tactic was repeated in July 1997. One wonders how the sound of the helicopter affected those Mayas who know the helicopter only as an instrument of sudden and violent death.

In late 1996, owners began to fence the perimeters of the groves, and the migrants were forced deeper into the center. Since the land had become valuable for housing development, many citrus orchards sprouted "For Sale" signs. In 1997, increases in the number of INS agents and anti-immigration public sentiment brought an intensified campaign to close the migration route down. A 3:00 A.M. raid with dogs on Good Friday in March 1997 netted two van loads of prisoners. Increasingly frequent raids after that limited the willingness of the migrants to use La Huerta at all, and other routes were established, especially after July 1997, when Border Patrol vehicles, parked for twenty-four-hour periods at all nearby crossroads, made it impossible to use the area as before.

The number of Maya people who entered the United States weekly through La Huerta during the peak years is astonishing, given that this is only one collection area and served only the western Arizona border. The Arizona connection with Florida was a factor in the great concentration of Maya people there (see Burns 1994; Wellmeier 1998; Miralles 1987 for descriptions of the Maya population in Florida). Florida managed to absorb all this labor, and recent research in Florida seems to indicate that it serves in the manner of a traditional Maya community center, from which people disperse to agricultural work all over the country and to which they return when it ends. This indicates a blending of the Maya dispersed settlement pattern with the previous Mexican migrant labor stream that has historically provided the labor power for U.S. agriculture.

The phenomenon of La Huerta lends itself to reflection on the problems it presented. The volunteer services kept it viable as a transportation hub, a collection point for entering migrants, and a convenience for the coyotes who always knew where to find customers. Closing down would have meant denying food and clothing to transient Mayas who desperately needed it. Volunteers had to overcome their uneasiness about the technicalities of the federal law, which makes it a crime to shelter, transport, or otherwise aid undocumented persons in the United States. At the same time, there were and are few alternatives for those who are called in the literature "cross-fire refugees," those who cannot prove that they were personally targeted for persecution (Ferris 1987:36–38; Aguayo 1986:103, 109, 119). There is no process by which they can be admitted into the United States in advance; they must get here first, then either present themselves to the authorities with a voluntary political asylum case, or wait to be arrested and make application for asylum at that time. Most Guatemalans who applied for asylum in the late 1980s or early 1990s are still waiting for a hearing and a decision in their cases. New legislation changes the rules of the process almost monthly, and a nonliterate agricultural population whose first language is not a major Western language finds it almost impossible to navigate the paperwork. Even with some positive changes, legal permanent residents with good jobs have expressed their reluctance to go ahead with plans to purchase homes, afraid that their children will be kept from public schools, and concerned about the lack of access to health care.

At this writing, some solutions are being discussed, including a new "bracero" program to ease the labor shortages, a new amnesty for some Central Americans who have been in the United States for more than ten years, and targeting employers and transporters rather than the migrants. In the long term, basic changes in Guatemalan society must be made, so that the indigenous majority is no longer seen as a threat to the privileges of either the poor and middle-class ladinos or to the wealthy landowners and military elites. The Maya people who until recently were streaming to the United States through La Huerta were either the most ambitious and adventurous of their society, or the most desperate. Their presence here has enriched the society of the United States and those who have become their friends, but it would be better if their own Maya homeland were able to be home to them again.

NOTES

1. The personal names are fictitious, and some places in the United States are indicated only in general terms in order to protect the security of the Maya, many of whom are not documented even after many years in the country. Guatemalan place names, however, are real.

2. La Huerta was not the only entry point but was one of the most frequented because of the great expanse of unpatrolled and unpopulated desert terrain. Although the Maya who came to the United States often came for different reasons from those of the Mexican migrant laborers, they inherited their pattern of trails, connections, and contact points. The citrus grove described here was a collection and distribution point for Mexican migrant laborers long before 1980. Thus historic patterns of economic migration from the south to the United States had a great influence on the later "conflict migration" (see Ferris 1987:9 and Aguayo 1986:109, 115). This includes the infrastructure of migration, including safe houses, smugglers, rest and collection points, providers of false documents, and the increase in provision for social services in Spanish in the public health, safety, and education sectors—which have also benefited the later wave of Central American refugees (see Conover 1987:37–64 for a detailed account of this infrastructure). Guatemalan Mayas have also benefited from immigration legislation that in 1986 provided an opportunity for most undocumented Mexicans who had lived in the United States for many years to acquire legal standing and move into better employment in the visible economy. This left open the underground employment sector: agricultural piece work, sweat shops, day labor in construction, etc., for the new immigrants to fill. Many moved right into the traditional agricultural migrant stream that most Mexicans were simultaneously abandoning (Ashabranner 1986:4, 7; Burns 1989b:46; Burns 1988:41; Miralles 1987:12).

3. They would be taken to the Mexico-United States border if they succeeded in "passing" as Mexicans. If discovered to be Guatemalans, they are detained and sent by planeload to Guatemala City. The Border Patrol uses investigation techniques based on knowledge of geography and vocabulary differences to discover national identity.

4. I provided services on at least a weekly basis in La Huerta from the summer of 1988 through 1997, when the services were discontinued due to increased pressure from the Border Patrol.

5. The civil patrols were officially disbanded after the signing of the Peace Accords in Guatemala in December 1996.

6. As of this writing in the fall of 1999, there was indeed fieldwork available in South Florida, less in Arizona. Several service centers provided help in obtaining work permits in Florida citrus, sugar cane, and vegetable areas from 1983 to 1995. But recent immigration legislation has made it more difficult, if not impossible, to obtain legitimate work permits based on claims of political asylum. The response of most newcomers is to seek forged permits.

7. At the Federal Detention Center in Florence, the INS has 425 beds for detainees; 100 of these are reserved for noncriminal Central American "aliens." The staff at the Florence Immigration and Refugee Rights Project interviews sixteen detainees per day to determine asylum eligibility.

8. At least five of the volunteers have made trips to Guatemala to learn about the culture firsthand and to visit families of people they have befriended in Arizona.

ALLAN F. BURNS

10 Indiantown, Florida: The Maya Diaspora and Applied Anthropology

IN 1982 nine farm workers were picked up by the Immigration and Naturalization Service (INS) in south Florida as part of a sweep of farm labor camps and small agricultural towns at the end of the harvest season. When INS officials found that the nine had no visas or immigration papers, they were detained at the Krome Detention Center in Miami. Krome Detention Center had become famous in the early 1980s as the place where Cubans from the Mariel migration and Haitian boat people had been housed, so it was an appropriate place for the newest diaspora community of Florida, the Q'anjob'al Maya, to begin their experience in the state. The detention center was named after the street on which it was located, Krome Avenue in Miami, and was well known as a difficult place for people awaiting deportation because of overcrowding. This was one of the first institutional culture shocks that the Maya had in Florida, one that would be followed by many others in the institutions of education, health, work, and government.

The eight men and one woman from the highlands of Guatemala did not identify themselves in either Spanish or English and so were listed as "eight John Doe's and one Jane Doe" on the intake forms. They were unknown and undocumented aliens, people who looked Hispanic but were not like the Cubans, Salvadorans, or Mexicans normally seen in south Florida. The nine people had fled the Cuchumatán Mountains of northwest Guatemala during the height of the counterinsurgency campaign of the Guatemalan government, a campaign that was especially brutal and unremitting in its destruction of small settlements of Maya people hidden away in the highlands (Manz 1988a). These nine had made their way through Mexico to Arizona, where they worked for several months before a labor contractor persuaded them to come with him to find work in Florida. Like many labor contractors who prey on people desperate for work and a chance to make a living, he charged them each several hundred dollars for the trip, then left them working in the fields in an unknown state without housing or support of any kind.

Bewildered and without friends or family, the nine were easy to spot as undocumented aliens. They were physically shorter than many other migrant workers, wore clothes more typical of rural Guatemala than of the U.S. migrant stream, and had not learned how to play the "*migra* game" of effectively escaping INS sweeps. These sweeps often occurred on payday when people were assembled to collect their wages. The strategy was efficient and also helped owners; since raids often took place before wages were paid, workers were not only rounded up but deprived of their pay.

The goal of this chapter is to show how the Maya have strategically adapted to the small agricultural community of Indiantown over the first ten years of immigration to the United States. The case of Indiantown shows how the crucial social experiences of Maya people in the community have resulted in an emerging Maya identity in Florida (Burns 1989a). This identity is based on differing representations of the refugees as well as the increasing numbers and variety of people who continue to immigrate to Indiantown. Finally, this chapter addresses the role that anthropology played in the community through long-term collaboration between some community members and anthropologists.

The Maya of Indiantown, Florida, changed both as they spent more time in the United States and as changes occurred in Guatemala. The original nine people became the nucleus of a community of Q'anjob'al Maya that became an important population in a particular agricultural town, Indiantown, in south Florida. Later the community spread as more and more Maya and other Guatemalans fled their country and came to Florida looking for work and refuge, until their numbers rose to over twenty thousand. By the late 1990s Guatemalan Maya people were well established throughout the state. Their children attended schools and universities, they opened stores and businesses and even began broadcasting Mayan language radio programs. By the late 1990s it was common to see and talk to Guatemalan Mayas in small towns throughout the state. While Indiantown first functioned as a center to the Maya community of Florida, it later became more a symbolic center, or an entry point through which many Mayas passed upon arrival in Florida. A community-based social structure developed there. Later, as families and individuals left to seek work elsewhere in the state, the social structure of the diaspora group became more family-centered and less community-oriented.

Unlike enclave communities (Portes 1985), diaspora communities have a characteristic scattering of people and institutions across wide geographic areas. The Greek word refers to the dispersion or scattering of seeds, and the Maya of Florida have spread both physically and culturally throughout the state and the continent of North America. Another characteristic of diaspora communities is that people in them easily relocate between different locations within the diaspora; the community is everywhere but home. The different locations are like spokes on a wheel around the hub of the home community. Movement to different communities on the perimeter, be they in Mexico, the United States, or Canada, takes place either through travel back to the central hub or through travel around the edge from one community to another. A final characteristic of diaspora communities is that the migration chains established in the diaspora cannot be activated equally by all people. The pioneering families who came to Indiantown soon after the first nine brought their spouses and children, but by the late 1980s, single men in their late teens and twenties had become the primary immigrant population from Guatemala. When civil unrest ended in that country in the early 1990s, a diaspora had already been established, so that the return of official refugees from Mexico did little to change the out-migration from Maya communities.

When the first nine Q'anjob'al people were finally released one week after their apprehension, it was to an activist Catholic priest, Frank O'Loughlin, whose parish of Indiantown was a major center for farm workers in the citrus and winter vegetable fields of the area (Santoli 1988). O'Loughlin promised that the nine would be in his care. Once he began talking to them, he found that they indeed spoke Spanish, and the stories they told about the violence that drove them out of Guatemala were among the most horrific he had heard. As he said in an early interview, "They had no sense of any goal towards which they were headed. They were literally just responding to the terror behind them. . . . That defined refugee for me all over again. People with absolutely no goal, no place to go, but just simply something to be running from" (Burns 1993a:17).

O'Loughlin took it upon himself to educate his parish and those around it in southeast Florida about the civil war in Guatemala and the attacks on native peoples. To the residents of the south Florida area during the mid-1980s, the Maya were an enigma. While anthropologists and travelers knew that descendants of the great Maya civilization were still living, it was commonly believed that the Maya people had "vanished" with the collapse of that civilization in the tenth century. O'Loughlin's task with his parishioners was twofold: He had first to convince people that these immigrants were the "living Maya"; and he had then to educate them about the tragedy of their plight. In addition, he had to ensure that these first nine people and the others who joined them later would not be deported until they had the chance to apply for political asylum. To help with this, he contacted lawyers from Florida Rural Legal Services to begin documenting the stories of torture and escape from Guatemala, and he used the church's social service office, "El Centro," to refer the new Maya of Indiantown to appropriate counsel.

The name Indiantown predated the arrival of the Maya. The town was built near the end of the nineteenth century at a railroad camp situated on an old Seminole Indian village. By the time the Guatemalan Maya arrived in 1982, there were no Seminole people living in the area. Later efforts by Maya activist Jerónimo Camposeco to contact the Seminole failed, even though the Maya of Florida did have connections to other American Indian tribes. In 1986 the marimba band from Indiantown was invited to a Native American pow-wow in North Carolina, where they performed with Native American musicians from across the country. There, some of the ideas of pan-Indianism were introduced to the Maya diaspora community and became part of its cultural ideology. One of the ironies of that pow-wow was that the Maya marimba band wanted to dedicate something to the other Native Americans at the event. They chose a song from the migrant worker days of the 1930s written by Woody Guthrie, "This Land Is Your Land."

The nine refugees were the first people from San Miguel Acatán in the Guatemalan Department of Huehuetenango to make Indiantown their home. Chain migration of relatives and others quickly boosted the number of Maya in the community. By the 1990s, during the peak winter harvest season, there were four to five thousand Maya on the farms and citrus orchards surrounding Indiantown, and another fifteen thousand throughout the state. Although the Maya community remains predominantly Q'anjob'al, it is also home to speakers of other Mayan languages, including Akatek, Jakaltek, Mam, and K'iché. The town has become known throughout the human chain of refugees and other immigrants from the highlands of Guatemala by the Spanish translation of the name, "El Pueblo de Los Indios," a name easy enough to remember because of the irony of there being a town for "Indians" in Florida. The name led to misconceptions among Mayas still in Guatemala that Indiantown was a community deliberately established to welcome indigenous people migrating from Guatemala to the United States. The name Indiantown also spread through the academic community. I once heard Spanish anthropologists in Granada speak of it as a colony of Maya refugees in the depths of the Florida wilderness.

The name is at once ironic to the Maya and a recognition of the importance of the Maya diaspora in shaping a new identity. The irony comes from the term "indio," which in Guatemalan Spanish is still a derogatory term, reflecting the lumping together of the several indigenous communities of Guatemala in one racial—and racist—category. Such a simplistic reduction is especially offensive as it flies in the face of the overt cultural value placed on the distinctiveness of individual towns and communities in highland Guatemala. Craig (1977), among other linguists who have worked in the Cuchumatán homeland of the Maya of Florida, has commented on the inability of speakers of closely related languages to understand each other or even admit to a linguistic commonality. This has led to the proliferation of recognized Mayan languages and is a source of division between Maya people. But it also reflects a positive cultural value, the value of expecting cultural differences in the world rather than cultural uniformity. As Manning Nash has written, "The important axis of this worldview, in relation to persons and culture, is that Maya Indians see cultural differences as 'natural.' Cultural variety is a fact of nature. Different customs are both characteristic and appropriate for different people. . . . Furthermore, these cultural differences all exist at the same level of human validity. They are not ranked. Differences are neither better or worse—just different. They are in the scheme of things, not to be obliterated, overcome, or discarded" (Nash 1989:108).

José Antonio, an immigrant to Indiantown, explained this concept to me in terms of how United States citizens expect cultural assimilation from immigrants. He was visiting me at the University of Florida and was impressed with the variety of students from different parts of the world he saw on campus. Later that day, he was telling me how stressed he had become working for the Maya organization in Indiantown, and how tired he had become of hearing non-Maya people tell him that he and his family had to "become more American." "Why is it," he asked, "that Americans want us to be absorbed and become like them? We don't ask them to become like us; we don't ask them to wear clothes like us. They are supposed to be different from us, and we are supposed to be different from them as well."

So it was by an accident of history and geography that the town of Indiantown, "El Pueblo de los Indios," became home to an increasing number of the Maya. The separate identities of different *aldeas* and municipalities in Guatemala are being submerged under the creation of this new identity as Maya Indians in a North American context.

LEGAL AND SOCIAL STATUS: REFUGEES, IMMIGRANTS, AND MIGRANT WORKERS

The twenty thousand Maya who have come from Guatemala to Florida since the early 1980s are refugees from the political and civil violence of the region. The term refugee itself is highly charged, especially as the number of refugees throughout the world continues to rise at a rapid rate (Zetter 1988). One common distinction is based on criteria from the United Nations Geneva Accords, which state that someone escaping a well-founded fear of persecution is defined as a political refugee, while someone escaping the economic or social disintegration of his country is an economic refugee. Governments throughout the world are quick to adopt this distinction, as it allows for tighter control of immigration and denial of legal immigrant status to those determined to be "economic migrants." Although commonly accepted in governmental circles, the experience of the Guatemala Maya who leave their homeland and travel through Mexico and the United States suggests that the term needs reevaluation. I use the term "refugee" in a broad sense because it is important to recognize that there are degrees of "political persecution." Someone who is officially designated an "economic migrant" or "illegal alien" can often have his or her status changed to "political asylum refugee" by the good fortune of finding a good attorney or by events beyond his or her control, such as the ruling in the 1990 case brought by the American Baptist Churches against the INS, or the "ABC" case, as it came to be known. The ruling, based on a case filed by several church groups collaborating with the American Baptist Churches, successfully argued that political asylum decisions for Central Americans had been based not on the merits of each case but rather on U.S. foreign policy during the 1980s. The ruling in favor of the churches allowed political asylum applications that had been turned down over the previous ten years to be reopened. In the wake of the ruling, hundreds of thousands of cases for political asylum from immigrants throughout Central America had to be reviewed. By the late 1990s, the chances of even being called for an asylum review had become so slim that new legislation was enacted to allow the State Department to deport asylum seekers from Central America once the conditions that led them to flee their countries had improved. So the category of "refugee," while seemingly clear from a legal or commonsense perspective, is ambiguous among the Maya. It is better thought of as a point along a continuum of the legality of migration, a status that one can achieve in part or whole and that is related to others (Hagen 1994). When the 1986 Immigration and Reform Control Act allowed for the legalization of undocumented immigrants who had either been in the United States for over five years or had performed agricultural work in the years prior to the law, the Guatemalan Maya of Florida quickly applied for status as residents in addition to continuing their claims for political asylum as refugees. The uncertainty of legal status was reflected in the statements of immigrants. Many of them, proud of their ability to work hard and adapt to new employment opportunities, told reporters and others that they came to the United States "to work hard." While this kind of answer helped in establishing farmworker status under the 1986 immigration law, it was detrimental to political asylum cases.

One of the survival strategies that developed in the Maya diaspora community was the use of multiple nationalities. In California, false birth certificates and identity papers have long been available to migrants from Mexico and Central America, and young Guatemalan Maya men quickly learned that in the late 1980s it was easier to cross the border into California as a Guatemalan because one could easily claim to be a political refugee, but that, once in the United States, it was easier to move about with Mexican papers.

THE COMMUNITY OF INDIANTOWN

Longtime residents of Indiantown did not invite the Guatemalans into their midst, and many resented Priest Frank O'Loughlin and the

Catholic Church for welcoming them to the town. Indiantown was a small agricultural community of just over three thousand people in the early 1980s, a decade that saw some three thousand immigrants from Mexico and Guatemala stretch the capacity of the town's services to the limits. Indiantown is located inland from the southeast coast of Florida at the crossroads of several agricultural and labor markets. The land immediately around Indiantown includes thousands of acres of rich citrus groves and at one time was the major lemon-producing area in the United States. The town is at the southern end of the large Florida cattle lands and borders on the immense winter vegetable fields of southern Florida. But agriculture is only one important part of the attraction of Indiantown for people looking to survive in the U.S. labor market—the community is on the edge of the construction boom area of coastal Florida as well. Professional golf course communities and the ever-increasing spread of planned communities on the coast create a need for unskilled laborers. Day labor, construction jobs, and industries that support construction are all areas where the Maya can seek employment in the Indiantown area. It would be a mistake, however, to view the area as an economic Mecca of abundant good jobs. Much of the work is temporary, seasonal, and often without benefits. Temporary unemployment and underemployment are very high, and the seasonality of the agricultural work puts many of the Maya into the migrant stream, so that Indiantown is but one in a series of small towns where agricultural laborers live during the year.

The town is unincorporated and in fact is made up of several settlements in close proximity to one another, such as Booker Park, Indianwood, and Indiantown proper. Indiantown proper is centered on the one traffic light of the community and is a primarily middle-class community. A retirement community of manufactured homes, Indianwood, was developed in the 1980s. It offers a golf course and a chance for retirees to settle in southern Florida at a fraction of the cost of coastal areas. Booker Park is the poor part of town, home to the majority of the African American, Hispanic, and Maya people who have been attracted to the availability of farm work in the area. A few other farm worker settlements, or camps, are located on the fringes of the community and are known as "white camp" or "yellow camp" according to the color of the small housing units at each.

The county seat, Stuart, is located on the coast, and Indiantown has always been thought of as a kind of rural agricultural area rather than an important county location by people living on the coast. The community of Indiantown has a western, agricultural ethos. Farmers and ranchers come to eat in the local cafe every morning, and the rodeo grounds are busy throughout the year with various competitive events. During the 1970s, townspeople worked in the surrounding citrus, ranch, and winter vegetable corporations and many commuted to a Pratt and Whitney helicopter factory located fifteen miles to the south. So when the Guatemalan Maya immigration began in the early 1980s, many residents felt that the calm and tranquillity of small-town life was being threatened by an invasion of people who spoke unfamiliar languages, lived in poverty, and seemed to be arriving in ever-increasing numbers.

The long-term residents make up a community as diverse as many small U.S. towns. Differences in economic status, religion, age, and occupation make Indiantown a complicated social arena. The town proudly boasts a group of civic-minded people who form a permanent core of what they themselves refer to as the "helping community." This network includes volunteer emergency medical personnel who run the ambulance service, volunteer teachers and aides in the schools, and families from different churches who take it upon themselves to teach English and make personal efforts to incorporate Maya refugees into the social structure of the community. This core group is augmented by social workers and social service volunteers, an order of Catholic nuns and lay teachers who run a school for migrant labor children, legal assistance lawyers and aides, hospital and clinic workers, as well as journalists, students, and union organizers. This part of the "helping community" makes the town their home for months and often years at a time. Because Indiantown is relatively small, these people are more visible and more influential than they might be in a city or larger community.

The "helping" institution that has most affected the Indiantown Maya is the private school for migrant children begun by the Catholic Church. Hope Rural School is the only school of its kind in the state. Migrant children are supported in their education there through the church, and special attention is given to the fact that most of them do not stay in the community year-round. One of the first Maya activists to arrive in Indiantown was employed by the school to work on extracurricular activities. He began a garden project where families planted traditional crops from Guatemala, an alcoholic recovery program for young adults, sports programs for children, and other such initiatives. Hope Rural School became an important institution for the Maya of Indiantown and a haven from the discrimination they encountered in other areas. Not everyone in Indiantown is as hospitable to the Maya as this "helping community," nor is there uniformity among this diverse group in terms of goals, methods, or knowledge about the refugees (Dorman 1986). Still, the "helping community" is a new social factor in the lives of Maya immigrants, one that is significant in both their adaptation and their identity in Florida.

Residents of Indiantown never imagined that their town would become the destination of so many people from Guatemala, and the community has been hard pressed to provide for their health, educational, social, and emotional needs. But the availability of agricultural labor, the small-town atmosphere, and the hospitality offered by the Catholic Church put Indiantown into the migration network of the Maya diaspora.

The Maya have had to adapt to the multiethnic migrant worker community of Indiantown as well. In Guatemala distinctions between different aldeas or towns were important in the Department of Huehuetenango, as were distinctions between Maya and ladinos (Nash 1989). Even when the Maya went to the coastal plantations of Guatemala to do seasonal work, they tended to stay with friends and townspeople from their own language and community groups, and so had little experience with the multiracial and multiethnic diversity of a small U.S. town. But in the years since 1982, when the Maya began arriving in Indiantown, their social world has widened to include groups found in U.S. migrant work elsewhere: African Americans, whites, Haitians and other people from the Caribbean, Mexicans and Mexican Americans, and other Central Americans.

Like many small towns in the United States, low-paid work such as that found on farms and in citrus groves has attracted a multiethnic work force. Over time, different groups have gravitated toward different employment sectors. In Indiantown, Mexicans and Mexican Americans tend to work in the citrus industry, African Americans in construction or the pre-grown lawn industry of the area. The Maya began working in the citrus industry, but many quickly moved into vegetable farm labor, the nursery industry, and unskilled construction. Maya men have had success in the golf course construction industry. Their careful attention to the delicate grasses and layout of golf courses and their willingness to work long and hard has made them sought-after employees.

HOUSING

The influx of Guatemalan Maya to the community has caused tremendous strains in the social fabric of Indiantown, first among them a housing shortage. In a town used to migrant workers living on the outskirts during the citrus and winter vegetable harvests, temporary housing in apartment buildings, farm worker "camps," and rented rooms was a long-established pattern. But the Guatemalan Maya presented new problems. They were substantially poorer than previous immigrants, spoke unrecognizable languages, and filled available housing to the limit. A 1989 U.S. Labor Department study found an average household size of twelve people among Guatemalan Mayas in Indiantown, with many dwellings housing more than twenty. Mexicans and Mexican Americans, by contrast, averaged only five people per household. The pressure on housing in the community has been phenomenal. Anglo residents complain about the decline in housing values—and the overloading of the town's sewage system—brought about by the immigrants.

The lack of housing and the need for it during peak periods of the agricultural cycle drive rents up astronomically. Rents of $300 to $400 are common for unfurnished two-room apartments, with a "surcharge" of $25 per person per week for each person above the maximum capacity of five. Those who cannot afford such rents can pay $25 a week to sleep in an abandoned car or bus on private property. A few Maya immigrants have been able to purchase their own modest homes in the community, but there are extremely strong pressures on anyone who owns or even rents a house to take in boarders. Relatives, friends, and those who arrive in Indiantown homeless all seek out people who live in houses and ask for temporary shelter.

Housing is such a critical and visible need for the Guatemalan Maya of Indiantown that it overshadows many other issues. The community has been able to develop low-income housing for farm workers through a nonprofit housing authority and the involvement of Habitat for Humanity. But the continual influx of people, whether returning each winter or immigrating for the first time, puts an intolerable burden on housing resources in Indiantown.

INTERETHNIC RELATIONS

Interethnic relations in Indiantown are problematic. While individual friendships and relationships between the Maya and their neighbors do occur, to a large extent the barriers of language, national custom, suspicion, and violence keep interethnic associations from developing. The Maya are especially subject to personal violence in Florida. They are often assaulted and robbed because of their small stature and the fact that they are known not to be armed. A paralegal worker noted that when he talked to the Guatemalans in Indiantown about guns, they responded with horror. Even the tendency of the Maya to walk rather than ride in Florida sets them apart from long-term residents. The sight of groups of five or six Maya walking down the main highway is new to the town. One resident said the town is no longer Indiantown but has become "Guatemala town."

The workplace is often viewed as the setting where the "melting-pot" ideal of U.S. society operates best. The experience of laboring together, the structure of industrial relations, and the camaraderie developed on the job are all believed to help newcomers of different backgrounds assimilate into the mainstream culture. But interethnic relations in Indiantown tend not to improve at work, in part because most occupations remain segregated. Among migrant workers in Indiantown there is a strong motive to seek work, and other help, only from one's own kind. Only occasionally is it necessary even to communicate with someone who speaks a different language.

In addition, the extreme physical demands of immigrant work discourage socializing. One Haitian man tried to learn a few phrases in Spanish so as to communicate with a Spanish-speaking man who had been hired onto his landscaping crew; but after a few weeks he stopped trying. He had not been able to form a friendship with the man, he said, because there was so little time to talk while working. Even lunch breaks were not much used for socialization, because the men needed to eat and get back to work.

CHANGES AND CONFLICT IN THE COMMUNITY

It would be inaccurate to describe Indiantown as a transplanted "closed corporate community" (Wolf 1957) or as a refugee camp (Carmack 1988). The Maya diaspora to Indiantown has been a process of both annual and cumulative change, so that what might be true one year is often radically changed by the next. Yearly changes in the agricultural work availability in Florida due to freezes or changes in the international market have resulted in a movement of the Maya into more settled work such as nursery and landscaping jobs. The problems of crime, housing, and increasing sophistication have also motivated many Maya to leave the community for other parts of Florida. From 1982 through 1985 Indiantown was a center of Maya settlement in Florida, but since 1985 thousands of Maya have moved to other communities, often dispersing by family rather than congregating by the hundreds in a single town. Probably less than a fifth of the Maya of Florida still lived in Indiantown by the late 1990s.

The demographic profile of Indiantown has also changed dramatically since 1985, when more single men began to arrive. The first wave of Maya refugees was predominantly made up of families, but as emigration from Guatemala has become more difficult, and as Mexico has increased its efforts to capture and deport undocumented Guatemalans (USCR 1991), it is primarily young single men who can now make the trip. Mexico's interdiction of Central Americans has resulted in younger immigrants, fewer Central American immigrants, and an increase in Mexican illegal entrants.

The increasingly complex background and makeup of immigrants to Indiantown has also changed the Guatemalan community there. The Q'anjob'al from San Miguel Acatán are the predominant group in the community, but ladinos, other Maya, and other Central American immigrants are now common as well. Refugees from the early 1980s complain that the new immigrants have different reasons for immigrating than they did. The American Baptist Church ruling resulted in a surge of several hundred thousand cases in the United States awaiting documentation of refugee status. Conflicts have now had time to emerge in Indiantown, conflicts that often had their origin in events of Guatemala. People are accused of affiliation with different guerrilla insurgency or of collaborating with the Guatemalan army. The identity of people in the town as "Maya" or "Guatemalan" has become an issue of great conflict, as have the identities of Q'anjob'al, Mam, and K'iche'. Even the spelling of these names has become a source of divisiveness. More recent immigrants use the Academy of Mayan Languages' official spelling of the different languages, while older immigrants are more accustomed to the traditional Spanish spelling of Kanjobal and Quiché.

Church affiliation, whether evangelical, Catholic, or *costumbre*, is yet another area of contention that has arisen more and more in the community. Finally, and perhaps most perniciously, envy and denunciations of those Maya people who work in social-service roles in health clinics or nonprofit organizations by other Maya are now common. Individuals in leadership positions in particular are the targets of tremendous envy. This envy has led to the creation of several other Maya organizations in addition to the original CornMaya, the first Maya community group established in Indiantown.

INSTITUTIONAL CULTURE SHOCK

As the community evolves, more and more refugees experience institutional culture shock in the offices of government bureaucracies. Police, the courts, and the INS are obvious arenas where the Maya confront new problems, but experience in Guatemala with similar institutions at least makes these comprehensible. Other institutions, such as state health programs, present new problems. Maya young people, especially, are in turmoil in Indiantown. The birth rate among teenage girls is very high, and child spacing very short. Many of the Maya have now grown up in the United States from early childhood, and the gulf between their experiences and those of their parents is great. While many health workers assume that there is a tradition of health knowledge that young mothers bring to the United States, many of these women have spent the majority of their lives in the culture of communities like Indiantown. Their acculturation and that of their husbands and boyfriends has taken place in the underclass poverty of agricultural and construction work. In a recent case in another Florida community, a fifteen-year-old unwed Maya mother had her child taken away by the state because she was a migrant worker who, according to nurses in the hospital, had "failed to bond" with her infant. At the court hearing, the girl quietly answered "no" when asked if she wanted her baby, and "yes" when she was asked if she wanted to return to Guatemala. Her limited Spanish and the fact that she was an undocumented immigrant suggest that she thought she was at a deportation hearing, not a child custody hearing. Her statements that she wanted to return to Guatemala but did not want her own baby suggest that she thought she was about to be deported and was trying to save the child from the same fate. Several months later, after talking with child welfare advocates and Jerónimo Camposeco, she petitioned to have her child returned to her. Eventually the child was returned, but only after it had spent the first year of its life away from its mother.

Another case was even more striking. Soon after she gave birth, one of the Maya women of Indiantown went into postpartum depression. She left her infant with her husband and got a ride to a nearby community, where she was picked up by the police and questioned. Since the police spoke little Spanish and no Mayan, she seemed to them incoherent. She was taken to a nearby city, hospitalized, and put under psychiatric care for two weeks until someone from Indiantown tracked her down. Hospital personnel said that she was "speaking in tongues." Because of her stress and depression, she was able to speak only Mayan, and the hospital was far enough away from Indiantown that health workers had no idea that she was in fact speaking a real language.

The institutional culture shock experienced by Maya in Florida adds to the interpersonal culture shock they undergo in their everyday lives. The frowns of longtime residents of Indiantown puzzle immigrants who expect hospitality or at least neutrality. The demeaning nickname of schoolchildren for the Maya, "Watermelons" (a corruption of the Spanish pronunciation of "Guatemaltecos"), and the belittling label that many Mexicans give them in the fields, "Inditos" or "little Indians," all add up to a burden of interpersonal culture shock that compounds the institutional culture shock of life in Maya immigrant communities like Indiantown. Even more horrific is the kind of violence that the Maya have encountered in the poor areas of Indiantown and nearby cities such as West Palm Beach. Robberies and assaults on Maya people became so common that several community task forces were begun in West Palm Beach in 1994 to discuss increasing levels of crime between African Americans and Guatemalan Maya. The task forces did not solve the problem, but at least the vulnerability of rural Maya in inner-city West Palm Beach was recognized.

Collaborative Research in Indiantown

In 1983 I met Jerónimo Camposeco through a mutual friend who had begun a local chapter of Habitat for Humanity in Gainesville, the site of the University of Florida, and wanted to start one in Indiantown. I was teaching at the University of Florida a course on applied anthropology and the Maya, and Camposeco had been one of the very few Jakaltek Maya at that time to have received political asylum in the United States. I invited him to campus to give several lectures and to explore the possibility of his continuing his university education in Florida. Camposeco had been trained in anthropology and education in Guatemala, and so stood in the unique position of a culture broker and spokesman for the new Maya arriving in Florida. Unlike so many others, his position was safe, and he could not be deported or subjected to harassment here in the United States for speaking out on the situation in Guatemala. In addition, his contacts with Native Americans, and especially with the Indian Law Resource Center, provided a means by which he could assist Maya immigrants with asylum and immigration issues.

In 1984 we began a program of applied anthropology in Indiantown, using a network of students and other colleagues at the University of Florida, social service offices such as the Catholic Church's El Centro in Indiantown, and institutions concerned with immigration, asylum, and social justice issues. Over the years since our first meeting, we have developed a program of community organization and action; done primary research on questions of employment, health, and education; created public television video documentaries on the community; and implemented programs of cultural expression through marimba performances at museums and universities. Not all of these activities have met with equal success, nor have we been the prime movers behind all of them. These are not the only projects in Indiantown, either. Many other people have developed very useful social programs with the Maya there. Still, with the changing nature of the Maya community in Indiantown, our own work has contributed to both the legitimacy and adaptation of its Mayas.

One of the collaborative activities in which we have engaged is the nonprofit community organization CornMaya. CornMaya was initiated by Camposeco and anthropologist Shelton Davis in 1982 as a way to give Maya immigrants a voice in the United States. In 1986 Camposeco traveled to Los Angeles and helped organize a sister association there, IXIM. The CornMaya association in Indiantown was at first under the auspices of the Catholic Church, but as funding became available for political asylum and social service help through the World Lutheran Council, it developed into a completely independent organization. It took several years to gain expertise enough to file for nonprofit and tax-exempt status, but the experience of doing so gave participants skills for dealing with U.S. bureaucracies and governmental agencies. Once again the resource base of the University of Florida was useful in that colleagues from the College of Law assisted with the applications for nonprofit status. The process of working through the state and national bureaucracy for nonprofit status also helped subsequent leaders of CornMaya by building their confidence to approach county commissions, zoning boards, and other associations in the community. In the early 1990s the association found funding to rent a storefront on the main highway running through Indiantown. This gave CornMaya a physical location distinct from the private homes where it had been housed previously. The public location of CornMaya was important in providing both legitimacy and visibility for the Maya of Indiantown. But the lease on the storefront brought to the fore divisions within the organization and also led to regular financial crises, since monthly rent now had to be paid. CornMaya underwent a period of intense criticism, from both within and without the organization.

Some Guatemalan and Maya immigrants criticized the association because it was so closely tied to the activities of Camposeco and myself. One complaint, for example, was that it contained the word "Maya" and thus did not represent the newer immigrants to the community who were from Guatemala but were not indigenous Maya. In the 1990s, other organizations formed that stood in opposition to CornMaya and yet ironically, as so often happens, profited from the experience of the association. By the mid-1990s CornMaya had suspended operations and the storefront location on the main street of Indiantown was abandoned. Some of the early leaders of the organization opened different kinds of profit-making businesses, such as importing Guatemalan clothes and foods or arranging for the transfer of money to Guatemala, and had little time for the ethnic organization. By the late 1990s CornMaya had been incorporated into a larger pan-Mayan diaspora organization that linked Indiantown to other Mayan communities in Los Angeles and other parts of the United States. A second set of collaborative activities that resulted from applied work was the creation of several video productions. Early in our friendship, Camposeco and I decided that it would be useful to have a half-hour video program about the Maya who had come to Indiantown. This would take some of the pressure off Camposeco and others who were regularly asked to speak at churches and other groups in the state to explain why Guatemalan Maya people were coming to Florida. Camposeco had an extensive slide collection from his years as a teacher and researcher in Guatemala, and these images were an excellent way to present the case of the refugees to the American public. I enlisted the help of a professional film team from the public television station in Gainesville and together we made the first of several programs. *Maya in Exile* was shown on PBS stations in Florida as well as sold to schools and anthropology departments. All proceeds from sales and rental of the program went to CornMaya. All in all, however, the program lost money. Sales and rentals were few and were never enough to recoup the costs of renting equipment and paying a professional film team to make the program (Burns 1993b). But the program was well received, and we decided to make a second video a few years later. This one focused on the San Miguel fiesta that was now held in Indiantown both as a remembrance of San Miguel Acatán in Guatemala and as a public event for both the Maya and non-Maya of Indiantown. Several years later we were asked by the March of Dimes and the Presbyterian Women's Ministry to make a video for Maya women on prenatal care and nutrition. We made two, focusing on the changes in food, housing, and institutions that young mothers face in the United States. While these videos had the least appeal as general documentaries, they were the most widely distributed. Interest in immigrant women's health care was widespread throughout the United States, and the videos were distributed by the funding institutions through clinics in many states.

Like the documentary programs, the two health videos depended on the help of experts who were willing to work with the community for little or no remuneration. The health videos were produced by Randi Cameon, a physician's assistant with an advanced degree in public health, and Maria Rocha, a graduate student in anthropology. In Indiantown, the demands on local people as volunteers in social service programs often led to exhaustion or "burnout." Fortunately, the University of Florida possessed a large population to draw from so that highly motivated students and colleagues could bring their expertise to projects such as these for reasonably short periods of time.

Health concerns continue to loom large in the diaspora community of Indiantown. A Guatemalan service center in nearby Lake Worth received funding to produce a video in Maya and Spanish about the spread of AIDS in the immigrant community. The effects of pesticide and other chemical poisoning from farm work now haunt the Florida Maya. The rate for babies born with malfunctioning hearts was four times that reported for other groups in the mid-1990s. The applied work Camposeco and I began in the 1980s moved quickly into areas of health and disease, especially as more long-term effects of pesticide and other chemical poisoning began to appear in the latest generation of the diaspora.

CONCLUSIONS

The situation in the diaspora community of Indiantown is much more complex than that in other refugee communities officially designated by government or United Nations agencies in the world. Indiantown is a place to which refugees chose to move and not a place where they were involuntarily resettled. In the years since the Maya began immigrating there, the community has adapted to them, while at the same time the characteristics of the immigrants have gradually changed. Indiantown is now one of many places in the Maya diaspora through which Guatemalan Maya people move on seasonal and episodic cycles.

As communities like Indiantown become linked through networks of kinship, work, the hospitality and also hostility of local residents, and the presence of scholars, the Maya of Indiantown take on some characteristics of other Native Americans. This idea is better put by Jerónimo Camposeco, who wrote,

> The situation in San Miguel is no longer what it was. Difficult as it is to face, a return to the tranquillity, to the traditional and peaceful community that existed before is now only a dream. The Migueleño, Jacalteco, Solomero, Mame, Quiché, Aguateco, Kanjobal, and other refugee Maya in Florida and other states, as a community, as a nation, or as a group, will not return to Guatemala, although a few individuals may do so temporarily or permanently.

Practically speaking, there is a new Indian nation in North America—the Maya in Exile. In light of this, from now on we face a tremendous obligation, a formidable task, a constant struggle, and a continuous fight for respect, recognition, and survival. (Camposeco 1993:xlvii)

The Maya diaspora in Indiantown reflects the experience of other groups who have been forced to leave their homelands and develop extensive communities where they could find employment and security. Maya communities in the diaspora give evidence of acculturation to different North American models—Chicano, Anglo, and ethnic enclave are the most common. But Maya and their U.S. research partners increasingly recognize that the diaspora communities in Florida and beyond are the crucible of new cultural formations that have conscious Maya characteristics. At the same time, however, these new cultural forms are less Guatemalan than they are American.

Jerónimo Camposeco

11 A Maya Voice: The Refugees in Indiantown, Florida

THIS BRIEF paper addresses the situation of Indiantown, Florida, but the same situation exists in other towns in the Florida countryside, like Immokalee near Naples, another area with three to five thousand Maya at the picking season for oranges, tomatoes, and vegetables.[1] We Maya are also located in areas like Homestead, south of Miami, a very agricultural region, and in the areas around Indiantown, West Palm Beach, Lake Worth, Boynton Beach, and Fort Pierce, places where there is a variety of work in citrus and vegetable farming as well as in construction, golf course jobs, and other manual labor.

Currently the Maya are working primarily in the lowest-paying jobs. Many Guatemaltecos in this region were unable to secure their migration papers through the Immigration Reform and Control Act of 1986 (IRCA). Later many who had come to this area—especially single young men and some women—did not qualify for the IRCA program because they did not arrive in the United States before the cut-off date for application. If they apply for their papers now, they do so in a very haphazard fashion and are often exploited by certain notaries public in Miami when they try to get a temporary work permit. The majority do not have papers because they cannot make a good case for political asylum. Therefore, because of the Employer Sanctions sections of the IRCA program, many employers cannot offer jobs. As a result, these undocumented people must look for work with some crew leader who gives them a day's work and then tells them they have to find another job, because he has to protect himself from the immigration laws. I believe that employer fines run as high as $10,000. By doing this underground, clandestine work, Maya workers must agree to receive below-minimum wages. Sometimes they find only two or three days' worth of work a week. They can hardly survive in their houses and apartments and in the fields. They pay very high rents; sometimes they must share space with ten to fifteen other people. There is very little money

172

eft for food. Their lives are among the most difficult of all agricultural workers.

Drug addiction has already begun to be a problem among the young people living here in Florida. Not surprising, there is also alcoholism, a social phenomenon of refugee life. It is very high among the Q'anob'ales and Maya of Florida and it leads to more specific problems like arrests, jailings, traffic violations, car accidents, and other problems of violence.

Identity is another problem for Maya people in the United States. The original refugees in Florida were almost totally Maya, but later they were joined by ladinos from different parts of Guatemala. Now we identify ourselves as Maya in order to maintain our identity or to obtain better treatment from U.S. society or as a strategy for gaining political asylum, or to obtain better treatment from immigration authorities. But this often means distancing ourselves from other Guatemalans who have different claims. One aspect of our claims emphasizes the racial and cultural discrimination to which we were subjected in Guatemala. But these issues are being questioned by the ladino refugees and they, without knowing the basis of our strategy, consider us racists.

We also experience violence, which has caused about fifty fatalities in this region, most of them in Indiantown, due to drunken brawls caused by non-Guatemalans who came here looking for easy money to buy drugs. And among our own friends and family there have been serious problems as well.

As we now look ahead to the future, we are questioning our identity. What will the future of the Maya in Florida be like? There are already many different groups here. In the beginning there was unity, but now factions have divided the community. One faction wants to Americanize, to give up their Maya identity and become more American. This is a small group of people who originally saw themselves as Maya but now feel less Maya because the press, they say, and other persons who have come from outside, identify us as dirty, ignorant, and living crammed together in small apartments. To them we appear to be the scabs of society. Outsiders now identify these qualities as part of our ethnic Maya identity, but they are wrong. Ladinos, on the other hand, pressure us to reach equality not as Maya but in a different, more Guatemalan, way. Given these problems, adaptation to our new home in the United States is not easy for us. What are we going to do? There is already a Maya population, one could say a nation-in-exile, in the United States. Will we continue, will we reinvent and seek our identity as Maya, or will we look to integrate and adapt our community to that of the larger society? And by doing so will we lose our life's purpose which lies in being Maya, our inheritance from our forefathers?

NOTES

1. This is a transcript of an oral presentation given at a panel entitled "The Maya Diaspora" at the Latin American Studies Association Congress in March 1991. Translation by Elisabeth Sirucek, edited by Marilyn Moors.

LEON FINK AND ALVIS DUNN

12   The Maya of Morganton: Exploring
      Worker Identity within
      the Global Marketplace

BEGINNING IN 1991 and culminating in a four-day strike and
successful union election campaign in 1995, a series of labor conflicts
rocked the town of Morganton, North Carolina, a usually quiet industrial center (population 16,000) perched at the edge of the Great Smoky
Mountains.[1] The events place two recent socioeconomic developments
into bold relief. First, the poultry industry stands as a symbol of an
exploding new wave of low-wage domestic food-processing industries,
a highly competitive manufacturing center, generally bitterly resistant
to unionization and collective bargaining. Second, the 550-person Morganton workforce, estimated in 1995 as 80 percent Latino (of which 90
percent were Guatemalan immigrants), and 80 percent male, highlights
the crucial role that a new Hispanic migration is playing in the U.S.
labor force, a role that requires a revised exploration of "working-class
community" as well as a new assessment of both potential resources
and obstacles facing organized labor in a changing political climate.

In this chapter we hope to set the Morganton organizing experience
in its global context. After attending briefly to the structure of the industry and the nature of grievances besetting the Morganton plant over
several years, we turn to the experience of the workers themselves,
especially the Guatemalans, for an explanation of the pattern of protest
and organization that has taken shape in Morganton. In doing so, we
are struck by the mixture of faraway forces—regime changes, economic
pressures, and immigration policy—and distinctly local peculiarities at
both ends of a transnational journey, in setting the terms of conflict.

That poultry processing plants have proved a magnet for a new
immigrant labor force is a testament to the peculiar dynamism of this
post–World War II industry. Prior to that time, as Herbert Hoover's "a
chicken in every pot" campaign promise suggested, chickens generally
needed extended stewing. But postwar entrepreneurs like Arthur W.

175

Perdue combined new processing techniques, name-brand recognition and integrated control of egg growers, farmers, feed producers, and processors under one corporate roof, to revolutionize what became known by the mid-1960s as the "broiler" industry. In subsequent years the advent of fast-food chicken and rising health concerns about red meat created an explosive demand for chicken products that continues to the present day. Market success, however, has also bred a demand for labor not easily satisfied through conventional sources. For one thing, a search for a uniform-size chicken—required for both assembly (or rather disassembly) line production prôcesses and for fast-food automatic frying vats—has placed a continuing premium on locating processing plants near rural growing areas. Second, an intensely competitive industry (the four leading firms controlled only 42 percent of the broiler market in 1994), has been determined to keep a tight lid on wage costs and has succeeded in keeping the poultry wage at roughly 60 percent of the U.S. manufacturing average since the early 1970s. From the beginning of the industry's development in the 1950s and 1960s, low land and labor costs favored location in southern states, and that trend continues. Once the surplus labor of depressed, southern farming areas was tapped out in the 1980s, however—and against the backdrop of a generally booming Sunbelt economy that offered other, usually more pleasant as well more remunerative options to the traditional factory labor force—poultry employers proved both desperate and adventuresome in seeking a new low-wage recruitment base. The answer came swiftly. Latino workers represented less than 10 percent of the overall poultry labor force in 1988; by 1993 this aggregate figure had jumped to 25 percent. In Morganton, and in other poultry centers like the tri-state Delaware-Maryland-Virginia peninsula (home to Perdue Farms), the demographic change was even more dramatic. Here, Mexicans and Central Americans, especially Guatemalans, became the employees of choice.[2]

Aside from the possibility of steady employment free from war-related violence, Morganton's natural setting at the edge of the Great Smoky Mountains was its most attractive feature for new Guatemalan residents. With only the occasional exception, the Guatemalans in Morganton are indigenous people of Maya descent who claim the modest-sized *pueblos* (towns) or tiny *aldeas* (hamlets) that dot the sides of the towering peaks of the Cuchumatán mountain range in the Guatemala's northwestern Department of Huehuetenango as their home. Although the indigenous peoples of Guatemala number over twenty distinct language groups in all (and six in Huehuetenango alone), two groups made their presence most felt at the Morganton poultry plant—the Q'anjob'al and the Awakateko. The first to come were Q'anjob'al from the remote area (remote even by Guatemalan standards) surrounding the towns of San Miguel Acatán (population 16,000) and San Rafael La Independencia (population 8,000), an area situated well over a mile high on a rocky plateau.[3] Positioned as they are in one of the most difficult-to-homestead ecosystems in the world, these people grow the holy trinity of corn, beans, and squash, supplemented by the raising of some livestock, mainly sheep for wool. Many of the Q'anjob'al are virtually monolingual, speaking only a few words of Spanish in addition to their own language. Amnesty International and other human rights reports are replete with accounts of massacres in this region during the late 1970s and early 1980s, including at least seven incidents in San Miguel and two in San Rafael (Davis and Hodson 1983).[4] On 19 August 1981, for example, the army entered Suntelaj, an aldea of San Miguel Acatán, and killed fifteen people identified on a school subscription list after forcing them to dig their own graves; only months before, following the public appearance of guerrillas in Lajcholaj, an aldea of San Rafael, a large group of men was rounded up, locked in a house, and burned to death (Davis and Hodson 1983).[5] In response to such atrocities, the Q'anjob'al began to move northward en masse (Hernandez Castillo 1988).[6]

Like San Miguel Acatán, Aguacatán (population 34,000) is nestled between steep mountain ridges. Yet the proximity of this verdant, well-irrigated valley to the departmental capital (also named Huehuetenango) makes it a more bustling agricultural and commercial center than the more remote towns of the Q'anjob'al. According to anthropologist Douglas E. Brintnall (1979), the local campesinos, long caught in a vise of forced day labor on coffee plantations to supplement the meager crops they could grow on their own, were able to take advantage of the end of the Vagrancy Laws (officially abolished by the progressive national government in 1944) to engage in commercial agriculture, especially garlic cultivation, when a road to the valley was completed in the early 1950s. For the first time a small, indigenous middle class appeared, people stayed in the village, schooling was extended, and, simultaneously, an older religious regime of *costumbres* or folk Catholicism gave way to a religious division between missionary Catholicism and evangelical Protestantism. These economic and cultural developments, moreover, also slowly eroded an early ethnic division within the town. Substantial numbers of K'iche' settlers (31 percent) had moved in from the east along the highland slopes leading out of the valley. There was a tiny pocket of Mam-speaking emigrants (1 percent) as well, and the ladinos included both a landholding elite and a laboring-class element (13 percent) of the population. The Aguacatán community was traditionally divided internally into ethnic halves, based on a nineteenth-century amalgamation of two valley villages into one. On the eastern side of the village plaza and church courtyard lived the "Chalchitekos" (41 percent); to the west lived those who called themselves the "Awakatekos puros" (14 percent). Undistinguishable to the outsider, until the past few decades the two groups had maintained separate community governments (or *comités*), endogamous marriage patterns, some small differences in vocabulary, and different brocaded designs on the women's *huipiles* (traditional blouses), not to mention attitudes of mutual suspicion (Brintnall 1979).[7] But the combination of new religious identities and war-related disruptions exercised a corrosive effect on earlier communal separatism. For example, the fact that General Ríos Montt was a former resident of Aguacatán did not save it from the army's scorched earth policy toward guerrilla infiltration in the early 1980s.[8] Morganton residents tell stories of violence in the aldeas surrounding Aguacatán, including government firing squads operating in the guerrilla strongholds of Pichiquil and La Estancia and of a massacre in Llano Coyote that included the tying up and machete death of an entire family.[9] If they accumulated more slowly than among the Q'anjob'al, the strains of the war-time siege ultimately pointed many Awakateko men in the same direction.

The outright terror of war combined with the simultaneous devastation of local economies produced a new wave of Guatemalan emigrants into the United States in the mid-1980s. While the fighting in the countryside of Huehuetenango gradually subsided, poverty and unemployment did not. Thus a stream of "war refugees" quickly gave way to a chain migration process of "economic refugees" drawing on family and village ties. These new migrants frequently first made their way across the border of Texas or Arizona, then headed west to pick crops in Cali-

ornia or east to do the same in Florida, where the village of Indiantown
near West Palm Beach became a prime catch basin of Guatemalan settlement (Burns 1993a). There they harvested tomatoes, cucumbers, and
oranges and worked in construction or yard—especially golf course—
maintenance until greater opportunity elsewhere beckoned. It was just
such a pledge of better pay, "inside" work, and more familiar physical
surroundings that led many to Morganton and the Case Farms poultry
processing plant.

Two cases serve to illustrate the early migration to Morganton.
Among the earliest Maya arrivals there was a young couple, Andrés
and Juana Pascual, from Suntelaj near San Miguel Acatán. According to
Andrés, his uncle was killed by the army in the period of the massacre,
and he himself had been abducted, stripped, and questioned in the middle of the night by guerrillas. Fleeing his home, Andrés hid out in other
pueblos before crossing the border to Mexico in 1984. For months he
worked construction jobs while slipping back and forth across the border to see his family. Later that year, he was summoned by a friend in
Indiantown. After weeks of walking across the country, he crossed the
U.S. border in a van at Nogales, Arizona, and went straight to
Indiantown, where his wife joined him a year later. Four years later a
call from Juana's sister, Melchora, already in Morganton, invited them
to come to North Carolina. Mátias Tomás, a native of Lajcholaj, an aldea
of the Q'anjob'al town of San Rafael la Independencia, had worked on
the coffee plantations of the coast from age ten to twenty-two. After his
father-in-law was "disappeared" by government counterinsurgents,
Mátias traveled directly from Lajcholaj to Arizona in August 1987 and
then quickly decamped to Florida. After two years of work in construction with the intent to return home, a cassette in the mail warned him
that his life remained at risk. A friend from Indiantown, Andrés Tomás,
had traveled to Alabama and then to North Carolina in search of work
in 1989. Andrés, with Case Farms' blessing, returned to Indiantown to
recruit Mátias and other friends to Morganton. Mátias himself performed the same feat a year later, returning by van to Indiantown to
bring more Guatemalans to their new mountain home.

At Case Farms, a small firm in a very competitive industry, labor
loomed as one of the most unpredictable factors of production. In 1986,
Tom Shelton, fired from the presidency of Perdue Farms after a falling
out with the owner, acquired the independent Case Farms company in

the Amish district of Winesburg, Ohio (where it produced its "Amish Country Pride" brand label); a year later Shelton added Breeden's Poultry, an old family firm in Morganton, to his enterprise. Shelton's own background was in the agricultural side of the business (that is, raising the birds), and from the beginning he approached the challenge of an efficient processing factory strictly as a technical issue. Denny Hughes, who oversaw the chicken-growing and sales operations at Case Farms from 1988 to 1991, remembers the struggle to increase both the poundage and number of birds killed per week: "We had labor [scarcity] problems galore then. We didn't have the labor force to kill the birds. So we might plan, let's say we were gonna need a half-million birds [per week], well the labor was so bad here in this area that maybe you've got 200,000, now I'm exaggerating [but] you had customers out here and you couldn't fill the orders."

According to Hughes, sometime in 1989 Norman Beecher, Case's human resource manager, received a tip through industry circles and a church group about a new source of labor. "Norm went to Florida . . . drove all night in a van . . . and picked up ten Guatemalans. And they put them to work in the plant and of course you know that week and the next week here was thirty or forty [more] and it just grew and grew."

Among management, as Hughes remembers, there was instant satisfaction with the experiment. "They showed up every day, of course somebody had to go get 'em [the company arranged a van pool and charged the workers for transport], but they showed up everyday. There was some humor, most of 'em . . . they're a little on the short side, you had to give 'em a job that they could reach [but] I think they were always satisfied with them, and I think they still are today, as far as I know. Dependable workers."[10] Initially, the Guatemalans possessed an employment advantage even over other potential Latin American recruits who had already made a significant impact on chicken plants in Georgia and Arkansas. Unlike frequently undocumented Mexicans, for example, whose status placed employers at potential legal risk, the Guatemalans, like other emigrants from war-torn Central America, for several years received nearly automatic temporary work permits upon application for political asylum (Hamilton and Chinchilla 1991).

Work in a poultry plant, under the best of conditions, presents a demanding and often unpleasant routine. The processing plants are organized so that birds enter one end of the plant and trucks carrying packaged and priced products depart from the other end. In the receiving or "live bird" area, workers in a dimly lit room (the dimness presumably has a calming influence on the chickens) pull live, scratching birds from plastic crates and hang them on hooks. Subsequent processing areas—for depluming, evisceration, chilling, "whole bird" trimming, and packing and shipping—become progressively cooler (ending up with the frozen coolers where birds are stacked for shipment), slippery with chicken fat, and wet from the constant hosing down—an environment requiring rubber boots, gloves, layers of clothing, and aprons (Griffith 1995:135). As to why an older workforce of local whites, blacks, and even Hmong refugees (several hundred of whom were resettled by church groups in the community in the early 1980s), provided an insufficient recruitment base for a poultry plant in Morganton, Denny Hughes explains, "It was just poor working conditions. It's not even the pay; to my understanding there's not that much difference between the pay in it and one of the [local] furniture factories. [But] would you rather go into a place that's clean and dry or wet and bloody and cool all day long?" In addition to the basic physical environment, poultry plants, including Case Farms, are notorious for unreported accident claims as well as for the third-highest reported rate of carpal tunnel syndrome among U.S. industries (Anderson 1995:26–28).[11]

Despite their motivation to find and hold a job, immigrant workers unused to the tight supervision and time management of the factory floor historically have often proven an obstreperous lot. It is worth noting that to the best of our knowledge, *not one* of the Guatemalans in Morganton had *ever* worked a factory job prior to entering the local poultry plant. In a structural sense, therefore, theirs was but another historical case of the tensions surrounding the raw inductees to "industrializing society" that Herbert Gutman (1976) so skillfully analyzed twenty-five years ago.

At Case Farms, particularly onerous and seemingly arbitrary work rules and penalties only fueled a buildup of resentments over the generally poor working conditions. As early as September 1991, some twenty Q'anjob'al workers left their night-shift assignment to protest the cutting of their overtime hours. A second eruption occurred in May 1993 when approximately one hundred workers, led by Awakatekos, stood up in the service area of the plant and refused to work unless a list of alleged abuses—including unpaid hours, lack of bathroom

breaks, poor working materials, and unauthorized company deduc-
tions for safety equipment like smocks and gloves, as well as inadequate
pay—was addressed. On this occasion, local police were summoned by
plant managers and fifty-two workers were charged with trespassing.
Of the arrested workers, all but a handful were Guatemalan. Following
mediation by local Legal Services lawyers and state labor officials, the
workers agreed to go back to work and the company dropped all legal
charges. But the conflicts sparked in 1993 continued to smolder.

A major confrontation came in May 1995. On Thursday, 11 May,
Aguacatecan workers in the "live bird" area stopped work when an
individual's request for a bathroom break was allegedly denied. After
briefly huddling together and refusing to resume their operations, they
quickly designated three of their number (later dubbed the "three
muchachos") to approach site manager Ken Wilson with a set of grievances unaddressed since the previous confrontation. Instead of talking
to the group of three, Wilson had them arrested for trespassing. After a
weekend of frantic meetings within the Guatemalan community, what
ensued beginning Monday was a plant-wide shutdown—announced at
a rally of some three hundred Guatemalans outside the plant gates—
lasting four days. Though workers agreed to return to work following
threats to replace them en masse, their strike produced the first tangible
responses to worker pressure from the company, including reinstate-
ment of the three arrested workers, dismissal of one particularly obnox-
ious supervisor, and installation of new microwaves and drinking
fountains for workers' convenience in the plant.[12] Even more importantly, news of the strike brought the Morganton workers to the attention of the outside world, including emissaries from both the United
Food and Commercial Workers (UFCW) and the Laborers' International Union of North America (LIUNA). By mid-July, after a self-des-
ignated committee of strike leaders chose to work with LIUNA, and
following successful application to the National Labor Relations Board,
workers voted 238 to 183 to unionize. There followed an exhausting
series of company legal appeals, wildcat and "quickie" strikes, harassment and firings of union activists, and continuing rapid turnover
within the labor force itself. Despite a series of legal rulings backing the
union's legitimacy, including a court-ordered year of contract talks,
Case Farms pulled out of negotiations in April 1999, shut down the
plant the following Monday, and encouraged circulation of a decertifi-

cation petition among the workers. More than four years after its initial election victory, therefore, the union (now LIUNA local 700) remains, as of this writing, in a perilous political state, with its survival still very much in doubt. Whatever the outcome of the Morganton union struggle, however, what is not in doubt is the capacity of a new immigrant community for a remarkable display of resistance, solidarity, and even sustained organizational development.

It is the internally varied—and even somewhat divided—dynamic of that community, however, that we want to emphasize here. The Q'anjob'al walkout of 1991, for example, bore the characteristic marks of a tight-knit group of war refugees who barely spoke Spanish, let alone English. At the prompting of a community "elder," Francisco José, whom the workers respectfully call "Don Pancho," the entire night shift not only departed the plant but quickly dispersed from Morganton back to their Florida roots (from which they had to be summoned by a company anxious to settle an issue blamed on miscommunication). Typically, it was neither a planned nor a very calculated affair. "Americans are used to paying [somebody] a wage and the worker working no matter what," explains Rosa Benfield, a nurse and native ladina from Guatemala City who had followed her husband back to North Carolina after his stint as a Marine guard at the U.S. Embassy and who was contacted through the St. Charles Catholic Church to help resolve this first dispute. But the Guatemalan Indians "were different," Benfield remembers. "It was not just money that was important to them. They just walked out if they didn't like the working conditions."

Indeed, with the Q'anjob'al, it was probably not just industrial "inexperience" but a very specific past experience that conditioned their response to workplace conflict. On the one hand, the Q'anjob'al workers reflected a traditional deference to their oldest members. Rosa Benfield remembers entering the apartment of Don Pancho and trying to engage the women of the family. They would not speak, and indeed all questions addressed to the workers were answered by Don Pancho—"he was the patriarch." Yet, Pancho's use of the term *huelga* to define his walkout at the time is also a sign of a heightened political awareness he was applying to his new American situation. There is other evidence on this score as well. Don Hemstreet, a veterinarian and thirty-year resident of Morganton, recalls with wonderment a late-night encounter with Pancho, a man he knew through his wife's helping efforts in the Guatemalan community:

It was one of those chilly mountain nights and as we cut through a back street, across a part of town that most considered to be a bit on the "rough" side, as we topped a hill, we saw Pancho. Now it was odd enough to see anybody walking around that time of night . . . but this was the strangest sight I ever did see. There he was, his five children filing along in a line in front of him. He was bringing up the rear, a long switch in his hand, herding them like an old banty hen. We stopped and asked him if anything was wrong. He answered in broken English, "Teaching how to walk." That was all, and off they went.

The other insight into the actions of Pancho emerged in conversations with his friends and extended family in the Q'anjob'al town of San Rafael la Independencia. There, he is remembered by more than one person as a guerrilla activist (but not a leader) who had to flee for his life. Don Pancho himself, it must be said, categorically denies involvement or sympathy with the *guerrilleros*. According to his testimony, he first traveled to the United States before the war touched his home, and it was only on a return visit that he witnessed firsthand the terror inflicted by the army on friends and family—a situation that propelled him into permanent exile. Whatever his allegiances at the time (and personal interest—in both the United States and Guatemala—argues strongly against latter-day identification with the guerrillas' failed cause), Pancho, like many of the war-torn Maya, did what was necessary to ensure the survival of his family.[13] "Pancho is tough," affirms Don Hemstreet. "[Pancho's daughter] once told me she lived in cardboard boxes in the woods [in Guatemala]."

Tellingly, however, it was not the fiercely independent and war-experienced Q'anjob'al—a people whose powerful but furtive protests remind one of the pattern of "primitive rebels" sketched by historian Eric Hobsbawm (1965)—but the culturally more "assimilated" Awakatekos who, at least among the Maya, were at the center of the unionizing experience in Morganton. Not only was the strike of 1995 an Awakateko-dominated affair, but the evidence suggests that a new leadership group among the workers had been established by the time of the 1993 in-plant disruption.[14] In part, of course, this ethnic angle on the Morganton events may simply reflect a temporary numerical preponderance within a chain of ethnic succession into the town over time.[15] Yet the evidence suggests that the explanation goes beyond mere numbers. For one thing, at the most general level, non-Maya observers of the Guatemalan community in Morganton readily contrast the relatively "urban" sophistication of the Awakatekos to the "backwardness" of their more isolated rural cousins. Marta Galvez, for example, a ladina from Guatemala City and Case Farms worker since 1973, observes that Awakatekos are simply "more civilized" and "more clever" than other indigenous groups. The Q'anjob'al, by contrast, who have "suffered more" from the guerrilla wars, seem comparatively "ignorant" and "illiterate" and "don't understand well" the world around them.

The first sign of a new leadership among the Case Farms workers was apparent in the 1993 plant shutdown. More than 60 percent of those arrested on 11 May were in their twenties or younger, but among the more "senior" activists were Paulino López, forty-eight, and Francisco Fuentes, thirty-five, both names that would be heard from again among the Awakateko community in Morganton. Paulino López, a campesino with only two years of schooling who had fled Guatemala in 1987 when he was mistaken for a guerrilla sympathizer, had worked in the United States as an agricultural laborer for five years before following some Florida friends to Case Farms in early 1993.[16] In 1993 Paulino López joined up with fellow Awakateko Alejandro López (no relation), Fuentes, "a few Mexicans," "and a Salvadoran" in leading the plant protest. Although no one who took part in the action, so far as Paulino knew, had had any prior political or labor experience, use of the term "huelga" was readily invoked. Paulino, for example, knew about strikes on coffee fincas, and on television he had seen news of teachers' strikes as well as the famous Coca-Cola strikes that spanned the decade from 1975 to 1985 (see Levenson-Estrada 1994). The 1993 event was a collective learning experience. Afterwards, says Paulino, "people were more awake, they wanted to know what were their rights." The next strike (in 1995) "had more strength because people had more experience," Paulino asserts, although it was not one in which he could directly participate, since following one of his migratory journeys home, he was denied reentry into Case Farms. Forced to take a factory job in a nearby town, Paulino nevertheless maintained close contact with his fellow worker-activists, whose struggle he identified with the larger community welfare. "It is a strike," he told us in August 1997, "that continues today, this is what I see."

Beyond employment in area industry, Awakatekos like Paulino López could draw on a variety of institutions to sustain their community self-identity. In addition to forming their own choir group in St.

Charles Catholic Church (as well as supplying worshippers to two local Hispanic evangelical churches), for example, local Guatemalans were divided by native town in a vigorous, all-Hispanic local soccer league. But one of the more sophisticated signs of community organization emerged only weeks prior to the unionizing strike of 1995 with the formation of a local Aguacatán burial society. The idea of an organization that would collect money from fellow countrymen to send bodies home to Aguacatán for burial sprang directly from Paulino López. When his own twenty-one-year-old son Remigio died of illness in Indiantown in 1989, "friends, countrymen, Awakatekos . . . gathered the money to send his remains to Guatemala. . . . There began the idea to organize." Following the death of Roberto Vicente in an automobile accident in Morganton in April 1995, Paulino López drew on his earlier experience to institutionalize the self-help network through a *"directiva,"* or leadership committee, on which he served as treasurer. From this experiment came the beginning of a nationwide network of Aguacatán directivas that regularly respond to local appeals for help. Requests for aid from non-Awakatekos are treated with sympathy but are held to be strictly "voluntary."

As the contact center between the home and diasporic community, the Aguacatecan directiva clearly carried an emotional and symbolic significance beyond its practical functions. As such, the fact that the secretary of the Aguacatecan directiva in 1995, José Samuel Solis López, was also on the strike committee and subsequent union organizing committee suggests the seamless connection between the Case Farms struggle and the "official" interests of the community. That José Samuel, moreover, was Paulino López's nephew also suggests the significance of distinctive family ties and influence within a larger field of social action. Samuel, in fact, was just twenty-six years old when he followed his uncle from Guatemala to Morganton via Indiantown some months after the 1993 strike. An avid reader and informal student of politics, he quickly identified with what he calls the *levantimiento* (uprising) of 1993 and instinctively linked himself to the events leading to the 1995 strike and its unionizing aftermath.[17]

If the Awakatekos clearly drew on ties forged in their home country, the migration experience seems also to have affected the definitions and boundaries of Aguacatecan fellowship. In particular, the traditional separation between "pure Awakatekos" and "Chalchitekos" all but vanished in the new land. Serving alongside José Samuel on the union organizing committee in 1995–96 was his nineteen-year-old housemate Mario Ailón, an unremarkable coincidence except for the fact that Ailón, unlike Samuel, is Chalchiteko. The Aguacatecan burial society makes no distinction by ethnic (as opposed to linguistic) origin, and the fine distinctions still apparent in the homeland simply no longer operate abroad. "We are in a country that is not ours," as Samuel put it.[18] The sense of immediate solidarity, of mutual support for the self- respect and welfare of family members, fellow countrymen, and other work mates, proved a strong bond uniting the union partisans at Case Farms.

While there seem to be both pragmatic and cultural grounds for understanding the solidarity of the Maya workforce at Case Farms, it is more difficult to generalize about the specific ideological and political understanding of the rank-and-file leaders. Among union activists at Case Farms, only the Mexican immigrant Juan Ignacio Montes, who did not arrive in Morganton until after the 1995 strike, and another late arrival, Roger Nuñez, a Nicaraguan with professed Sandinista sympathies, appear to have had any formal exposure to Marxism and socialist thought.[19] For some, like José Samuel (as we have seen), workplace activism offered an avenue for putting into practice basic democratic political ideals learned early in life. For other Case Farms union pioneers, like Marta Olivia Gálvez, a native of Guatemala City who fled the country after guerrillas abducted her and other passengers from a bus in 1989, practical political knowledge was derived from events very much "on the ground."

> I had knowledge [of organization]. Not of a strike exactly. I was in a group after the earthquake in 1976. . . . Many people died and our neighborhood became a ravine and we took a football field, we occupied it. We organized ourselves to keep this land. . . . We struggled with the government. We lived there four years. We improved that land with the help of the government. . . . Later, when the football players returned the government told us we had to leave. . . . We asked the government for other land. They sold us new land. We won. They built us facilities. I have this there today.[20]

The role of another Aguacatecan family pair—young Oscar Fuentes and his older brother Francisco—shows the inner complexity of such time-honored dichotomies as "resistance vs. accomodation" in a real-life setting. For reasons variously attributed to their looks and size (lighter skinned and taller than most of their Guatemalan compatriots), their combative instincts, confidence in Spanish, not to mention Awakatek, at least passable knowledge of English (a triple linguistic mastery uncommon among the Maya), and forceful oratorical powers, the Fuentes (both individually and together) are universally recognized as catalysts of the 1995 Case Farms strike. As José Samuel remembers, it was "Oscar Fuentes and his brother Francisco" who "called together the people—the Awakatekos." According to witnesses, more than two hundred Awakatekos showed up at a meeting outside Francisco's house on Sunday, 14 May and vowed that no one would return to work the next day. Oscar is most often cited as the "ideologue" and more powerful speaker; Francisco—who ran a van transport service (including runs to Florida for new factory recruits) as well as a production job at Case Farms—as a man with a larger authority within the community.

The shining moment for the Fuentes brothers, however, was brief. When union representatives arrived in town to try to turn the strike's momentum to permanent advantage, neither of the Fuentes brothers offered support. Instead, Francisco, the strike's instigator, actually returned to work, while Oscar soon left town for California. The reputation of the brothers Fuentes quickly suffered as workers tried to account for what many experienced as acute betrayal. "In the last hour they sold themselves to the company," says Carlos Salido. "The first thing Francisco saw was the money," explains José Samuel. "To be bought is the . . . devil. He sold his people and continued working." "He lied and deceived the people . . . it is his character to organize and then abandon the people," adds Paulino López. "Before he was Señor Francisco, now he is different."[21] Fuentes himself, not surprisingly, puts a different gloss on the Case Farms conflicts. He readily acknowledges that he led his fellow Awakatekos out of the plant to protest unfair treatment and intolerable line speeds. But, according to Francisco, he knew he could not formally lead a workers' organization because of his dependence on company personnel manager Ken Wilson, who had helped secure credit for Fuentes at a local bank. Once the strike was on, says Francisco, he therefore left his brother Oscar "in charge" of the events. Things might have worked out well, he suggests, if only the union had not stepped in to inflame the situation.

Yet, just as for the union "stalwart" López family, the experience of the "turncoat" Fuentes family bears an intricate and complex relation to events in Guatemala. To begin with, Francisco Fuentes is the only one of our Morganton informants who openly acknowledges an active, if limited, engagement with the guerrilla movement back home, including friendship with two men who were later executed by the army. Pressed into service in 1976 by a cousin who was already a guerrilla leader, Francisco, who used a pickup truck for delivering produce from the family plot in the Chalchitecan aldea of La Estancia to local markets, became a valuable "supply man" and "organizer" of new guerrilla outposts in distant villages. Yet even amidst the turmoil of armed struggle, Fuentes looked out carefully for his own survival. According to his testimony and that of his teenage son Max, Francisco maintained good relations with local men who had been recruited into the army and willingly complied when his truck was commissioned for army maneuvers. As Max relates (in English), "My dad was a leader with the guerrillas and then he was a leader with the army also . . . but when the army found out he was goin' both ways, they decided to take him out." On a leak from an army friend, Francisco quickly left Aguacatán for a less agitated residence in Chiantla. Continually pressured to return to guerrilla action or face the consequences, Fuentes finally exited the country for the United States in 1987. Although the guerrillas, according to Max, had promised his father that "they were gonna win and once they did they were gonna get the president out and then the guerrilla leader was gonna, you know, buy him a house in the capital . . . he knew they wasn't gonna win." In two very different circumstances, it would seem, Fuentes's mixture of popular sympathies and leadership skills on the one hand, with suspicion of "outsider" authority (be it army, guerrilla, or trade union), and fierce determination to make it on his own, on the other, helped to shape a common response to historical contingency.

By one measure, the story of the Maya (as well as other Hispanics) in Morganton is a classic labor history of competing poles of solidarity and fragmentation within a diverse workplace—but with a twist: Both qualities derive succor from opposite poles of alienation and integration within the immigration experience. The forces of fragmentation, for example, thrive on the intimidation that strangers—particularly those without secure citizenship—suffer in a new place. Local teacher and translator Daniel Gutiérrez thus cites the fears that the company could provoke simply by threatening to call the police in a workforce reared on the Napoleonic Code, under which the accused is guilty until proven innocent. Likewise ignorance and the hostility (implicit or explicit) of the native population could have a chilling effect on new immigrants. A Morganton police officer recounted his experience several years earlier with a new Hispanic translator in breaking up a fight between two local Guatemalans:

> When the two men [initially] refused to cooperate, the translator took [one of the men] into a separate room without the police. In a few minutes the man was happily recounting the details of the story. . . . The investigator asked the translator what he had told the man that made him open up and tell his story. The translator replied: "I told him that you were going to have him executed if he didn't tell the truth." Well, immediately we no longer used that translator.[22]

Yet if distance from the host culture is a source of intimidation, it is also a basis of unity within the expatriate Maya community. Back in Aguacatán, Padre Gabriel Rodríguez (who visited Morganton in 1996) is not surprised by the union movement among those he calls his *paisanos*.

> The lifestyle of the U.S. is much more individualistic, the community is different. . . . [Here] a person doesn't want to be separated from the group. . . . For us, life is *par* [pairs], just "you" does not exist. . . . We don't use the word *syndicato* [or trade union]. Here we use the word *communidad* (community). The idea is the same, no? . . . Build a bridge, it is community. Build a school, it is community. If there is a disgraceful event in a neighborhood, the community has to fix it. For us all is par, two, three, or four, they are the same.

Victoriano Raymundo, assistant principal of Aguacatán's Instituto Mayense, a bilingual school started with Norwegian funds in 1971, echoes Padre Gabriel with reference to the colloquial use of the first person plural. "Everything is a chain," explains Raymundo, "I don't put myself in my own place but rather I put myself in the place of others. Before making my own decision, I ask for the opinions of others. For that reason we use the plural and not the singular." In the same spirit, Jesús Acevedo, a Spanish-born UN peacekeeper stationed in Huehuetenango in 1997 explains the indigenous resistance to the Guatemalan military with reference to "a spirit of groupation. . . . They have a concept of justice, not so much Judeo-Christian, through which to resolve conflicts and they have, although we still have to discover this, leaders with the talent for this. Theirs is a code to which an individual submits himself." From this angle, the union—like the *directiva* or the widespread Guatemalan participation in local churches—is simply the latest means of maintaining a moral order within a traditional community.

Yet even as the tension between the values of immigrant and host community offer one index to local political outcomes, it would be a mistake from either side of the ledger to paint the comparison between Morganton and its international feeder communities as a study in contrasts between capitalist individualism and premodern communalism. On the one hand, in receiving and accommodating, however grudgingly, yet another foreign workforce, the town of Morganton eludes easy stereotypes of a "southern town." Although outside the scope of this presentation, the local Catholic Church (which opened its doors to union meetings), as well as the offices of a resident labor and immigration attorney, have clearly had a material influence in sustaining the Case Farms union drive. On the other hand, we should not discount the "globalizing" effects of change on the home communities of the workers themselves. The combination of poverty, militarization, and out-migration in Guatemala (let alone Mexico) over the past decades has already broken down much of the traditional hierarchy of a preindustrial society. Acevedo thus speaks of an internal conflict "which the communities [in Huehuetenango] do not have the instruments to resolve." Padre Gabriel refers even more darkly to an ongoing "disintegration" of the traditional Maya family and community structure as more and more young men leave Guatemala for economic reasons. In Morganton Father Ken Whittington of St. Charles Church sees the process only further accelerated in a new setting: "The elders don't have the sway that they used to. . . . Largely, it's a community that's being broken down."

But the changes affecting the Maya peoples might be seen as a reconstruction as well as a destruction of ancient community standards. At the Recovery of Historical Memory (REMHI) project sponsored by the Catholic Church in Huehuetenango, lay worker Edgar Hernández, who in 1997 oversaw a team of twenty-five social workers spread out in indigenous communities, offered a surprising commentary on the effects of the Guatemalan civil strife: "When we have asked the people [about] this war, this violence, all this suffering, what has it given you, the answer is generally positive. 'Thanks to the war [they say] we have promoters of health among us, we have agricultural agents, we have organizations.' You are going to discover a transformation of the Maya culture of survival." In the United States as well there is evidence of a most creative Maya adaptation to new circumstances. A recent study of the transplantation of settlers from rural Totonicapán to Houston, Texas, notes that "the Maya have developed extensive community-based networks while maintaining strong cultural and economic ties with the home community in Guatemala." "These well-developed organizational forms not only regulate migratory flows but also explain the successful Maya settlement experience" (Hagan 1994:10).[23] Among transplanted indigenous communities, Morganton probably presents an exceptional situation given the predominance of a single employment magnet and the accompanying preponderance of young men over family units within the immigrant population. Perhaps precisely for these reasons, the poultry workers union offers a special case of regulation and adaptation across borders. For workers who have few other avenues of assimilation or, for that matter, few other welcoming social spaces of any kind, the union has emerged as a kind of alternative extended family—a symbol of communal pride as well as a potential source of economic security. Thus, while seizing on different institutional bases from those in Houston (where initial economic mobility beckoned through the ranks of an upscale, and reportedly solicitous, grocery chain), the Maya of Morganton appear to be facing an uncertain future in the United States with remarkable energy and resolve.[24]

Among the survivors with a positive view of the future is Paulino López's son, Felipe, a former Guatemala City law student who fled his native country for political reasons in 1991, returned after the Peace Accords to frustrating unemployment, and arrived in Morganton in the summer of 1997 anxious to put his talents, either as a lawyer or a community organizer, to new use. To Felipe López, the explanation for the Morganton poultry workers union is obvious, but it is not a matter of traditionalism vs. modernism. "One reason is that we have suffered a lot here in Guatemala, more than the people in the U.S. . . . We have learned how to defend ourselves. Many of the people were members of the guerrillas, they trained them, they taught them how to organize, to fight for their rights. Other people were in the army and there they taught them how to defend their rights, how to organize themselves." Coming from a family with a love of politics (and perhaps a gift for reconciling the irreconcilable), Felipe might well have run for office in Aguacatán if things had worked out differently. When asked in Morganton if he could ever imagine renewing his political quest in his adopted country he replied matter-of-factly, "Yes, I like politics. I think I would join the Democratic Party."

INTERVIEWS

Acevedo, Jesús, 2 July 1997 in the United Nations compound in Huehuetenango
Anonymous Maya poultry worker in an Alabama plant, 2 May 1998 in Lajcholaj on a return visit to his family
Barlowe, Ray, 9 July 1997
Benfield, Rosa, 18 January 1998
Fuentes, Francisco, 19 April 1998
Gálvez, Marta Olivia, 1 June 1997, 28 August 1997
Gutiérrez, Daniel, 9 July 1997
Hemstreet, Don and Joy, 5 October 1997
Hernández, Edgar, 17 July 1997 in Huehuetenango
Hughes, Denny, 9 November 1997
Francisco, "Pancho" José, 25 May 1997
López, Felipe, 29 June 1997 in Aguacatán, 28 August 1997 in Morganton
López, Paulino, 10 August 1997
Merino, Yanira, 30 October 1997
Montes, Juan Ignacio, 7 September 1997
Palmieri, Phyllis, 8 March 1997, 10 August 1997
Pascual, Andres and Juana, 5 October 1997
Raymundo Raymundo, Victoriano Rubén, 20 May 1998 in Aguacatán
Rodríguez Yol L'un, Padre Gabriel, 28 June 1997 in Aguacatán
Salido, Carlos Alberto, 12 October 1997
Solis López, José Samuel, 25 May 1997, 1 June 1997, 17 August 1997, 18 January 1998
Tomás, Matias, 14 September 1997
Whittington, Father Ken, 8 March 1997

NOTES

1. This work is the result of an unusual working relationship between two scholars. As principal author of the project, Leon Fink, an American historian by trade and training, sought and found a most able research partner and cultural interpreter in Guatemalan specialist Alvis Dunn. Much of the research and interviews for the project have been conducted in tandem, and Dunn has contributed to the writing on Guatemala as well as transcribed many interviews in the preparation of this manuscript. The project has also benefited from the research assistance of Anna Fink, Amy Morris, David Sartorius, and Gregory

Kallis and from other technical help from Kris Ray. Acknowledgment for helpful criticism is gratefully extended to Miriam Cohen, Margaret Rose, and to the editors of this volume. All interviews with Guatemalan subjects, except for that with Rosa Benfield, were originally conducted in Spanish.

2. Information for this paragraph is drawn from Horowitz and Miller (1997) and Griffith (1995:129–52). In 1990 the five biggest poultry producers by state (in rank order) were Arkansas, Georgia, Alabama, North Carolina, and Texas (Griffith 1995:130). For information on the industry's competitive pricing structure and the resulting pressures on wage rates, see Bjerklie (1995:41–60). The gender division at Case Farms is peculiarly and disproportionately male for an industry which nationally is nearly evenly split (49 percent female) between men and women employees (Horowitz and Miller 1997).

3. The people from San Miguel Acatán, called Akatecos, speak Akateko, a language that is mutually intelligible with only slight alteration to that of a contiguous group known as the Q'anjob'al. The people from Aguacatán also have their own dialect, known as Awakateko, which is not understandable to a Q'anjob'al speaker (Kaufman 1976).

4. *Guatemala Nunca Mas*, the report of the Project for the Recuperation of Historical Memory, sponsored by the Human Rights Office of the Archbishop of Guatemala (ODHA), whose effective director, Monseñor Juan José Gerardi Conedera, was assassinated in a still-unsolved attack on 26 April 1998, two days after officially presenting a summary of the report to the Guatemalan public, attributes eight of the nine attacks mentioned above to the army or the state-backed Armed Civilian Patrols and one to the Guerrilla Army of the Poor (ODHA 1998).

5. Davis and Hodson (1983:51); interview in Lajcholaj with an anonymous Alabama poultry worker returning to visit his family, 2 May 1998.

6. To be sure, the Q'anjob'al have a history, predating even the guerrilla war, of migrating to Mexico in search of work and markets.

7. The population breakdowns are Brintnall's estimates, circa 1973, drawn from interviews with local officials. Chalchitán was officially incorporated into the municipio of Aguacatan on 9 November 1878 (Gall 1966:42).

8. Ríos Montt's father, who lived most of the year in the city of Huehuetenango, owned a sugar plantation in Aguacatán, and young Ríos spent summer vacations running the sugar mill (Anfuso and Sczepanski 1983).

9. Interviews were held with Paulino López in 1997; José Samuel Solis López on 17 August 1997; Felipe López on 29 June 1997; and Rev. Gabriel Rodriguez Yol L'un in 1997.

10. Griffith (1993:171) cites a general employer impression of Hispanics "as having a work ethic superior to most American workers, Black or White."

11. As late as February 1998, a Labor Department study of the nation's poultry plants "found that more than 60 percent . . . violated overtime laws" and "also found widespread safety problems, among them frequent back injuries that usually occurred when workers slipped on wet and greasy floors" *New York Times*, 10 February 1998.

12. This strike information has been compiled from the Charlotte *Observer*, 15 May 1995; the Morganton *News-Herald*, 15–18 May 1995; and interviews with Palmieri 1997; Gutierrez 1997; Carlos Salido 1997.

13. Francisco (Pancho) José, interview 25 May 1997. Pancho's story, like several other accounts of Guatemala's civil wars we have heard in Morganton, resembles the revisionist theme of a people caught "between two armies" (i.e., the left-wing guerrillas and the Guatemalan state), a popular feeling that "this is their affair, not ours," which anthropologist David Stoll first elaborated in *Between Two Armies in the Ixil Towns of Guatemala* (Stoll 1993, see especially xi–xvii, 305–13), and which was reaffirmed in *Rigoberta Menchú and the Story of All Poor Guatemalans* (Stoll 1999). While Stoll's thesis—challenging the depth of popular sympathy for the extended armed revolt in the Guatemalan countryside as well as questioning the authority of the country's best-known human rights defender—has touched off a fierce debate among Guatemalanists, we can only note here the conflicting local memories of the situation in the early 1980s and allow that we, like other post facto investigators pursuing such traumatic events, must be extremely cautious in assessing what may have been shifting political identities and sympathies across these years.

14. The Mexican Carlos Salido, who joined his uncle inside Case Farms just five days before the 1995 walkout, recalls being inducted into the strike action. "The only Mexicans that were in the strike were us—and the people from Aguacatán" (Salido, interview 1997). Likewise, LIUNA organizer Yanira Merino, who arrived at the tail end of the 1995 strike, recalls a workers' committee led by Awakatekos that also included Marta Galvez from Guatemala City, one man of K'iche' origin, and one Q'anjob'al (Merino, interview 1997). The identities of the three muchachos, Francisco Vicente (age nineteen), Juan Mendoza (twenty-two), and Victoriano López (twenty-one), were confirmed by an interview with José Samuel Solis López, 17 August 1997.

15. In this chain the Q'anjob'al came first, followed by Aguacatecos, and more recently by people from the Departments of Totonicapán and San Marcos.

16. Paulino's son, Felipe, recalls his father's flight into exile some six months after an uncle, Marcelino López, escaped to Canada. "They almost killed him, the army. Because a lieutenant was drunk and my uncle was drinking with a friend who at that time was accused of being part of the guerrilla and in reality he was . . . but they were doing business with my uncle and that lieutenant saw this and they tried to kill him. They caught him in the cantina and about 3:00 A.M. they took him to the mountains to kill him and he ran away, he escaped."

17. The one request José Samuel has made of his interviewers from Chapel Hill is that they lend him books of serious fiction and philosophy in Spanish.

18. Paulino's son (and José Samuel's cousin), Felipe López, who arrived in Morganton in late summer 1997 and immediately put his Guatemalan legal training to use as an assistant on immigration cases, explains the intermixing of Awakatekos and Chalchitekos in Morganton in only slightly different terms: "They are not in their [own] country so they have to stick together. They are all together [in Morganton]. But they know who's who."

19. Montes was elected local president of newly chartered Local 700, LIUNA, in 1998.

20. For more information on practical political knowledge, see Scott 1998.

21. This material is taken from interviews with Carlos Alberto Salido, José Samuel Solis López, and Paulino López. "He [Francisco] was a caudillo [labor boss]," recalls LIUNA organizer Yanira Merino. After his "turning" Francisco Fuentes was involved in repeated conflicts with his compañeros, including protests over exorbitant rents in buildings he owns and a dispute over a widow's insurance money, which Fuentes allegedly attempted to pocket for his own use.

22. In a survey of the poultry and other low-wage food- processing industries, anthropologist David Griffith (1993:195) concludes that, "while the Hispanic workers cannot be said to be carriers of the South's anti-union sentiments, they possess qualities, as new immigrants, that feed the continued weak positions of labor relative to capital. As long as new immigrants and undocumented workers permeate their networks, there are few incentives to organize, join labor unions, or resist plant authority in any capacity besides leaving the plant's sphere of control altogether."

23. Hagan's study, emphasizing the settlement experiences of Maya women, offers a valuable counterpart to our focus on a largely male work and political environment.

24. Information on Houston taken from "Mayans in Texas," a segment of the National Public Radio program *All Things Considered,* 30 November 1998.

Nestor P. Rodríguez and Jacqueline Maria Hagan

13 Maya Urban Villagers in Houston: The Formation of a Migrant Community from San Cristóbal Totonicapán

In this chapter we tell the story of the formation of a K'iche' Maya community in Houston, Texas. As is documented throughout this book, political strife and declining economic conditions in the Guatemalan highlands in the 1970s and 1980s forced thousands of Maya families to flee their highland villages and seek refuge in Mexico and the United States. The focus here is on the case of the K'iche' Maya migrant population from the Guatemalan highland *municipio* (township, but administratively more like a U.S. county) of San Cristóbal Totonicapán that settled in Houston during the 1980s. The municipio has a population of about twenty thousand inhabitants (Ministerio de Economía 1984). About four thousand live in the town of San Cristóbal and the remainder in surrounding smaller rural settlements referred to as *cantones* (hamlets) and *aldeas* (villages). Over 90 percent of the municipio's residents are Maya, and many speak K'iche' and Spanish. The migrants from San Cristóbal Totonicapán have traveled between two very different worlds. In sharp contrast with Houston's advanced industrial environment, situated at sea level, San Cristóbal Totonicapán is a setting of many handicraft workshops, family farms, small repair businesses, small and medium-size stores, communication and courier offices, located at an elevation of 6,300 feet in Guatemala's western mountain region.

Juan Xuc, a subsistence farmer and weaver, was the first migrant from San Cristóbal Totonicapán to make the undocumented journey north to Houston, where he arrived in 1978. His migration led to a large settlement in Houston of San Cristóbal migrants. By the time the senior author was introduced to Juan in the summer of 1985, the San Cristóbal migrant community had mushroomed to close to one thousand. Our study of the settlement experiences of this Maya migrant community thus began in the summer of 1985 and continues to the present. In the fall of 1986, the junior author moved into the community, renting an apartment in one of several large apartment complexes that house the San Cristóbal Maya. In addition, the senior author has spent about two weeks a year in San Cristóbal Totonicapán for ten years since 1988; the junior author has also visited and observed the migrants' community of origin. Much of what follows in this paper reflects the stories and experiences told us by members of the San Cristóbal migrant community.

Several research questions have driven our interest in the migrants and their family households both in Houston and in the municipio. The first question concerns the relationship between the social structure of the migrant community and the migrants' settlement opportunities. Do migrant-based social networks facilitate settlement opportunities by providing resources to newcomers in the community, or do these networks impede adjustment by limiting the development of relationships outside the migrant community?

Our second question asks how, given the obvious mobility restrictions of undocumented status, did the migrants manage to sustain contact with the municipio of San Cristóbal? Moreover, do these linkages, once developed, change as members of the migrant community in Houston become legal? Tracing the settlement behavior of the migrants through their participation in the legalization program of the Immigration Reform and Control Act of 1986 (IRCA) enables us to assess the importance of legal status in the settlement intentions of the migrants as well as its effects on social relations between the migrants' communities in Houston and Guatemala. The final research question emerged naturally from our second and concerns how migration to Houston, and to other U.S. localities, affects the municipio's economy and culture.

These questions are important, we believe, because they address the issues of how transnational linkages help international migrants sustain ethnic culture during the settlement process, particularly at the early stages. The questions also address the issue of how these linkages support social reproduction in the migrants' communities of origin, effecting or accelerating cultural change in the process. In migration research, Maya migrants represent a special case, we believe, because of their cultural and geographical remoteness vis-à-vis the well-studied cases of Mexican immigrants.

MAYA SETTLEMENT IN HOUSTON

One might intuitively hypothesize that Maya migrants, who come from traditional agricultural and artisan settings and thus possess few transferable job skills, would not fare well in an industrial milieu such as Houston. When compared to other undocumented Central Americans in the Houston area, however, the San Cristóbal Totonicapán Maya have adapted remarkably well to Houston's advanced industrial setting (Rodriguez 1987). We attribute their success to the strong community structure they have built in Houston.

The foundation of the San Cristóbal community structure in Houston was laid in the early 1980s after Juan Xuc made his way there. Upon arrival he encountered a booming economy and had little difficulty locating work. His first job was as a maintenance worker for an apartment complex, but within several months he joined the maintenance crew of an expanding local supermarket chain. The first San Cristóbal Maya to follow in Juan's steps was Tomás, Juan's brother-in-law, who arrived in the spring of 1979. Through Juan's work contacts, Tomás also secured a maintenance job in the supermarket where Juan worked. In the municipio, word of the high wages being earned by these two fellow Maya spread rapidly. Kin and friends in the municipio of San Cristóbal began writing to Juan, asking him about work opportunities. The social foundation for Maya migration from San Cristóbal Totonicapán to Houston had been laid.

By the time his family joined him several years later, Juan had been promoted to maintenance supervisor ("*el encargado*," as he is referred to by his Maya coworkers), and was earning $5 an hour. In this position he continued to recruit more workers from the municipio.

Juan's wife, Carmen, went to work as a domestic for one of Juan's supervisors at the supermarket. It was not long before word of employment opportunities for women in Houston spread through the municipio. During 1982 to 1983 the first stream of sisters and wives from the municipio arrived in Houston. As the women established more work contacts in Houston, they began recruiting other women from the municipio. By the late 1980s, many households in the municipio had social ties with migrant households in Houston. A small percentage of the households in the municipio had established social ties with migrants in other U.S. cities, including Los Angeles, Trenton, and Washington, D.C.

In Houston, the San Cristóbal Maya, along with other Maya populations and other Central American and Mexican newcomers, continue to
settle primarily in the western half of the city, miles away from the
established Mexican immigrant neighborhoods in the city's east side.
Owners of large apartment complexes helped promote this new settlement pattern in their attempts to rebuild declining white, middle-
income tenant populations with new Latino immigrants (Rodriguez
and Hagan 1992). In the western half of the city, Mayas from various
highland communities—Momostenango, Quetzaltenango, San Francisco el Alto, Santa Cruz del Quiché, San Cristóbal Totonicapán, San
Miguel Totonicapán, San Pedro la Laguna, and Sololá—have maintained substantial interaction that has eased the settlement process
through the sharing of social, cultural, and economic resources. The
migrants from San Cristóbal Totonicapán and Santa Cruz del Quiché
constitute the large majority of Maya in the city. Together these two
Maya groups have three to four thousand people. Each of these groups
constituted an independent migration stream, and they initially settled
in separate apartment complexes, apart from each other and from other
Central American newcomers.

The presence of a large number of kin and friends from the same
municipio has enabled the San Cristóbal Maya to form settlement pock-
ets on the outskirts of the larger Central American community. Hundreds of households, most within a short walking distance from one
another, serve as a rich setting for social interaction and cultural activity in the community. This residential feature serves an additional function in the formation and reproduction of Maya community in the
city—the provision of a variety of social, cultural, and economic
resources for newcomers (temporary housing, job information, transportation, preparation and sharing of traditional meals). Many social
networks have developed within the Maya neighborhood, ranging
from those that channel cultural information about community events
to job networks that direct newcomer males to maintenance jobs and
newcomer females to domestic work, the two main employment tracks
for the San Cristóbal Maya in the city.

The formation of Maya community organizations in Houston, such
as community churches and soccer teams, serves to ease the adaptation
experience of many of the Maya newcomers, as well as reinforce social
relations and cultural exchange in the more established segment of the

community. One community church, "Iglesia de Dios," espouses an evangelical doctrine that was embraced by some migrants before they left San Cristóbal Totonicapán. This church and a second evangelical one are perhaps the most important sources of institutional bonding among the San Cristóbal migrants. Membership in both churches is composed almost exclusively of San Cristóbal Maya, who bear the financial costs of maintaining the churches. Church members pay the rent on the church building, the utilities, and other costs of operating the churches. Several times a year the Maya women sell *tamales* to raise funds for the churches. These churches provide multiple opportunities for social interaction and are major settings for cultural events: Members meet for services on Sundays and Wednesdays; women and young girls participate in weekly Bible-reading sessions, and major life-cycle events such as funerals and marriages are often celebrated in the churches.

Soccer teams are a second type of organization that function to circulate information among the San Cristóbal Maya and provide regular social interaction. In the early days of their settlement in Houston, the San Cristóbal men met informally to play soccer; as more migrants arrived in the city, they organized teams, as other Central American migrants had done. Juan Xuc, the community pioneer, assumed a leadership role in the formation of the first soccer teams and for many years was a team captain. At the soccer fields, members of different households visit, new arrivals are welcomed to Houston, job contacts are made, and general news is exchanged. The soccer teams have met other community needs as well, including fund-raising for Maya migrants in difficult financial straits. On one occasion, for example, team players raised money to help pay the medical bill of a player who broke his ankle during a soccer game. In another case, team members raised money to help a widow send the body of her deceased husband for burial in Guatemala. Soccer teams have also raised money to sponsor events in the annual patron-saint celebration in the municipio.

The San Cristóbal migrants have been quite successful in adapting to a new society and culture. Their success can be explained by the strength of their community-based social networks, which provide a host of social and economic resources to newcomers from the municipio. Moreover, the development of community churches and soccer teams further strengthens and reinforces network relations among the

San Cristóbal community in Houston by providing an additional vehicle for community interaction. This feature has been documented for other immigrant settings as well (Massey et al. 1987).

DEVELOPING A TRANSNATIONAL COMMUNITY: ESTABLISHING THE MEANS OF COMMUNICATION AND TRANSPORTATION

As other groups of Latino migrants have done, the newcomers from San Cristóbal Totonicapán have evolved substantial transnational community relations. While a few have little contact with the community back home, most maintain substantial contact with kin and friends in the municipio through letters, phone calls, audio and video cassettes, couriers, visits, and even faxes. All of these means serve to circulate resources for ethnic cultural reproduction among the migrant households in Houston and their households of origin in the municipio.

In the early 1980s, the first migrants from San Cristóbal communicated with family and friends back home only by letter and telephone. Because they had no telephones of their own, they initially used the phones of their employers to receive long-distance calls from relatives in Guatemala. In Guatemala, relatives traveled to nearby Quetzaltenango to call Houston from the offices of the Guatemalan national telephone company (GUATEL), since practically no long-distance telephone service existed in the municipio during the first stage of the migration to Houston. The early years of migration were a period of intense political violence in Guatemala, and the thirty-minute trips to the GUATEL in Quetzaltenango were usually made during the day to minimize the risk of traveling at night. By the mid-1990s, private international courier and telephone companies like Rapido Express and Envios Urgentes opened offices in the municipio, enabling residents to reach family members in the United States much more easily.

By the mid-1980s many of the migrants started using audio cassette recorders to send "voice letters" to families and friends in the municipio. This was very practical, since some parents back home were illiterate and some spoke only K'iche', which is used primarily as a spoken rather than a written language in San Cristóbal Totonicapán. By the late 1980s, a few migrants had bought video recorders to record videos of family and community events in Houston and the municipio. In the late

1990s, new video-recording businesses owned by the Maya in Houston and the municipio were also producing videos, sent back and forth between Houston and Guatemala, of major family and community events such as weddings, *quinceañeras*, funerals, soccer tournaments, and graduations.

A number of Maya men routinely travel between Houston and the municipio to deliver letters and videos. For a fee, these carriers will also transport appliances, clothing, and other items from migrants to their families back home. Some carriers occasionally bring traditional items such as *cortes* (wrap-around skirts), *huipiles* (blouses), and *pan de fiesta* (festival bread) from the municipio to the migrants in Houston. A bakery opened in Houston in 1997 by San Cristóbal bakers sells Maya foods and colorful hand-woven cloth from the municipio in addition to traditional breads.

The Maya carriers have served as an important lifeline between the migrants in Houston and their families back home. The hazardous trip between Houston and the Guatemalan highlands takes three or four days, and the carriers face danger from bandits as they cross Mexico transporting household and personal items worth thousands of dollars. Before the passage of IRCA in 1986, which facilitated travel for legalized immigrants, the carriers played an especially important role in keeping cultural and economic resources circulating between the two communities.

MIGRANTS' ECONOMIC AND CULTURAL IMPACT IN SAN CRISTÓBAL TOTONICAPÁN

International migration to the United States affects conditions in San Cristóbal Totonicapán at various levels. For a significant segment of the municipio's population, the migration of family members amounts to dramatic social mobility that has transformed some patterns of the municipio's social structure.

Economic Impact

The economic impact of migration on San Cristóbal Totonicapán is evident at the individual, household, and municipio levels. At the individual level, the impact can be seen in the greater amount of food available (especially meat), in the increased ability to pay for the schooling of children (in secondary schools and beyond), in the purchase of more expensive clothing (both traditional and foreign-made), and in the greater affordability of health-care services (including care in Guatemala City). The individual effects depend on the amount and regularity of money sent home, and also on family priorities, which seem to vary by locality. Families in the town seem to spend a larger percentage on children than do families in the cantones and aldeas, who spend more on resources for production, such as land and vehicles for transporting products to market.

Televisions, radios, stereos, VCRs, audio cassette recorders, bicycles, and appliances—all from Houston—are common in the households with migrant family members. Indeed, these imports gave rise to a movement to convert the town's 220-volt European-style wiring to 110-volt U.S.-style wiring. Money sent from Houston is also used for home repairs and for upgrading adobe walls to cement block. Some households use the payments to expand their businesses. Households producing pants for wholesale, for instance, may replace single-stitch, foot-peddle sewing machines with double-stitch, motor-powered ones, which enables them to increase production and sell to larger markets in Quetzaltenango or Guatemala City. One household used an electric food blender sent from the United States to start a small business making herbal juices for naturalistic healing. The impact of money payments from Houston on municipio households may fluctuate substantially. A household with children working in Houston may enjoy considerable initial prosperity but then experience economic decline as their children start their own families in the United States and send less money back home.

At the municipio level, new businesses, new housing construction, and a growing presence of small imported trucks are among the most evident economic effects of migration to the United States. Some of the new businesses, such as long-distance phone services and international package carriers, cater almost exclusively to families with migrant members. Likewise, the few master builders in the municipio are supported primarily by contracts to build new homes for the families of migrants. Former migrants have also started new businesses, including a hotel, small eating places, medicinal shops, video recording services, and music amplification for family celebrations. The growing economic vitality of the municipio and the regular remittances to a large number of families no doubt played a major role in the opening of a bank office in the late 1990s.

The prosperity brought by migration to the United States has also produced some economic restrictions in the municipio. Some farmers face a labor shortage, as the promise of U.S. jobs lures young men away from the fields of San Cristóbal Totonicapán. With worker shortages, rural wages have more than doubled since the 1980s. In town households, the wages of servants have also increased, as young women from the cantones look to the United States as a source of employment. The impact of U.S. wage structures has also dramatically increased the price of housing lots in the town, restricting new homes mainly to families of migrants. Lots that sold for less than $10,000 prior to U.S. migration now sell for between $15,000 and $20,000. Some migrants spend $50,000 to $70,000 for a lot and construction of a new home.

While about a fifth of the adult population in San Cristóbal Totonicapán has migrated to work in the United States, the impact of international migration on the municipio's economy should not be exaggerated. Money sent by migrants in the United States helps energize segments of the municipio's economy by providing new business capital and creating new demand, but this money in itself cannot sustain the local economy. Far more important in this regard are the climates of the national and regional economies.

Cultural Impact

On one level, international migration promotes cultural change in the municipio, while on another level it reinforces traditional practices. The preference among the municipio's youth for clothing from the United States (for example, logo T-shirts, jeans, and stylish tennis shoes) is among the most visible cultural change promoted by migration. The demand for U.S. fashions is most significant among females, since their traditional garments are a major symbol of Maya culture (Smith 1988). In some households, young daughters occasionally use dresses and slacks brought from the United States in place of their Maya huipil and corte. Native and U.S.-born daughters who accompany their migrant parents on visits to the municipio use traditional Maya garments only for special ceremonies. Visiting and returning migrants also help promote Texas-Mexican music among the municipio's youth, at the expense of traditional marimba music. During the municipio's patron-saint fiesta in late July, Tejano and Mexican norteño music can be heard playing from the boom boxes and car stereos of visiting migrants. On one occasion a group of migrants contracted a Texas-Mexican musical group to play in the July fiesta.

In the cantones, gender relations have been affected by migration. The labor shortage caused by male emigration has forced some women to join their husbands in the fields for the first time. While some families hire farm workers to replace the sons who have left for the United States, there are still frequent labor shortages. But as with the economic impact of migration, in the area of cultural change—particularly in the case of dress and music—migration is simply accelerating changes that were already taking place in the highlands.

In several ways, migration to the United States has also reinforced the municipio's traditional culture. While some young females prefer U.S. clothing to Mayan garments, some mothers and older sisters of migrants use money sent from Houston to buy expensive traditional garments they could not otherwise afford, some costing hundreds of dollars. Using money earned in the United States to buy land for family farming or equipment for household artisan production also helps support the municipio's long-established work culture. It is the use of migrant resources to finance elaborate ceremonies (for example, house warmings, quinceañeras, and weddings), however, that has the most striking impact on the reproduction of the municipio's traditional culture. With money and managerial skills provided by migrant members, some families organize lavish social events, strengthening community relations in the process. Families that a decade ago could barely afford a family celebration involving a few dozen persons now hold fiestas to which hundreds of residents are invited. In 1993, for example, with the financial support of nephews in Houston, a family rented a municipal auditorium to conclude the celebration of their daughter's quinceañera with a meat-laden dinner for about two hundred guests. A few years later, a returning migrant invited some seven hundred guests to his wedding celebration in the municipio. It was a lavish celebration that cost thousands of dollars in food, music, and the bus transportation for hundreds of guests from surrounding cantones. At a time when political and economic problems had reduced the vitality of many highland areas, migration provided the means for many families to practice traditional celebrations on a grand scale.

ECONOMIC CONDITIONS, STATE POLICY
AND AUTONOMOUS MIGRATION

Economic and political problems in the highlands directly and indirectly restricted internal resources for social reproduction in San Cristóbal Totonicapán in the late 1970s and 1980s. Not all sources of the problems were local. A host of foreign developments affected Latin American economies starting in the mid-1970s and created a decade-long period of economic decline known as "la crisis" (Portes 1989). The major cause was a worldwide recession related to rising oil prices and restrictions of financial support to developing countries. Inflation, unemployment, and devaluation devastated the Central American isthmus (Pérez Brignoli 1990; Gallardo and López 1986). In the years of the crisis, migration to U.S. cities became a means by which many Latin American families survived the problems of long-term recession.

The regional economic and political crisis significantly restricted Guatemalan highland resources for the reproduction of community life in many Maya areas. In San Cristóbal Totonicapán, economic constraints (unemployment, low wages, and the shrinking value of the *quetzal*), worsened by the crisis drove many young men and women to migrate as undocumented workers to the United States. It is important to understand that from the beginning the migration from the municipio was very much a social process. The first migrants in the United States provided job and travel information to relatives and friends in the municipio, and families pooled monies to help pay for the journey north. This social process of migration spread from a canton to the town and to other hamlets in the municipio, becoming a general household strategy by the mid-1980s.

The evolving pattern of migration from San Cristóbal Totonicapán—large-scale acceptance of undocumented migration as a viable alternative, extensive cooperation among families with migrant members, approval from political, religious and other civic leaders, and so on—reflected a social enterprise of autonomous migration. That is, the community organized and implemented—independent of state agency—undocumented international migration as an economic strategy to help support its social reproduction. As a culturally and geographically remote case, the autonomous migration from San Cristóbal Totonicapán to the United States demonstrates the ability of peripheral communities to adjust through their own global strategies to structural constraints of the economic world system during moments of extraordinary stress.

State policies in the receiving areas can also influence transnational linkages and cultural reproduction in home communities, often in ways unexpected by national policy makers. The Immigration and Control Act of 1986 (IRCA) was designed to "cut the flow" and "redefine the stack" of undocumented immigrants in the United States. That is, INS would implement employer sanctions and reinforce the border with additional officers to curtail further undocumented migration. Simultaneously, a legalization program would be implemented for the pre-1982 undocumented immigrant population.

Because IRCA was implemented during the course of our study, we were able to trace a number of migrants through the legalization process and assess some of IRCA's effects on the San Cristóbal community. One of our most interesting findings during the post-IRCA period concerns the role of legalization in strengthening transnational linkages between the municipio and Houston Maya community. Such linkages are a result of two IRCA policy outcomes. One outcome was intended by policy makers; the other was not (Hagan and Baker 1993).

IRCA's framers anticipated that legal status would be a device used by migrants to integrate into U.S. society. After all, acquisition of legal status provides economic protection in the labor market and opportunities for increased interaction with U.S. institutions. We found that as legalized members of the San Cristóbal Maya have strengthened their foothold in the U.S. labor market, they have provided continued access for prospective undocumented migrants from San Cristóbal, especially since employer sanctions have had little impact on the job security of the undocumented Maya in Houston. Indeed, migration from San Cristóbal to Houston has almost doubled during the post-IRCA period.

Equally meaningful, but probably far more surprising to IRCA's framers, is the fact that legalized immigrants are reintegrating into their home communities. With permanent residency, formerly undocumented Maya can, for the first time, travel freely between the United States and Guatemala without jeopardizing their ability to work and live in Houston. Many legalized migrants from San Cristóbal Totonicapán travel frequently to the municipio. Some visit for two weeks or more during the July festival or during Christmas or Holy Week. Others have returned to live in Guatemala but make trips to the United States to sell goods from the municipio. And others have made Houston their home base but return to Guatemala for lengthy visits during which they work in their businesses back home. Regardless of the different settlement patterns adopted by the legalized migrants from San Cristóbal, our research strongly suggests a strengthening rather than a weakening of transnational ties as a consequence of IRCA's legalization provision.

The migration from San Cristóbal Totonicapán to Houston shows that for communities with large migrant populations, international migration leads to the globalization of everyday life, as daily household and community activities become at least partly dependent on resources obtained from migrants abroad. The case of San Cristóbal Totonicapán illustrates that international migration brings more than just economic resources to the international migrants' communities of origin. It also brings cognitive and material elements of global culture that are assimilated into the local social environment. From a class perspective, the case of San Cristóbal Totonicapán also demonstrates that working-class communities in developing countries can lessen the subordination of peripheral labor status through autonomous migration.

ZOILA RAMIREZ

14   A Maya Voice: Living in Vancouver

WHEN I came to Canada I thought that all my dreams had died.[1] But at the same time I could see that I had the right to talk, that I no longer had to worry that tomorrow the army would come for me or do something to my family. My physical protection is guaranteed here. There's freedom to express yourself here, a kind of liberty that is different than what we sought. We wanted the right to be Maya, to be *indigena*, but for this I need indigenous education and knowledge of what it is to be Maya. We have rights to speech, to look for work, human rights, but I don't feel I have psychological or mental freedom. I feel confined, surrounded by something that's not mine, something that belongs to others. I have also thought about my children and how now they could really succeed. So being here is a mix of good things and bad. For so long I felt lost, as if I had nothing left, no happiness. Now that we've been here thirteen years, I am beginning to see things differently, although there is still something inside that is empty.

The human mind is a lot like a computer. When we think or speak we return to the disk, remembering things that have happened, that will never be forgotten, that will continue to hurt us. So even when I hear that the war is over, that all is calm, until I see it for myself I can't believe it. It still affects me so much. We may smile but inside we're still crying. We have to be patient, but I've suffered so much. I wonder if I'm only getting worse thinking of what happened. It's hard to imagine that I'm going to live and die here, I really can't accept that. Even if I am an old woman with a cane in my hand, I have to return to Guatemala.

Here everything is driven by money. You can't go anywhere without spending money. It's expensive to go out or even to visit, especially if your friend lives far away. In my village, you could walk to other villages. We'd bring a dozen eggs and return with salt, and if you didn't have money you could bring something later. You could pick fruit as you passed by a tree, there was so much. Here you have to pay for even a small apple. Coming from a place where you barter or could go out and glean from the fields, it is so completely different.

It's hard here because the circumstances of this different culture close off my other options. If I wanted to organize a group I would need money. I'd need to show that I have a degree. I know about natural fertilizer and traditional gardening, but I lack a degree in agronomy, so I couldn't work in that field. If I wanted to teach Maya art or Maya cosmology, I couldn't. So these restrictions *me quitan los valores* (limit my options). If I were in Guatemala with my people, I could speak and practice together. But here, in this system, I feel oppressed.

All of my dreams are still based in Guatemala, and often involve forming groups, talking of how the war hasn't ended, and how we have to seek freedom for Indians and have the right to land, or we'll only stay poor. I also dream of friends who died in the struggle or who were never seen again. Sometimes I dream of building adobe houses or doing ceremonies.

Mothers dedicate themselves to their family in Guatemala, but here there are so many changes in that as well. I sensed from the start that this country would be difficult for me. People are too cold, hardly greeting you or visiting, lacking *corazón* (heart). Here you can be very isolated, even more when you don't know the language. I didn't ever think I would learn English. But there was no other way, so I knew I had to do everything possible. When I first went to classes, I didn't say a word for five months. Now that my children are older I have begun to learn to write and read, though it's so hard since my hands are used to working at home and weaving rather than writing. Thanks to God, after about three years I can begin to read and write. I am discovering what is between the covers of books that before were all that I could understand. There are such marvelous things within!

The struggle to keep my family together here is really hard. When my husband and I began our life together and had our first child, we had my mother's help and the advice of so many others to help us through our inexperience. But when we had to flee to Mexico, there started such hardship. A mother has even more responsibility than a father. All my life has been dedicated to my children. I never left them in day care, because I have always felt it was important to give them that care myself. At the same time, since we left in the middle of a war, I have had these wild ideas that if I left them somewhere something might happen. So the best I have been able to do is be a good mother, although this has meant having no relatives, none anywhere near.

When my children ask about their relatives, it is difficult for us to explain how some died and others have been killed. We tell them the truth, but it still affects us, like an endless film. Now that the children are growing, we think we should tell them because they don't remember. Guatemala is like a dream to them. But since we're in such a different society, where they spend so much more time in school than at home, there is never enough time to talk. Still we try to explain their past, how the Maya people have suffered for years, and that we're now in a country that was not ours, that we came to to save our lives. When they grow older and have their own children, we want them to remember that they came as refugees and be grateful that this country gave us a safe place to live.

Regarding my family, there is safety here. But if I hadn't taught my children about being Indian or Maya, they wouldn't have learned any of it, especially how the Maya have suffered since the time of the Spanish. Knowing this, they have a knowledge of being from a great culture, even if they don't speak the Mayan language. We practice Maya beliefs, the music helps us sustain our culture. We're doing this just barely, but the Canadian culture is so pervasive that it influences everything. Here children have so much freedom, they can go wherever they want. Their advice comes from their friends, and there are laws against their parents' disciplining them. I don't think this fits with what we wish for our children. So we tell our children that they have to respect others, to learn to have good friends, to learn about alcohol and drugs and the many problems that this society has. You see on television how teens are killing others, and we have to explain such things to them. We also teach them how everyone is different and to respect those differences. We're living in a culture that is so diverse that they must respect others. Our children have friends who are Chinese and Sikh. It is a great experience for us to have learned respect for others, in this country where there are so many differences.

What will happen if I return one day to Guatemala? Will I feel 100 percent that I am in my country? Or will I feel the same there as I feel here, realizing that my children will marry in Canada. So right now there's no real base for me. In Guatemala I had friends, *confianza*. I don't think I can recapture that if I return. It's like having to begin all over again.

I tell my children that if they decide to stay in Canada, they must not forget where they came from and what happened, even if it pains them.

They'll have a different way of considering such events, and perhaps other ways to understand them as well as to demonstrate who they are. We grew up being told we were animals, but now that indigenous people are rising up and the Maya are known throughout the world, it could be good for them in the future.

Now that I'm in school, I feel sad about leaving my youngest child. Yet by being able to communicate with others I am feeling better. Although I feel myself getting older, each day I now look forward to reading. Someday I want to write down everything that happened so that perhaps one of my children can learn from it. There are so many things to explain, but I want something to be left for my grandchildren.

Note

1. This is an excerpt from an interview with Zoila Ramirez, a thirty-nine-year-old Mam woman, now living in Vancouver, British Columbia, conducted by James Loucky and edited by Marilyn M. Moors.

James Loucky

15   Maya in a Modern Metropolis: Establishing New Lives and Livelihoods in Los Angeles

"WE FLED the violence there, but now here it is. Where do we go from here?"

For many Maya from Guatemala, such as this Q'anjob'al Maya man who recounts both the conflagration that consumed Los Angeles in 1992 and the everyday dangers in the barrios where he has lived for over fifteen years, flight to the United States meant moving from one war zone to another. More recent arrivals, Maya from the same communities as earlier refugees as well as growing numbers from other towns and hamlets throughout highland Guatemala, have been spurred to migrate more by economic and ecological devastation than by the kind of military and political repression that characterized the 1980s. For children and youth, some born in Guatemala and others in California, life in Los Angeles revolves around normative standards and institutions such as public schools that appear to have little connection to the homeland and experiences of their parents.

Whether uprooted by political violence or by economic turmoil, thousands of indigenous Maya have been dispersed from Central America to states and provinces across North America. The two largest concentrations of Maya in the United States are in south Florida and southern California. Los Angeles is home to over ten thousand Maya, primarily Q'anjob'al from northwest Guatemala, along with more recent immigrants from Quiché and other Maya areas. Most live in the crowded and impoverished barrios west and south of downtown, and labor long hours for low piece-rate wages in the garment district. Given their rural background, little prior English language ability (and for many a limited knowledge of Spanish), and few directly transferable job skills, most Maya appear to have adjusted remarkably well to the tremendous insecurities and changes inherent in this fast-paced and money-oriented global metropolis.

This chapter profiles the ways in which Maya respond to the multiple challenges associated with living and working in Los Angeles. There are striking contrasts between the context of exit, indigenous communities characterized by hoe agriculture, endogamy, and deep-seated cultural integrity, and the context of entry in Los Angeles. Yet the powerful dynamics of struggle and survival around which life in highland Guatemala revolves continue to guide their seemingly successful incorporation into urban U.S. society. Primary activities and core underlying values relating to work, social interconnectedness, and family priorities, as well as prior experience with hardship and even violence, enhance rather than inhibit their adjustment in Los Angeles. In particular, Maya resettlement in Los Angeles hinges largely on the intensive pursuit of available economic opportunities, social networks, including maintenance and re-creation of kinship and community ties, and shared concerns for family and children's well-being.

HUEHUETENANGO ROOTS AND UPROOTING

The state of Huehuetenango in northwest Guatemala is the homeland of several Maya ethnic and linguistic groups, including Mam, Chuj, and over 120,000 speakers of Q'anjob'al and the closely associated Akateko language. This extremely mountainous region has shared the political and economic experiences of the highlands, with the most arable lands being steadily expropriated or concentrated in fewer hands, and large numbers of people suffering poor health and living standards associated with insufficient landholdings and poverty. During the 1970s, efforts to modify existing land distribution included cooperative movements, notably large-scale colonization efforts in the lowland rain forests of the Ixcán along the Mexican border. As social conditions deteriorated, activities aimed at social reform became more widespread but also more dangerous. Underground activities grew, including those associated with guerrilla organizations whose message of ending poverty and repression resonated with the experience of many indigenous people.

The response of the Guatemalan military government was swift and brutal. Rivaling the Spanish conquest in scope and consequence, the army moved massively into rural areas in the early 1980s, applying a "Guatemalan solution" to both popular reform and the growing insurgency, one that included exemplary torture and indiscriminate massacres. Huehuetenango was hard hit, particularly the highland Q'anjob'al area and the Ixcán (Davis 1988; Falla 1994; Montejo 1987). Thousands of Q'anjob'ales fled, some to safer areas within Guatemala, others as part of a mass exodus of refugees into Mexico. Still more left during the period when militarization and population control mechanisms were established in the highlands following the scorched earth campaigns.

By the mid-1980s, the Maya population in Los Angeles had grown to several thousand. The refugees followed routes and networks that had been established by a small number of Q'anjob'al, mostly from the town of San Miguel Acatán, who had arrived during the 1970s. The first of these "pioneers" was a Q'anjob'al man, from neighboring San Rafael, who came in 1974. Generations of Q'anjob'al have migrated seasonally to the coasts and into Mexico to harvest plantation crops as well as for trade, and the initial movement further north appears to be an extension of that pattern. One of the first migrants from San Miguel, for example, had been picking coffee in Chiapas with a Mexican man who had worked in the San Joaquin Valley of California. After returning to Guatemala to pool money and find a travel companion, he traveled to the same California farm that he had heard about, and from there to Los Angeles in 1975. Others entered the rural labor stream in a similar fashion, migrating to cities in the off season. In Los Angeles, many found relatively steady work in the garment industry. With the subsequent arrival of women and children, there emerged a relatively cohesive Q'anjob'al community of about two thousand, primarily from San Miguel Acatán. They in turn represented a potential destination for the substantial number of refugees who arrived during the mid-1980s, and who comprised the second stage of Maya migration to the city.

A third stage consists of both Q'anjob'al and other Maya who have continued to head to Los Angeles in search of alternatives to declining economic options available in Guatemala. Almost all are taken in, at least temporarily, by relatives or others from their home community, although some appear with no more than a name or outdated address. As some earlier Maya immigrants have legalized their status in the United States, there has been an increase of re-visits to Guatemala in recent years. However, rather than signaling any long-term return migration, these visits (accompanied by gifts and other evidence of material gains), have instead merely stimulated even more migration.

Today there is a continuing exodus of Maya men, generally young and single, along with growing numbers of women, leaving communities across the highlands to try to make it (*a buscar su suerte*) in Los Angeles.

EL NORTE: DESTINATION LOS ANGELES

The film *El Norte* depicted a Q'anjob'al sister and brother who fled Guatemala only to find hardship and tragedy in Los Angeles. The reality for most Maya is even worse than that depicted in the film, since few immediately get the well-paying jobs or live only two to an apartment, as did the film's protagonists. Instead, most find an increasingly saturated job market, crowded living conditions, and a face-paced, atomized, money-driven society that contrasts sharply with the villages they left behind. The port of entry for most Maya is the garment district and the inner city, particularly the Pico-Union and Westlake barrios west of downtown and south-central Los Angeles.

Two streets symbolize the residential contrasts and the contradictions between international labor and international capital that confront the Maya in Los Angeles. Bixel Street lies on the east edge of Pico-Union. On the east side of the five-hundred block rise the gleaming corporate headquarters of ARCO Plaza. On the west, literally in the shadows of the downtown corporate and financial district, are decaying brick tenements crowded with Central Americans, the majority of them Maya The first and third worlds also find ironic juxtaposition on Los Angeles Street. On all corners of the 8th Street intersection lie the notorious sweatshops of the garment district, filled with sewing machines and piles of fabric worked by Maya alongside other Latino and immigrant workers. A block north are the twin towers of the extravagant Cal Mart building, the fashion center of the California apparel industry, closed to outsiders so that designers and marketers can produce and protect the next season's fashions, at markups many times what the machine operators are paid.

Both the day and the night settings in which Maya in Los Angeles work and live involve struggle, *la lucha.* People go to work much as they would to battle, beginning with a long commute on two or three packed buses and followed by long hours of repetitive tasks in loud and unsafe conditions, "driven" by contract deadlines as well as by personal economic need. Garment workers face uncertainty because of employers' changing labor needs, the exploitation and wage depression made possible by a large supply of undocumented workers, and sequential production squeezes of narrow profit margins and timelines that get passed on down the line, literally and figuratively (Loucky et al. 1994).

Living quarters for the Maya in Los Angeles usually mean a crowded apartment in a high-density building, where it is common for six or eight people to share a single room that can rent for $500 or more per month. The housing squeeze associated with the widespread lack of low-cost housing often results in two or more families "doubling" up. Compounding the contrast with the rural communities left behind in Guatemala, these inner-city areas have few open spaces. The few parks that exist are often locations for prostitution and drug sales. Dangers run highest at night, with crime rates and gang activity among the highest in the city (Chinchilla, Hamilton, and Loucky 1993). In the face of challenges of such magnitude, the question of survival—physical, economic, psychological, and cultural—becomes paramount.

MODES OF MAYA ADJUSTMENT TO LOS ANGELES

Recalling Tolstoy's observation that all families are happy in the same way but unhappy in their own ways, the Maya are both typical and exceptional in terms of their adjustment to Los Angeles. They harbor many of the same anxieties regarding needed but undesirable jobs, unsafe neighborhoods, and unwanted influences on their children that other immigrants do (Suárez-Orozco and Suárez-Orozco 1995). What may be "new" about these "new immigrants" is a deep-seated strength associated with shared experiences of hardship and hard work as corollaries of life in highland Guatemala. They also enter Los Angeles, particularly at the turn of the century, under changing political and economic conditions, specifically an "hourglass" economy and segmented society in which fewer people move up while many remain in a growing underclass, a situation compounded by anti-immigrant sentiments in which the Maya are apt to be viewed as so different as to be unassimilable (Scott and Soja 1997).

When the goal of bettering life for oneself and one's family confronts the reality of never-ending expenses in a city like Los Angeles, the need for money ends up driving much of Maya life. As one young Maya man expressed it, "Here everything means money, from the rent to your bus pass. You're more enslaved here [than in Guatemala]. From the biggest to the smallest thing, everything costs, and you spend it all too." This explains the willingness to take on work far in excess of forty hours per week and to return even to abusive working conditions under garment contractors who undercut wages and rights whenever possible.

Most Maya are quite aware of how bad their work conditions are. "It's getting more and more difficult," said one worker. "Garment work (la costura) is no longer much good. There is less and less work and poorer pay. Even if you know the real wage [per piece], you can't say anything since the owners can simply get someone else to work at that rate. I feel increasingly pushed to leave Los Angeles." In the face of this reality, Maya continue to exhibit competence and a sense of self-worth that is integral to the work ethic they developed during their childhood years of involvement in production and maintenance roles in the Maya household economy. They also actively assist friends and family members in locating better and steadier employment opportunities whenever possible. They recognize that international forces make garment work increasingly insecure, which has led to growing movement into other work sectors as well as other states.

A second way in which the Maya respond to the insecurities and dispersive forces of Los Angeles is through modifying and strengthening social networks. Networks of both family and friends are available from the earliest stages of migration. In Guatemala, both husbands and wives and wider networks of kin generally participate in emigration decisions by pooling monetary resources or borrowing money to raise the economic capital needed to migrate, with the expectation of receiving repayment or remittance later.

Once in Los Angeles, newcomers find "anchors" within formal and informal family and fellow-villager networks. These provide temporary housing, job leads, and social companionship, along with a kind of safety net to help prevent what relatives remaining in Guatemala fear most: becoming "lost" (perdido) in the big city.

Adjustments constantly occur in household membership and even in definitions of "family," allowing flexibility in composition and roles to confront the insularity of urban life while spreading resources and costs more effectively. Providing much the same support as do traditional extended families in Guatemala, these kin and ethnic support networks widen and are increasingly relied upon as Maya and their families grow older and increase their time in Los Angeles.

Community cohesion has been further developed by U.S. institutions as well as voluntary associations. The language, literacy, workers' rights, and legal education efforts centered in Los Angeles church congregations have provided technical skills and vital information that have helped many Maya learn to navigate new currents in the United States. Immigrant and refugee groups also provide these skills but serve as well to maintain cultural identity and mutual aid. One of the first indigenous Maya organizations, IXIM, was formed in Los Angeles in 1986, and since then about a dozen mutual aid associations, connected with different towns of origin as well as religious faiths, have been formed. Some function as sources of financial and emotional support in times of emergency or death, including funding the transport of remains of deceased members back to Guatemala for burial in the ancestral soil. Others promote sporting activities and cultural events, notably the commemoration of fiestas that are defining events in the life and collective identity of Maya communities. These organizations thus play a key role in the replication and re-creation of Maya modes of social organization, whether through conscious efforts to revitalize cultural "traditions" or through efforts to meet and consolidate in the face of shared problems of exile, such as commonly perceived threats to youth and families.

Apart from accommodating themselves to inhumane work schedules and establishing and utilizing social networks, a third arena critical to understanding the cultural persistence and relatively effective incorporation of Maya into new lives in Los Angeles involves emergent family roles, and particularly parental investment considerations (Bogin and Loucky 1997). The role of families in international migration has been overshadowed by the dominant focus on economic determinants of migration as well as a continuing presumption that migration is primarily a male activity, undertaken either by single men or young male heads of household (Loucky 1987). But global trends toward a feminization of the labor force have begun to inform migration theory, and the female immigrant experience has been addressed not only in terms of the search for employment but more recently in terms of role demands and familial responsibilities. Significant among these are concerns for bringing family members together (reunification), for keeping families intact, and for working out more egalitarian household statuses (see González de la Rocha 1994; Vlach 1992).

Rather than a set of individuals calculating the costs and benefits of any given action, the Maya in Los Angeles make most decisions within a family or household context, involving individuals brought into joint living arrangements as well as consanguine kin. In Los Angeles, they replicate many time-tested household patterns characteristic of the highlands. The axiom of interdependence is visible in the pooling of money in order to pay rent and other bills, or even in efforts toward home ownership. Collective accumulation of knowledge, skills, and money allows the Maya family or household both to support and to protect its members in the settlement process.

The presence of children brings a special dimension to the Maya immigrant experience. Not only do many parents base the act of migration on the increased survival and better health of their children in the United States, they make decisions and allocate time for work, residence, and education in large part on the basis of perceived benefits to their children. With lengthening time of settlement in the United States, parents, both those of children born in Guatemala and those of children born in Los Angeles, increasingly shift the focus of their concerns to their children. The impoverished neighborhoods in which they live pose substantial dangers. The American culture of consumption and individualistic values threaten long-established Maya age and gender norms, and these, in turn, threaten family unity. Maya priorities relating to children are seen in the physical moves a family undertakes when safety concerns mount. One family returned to Guatemala for several years when a teenage son began to hang out with a street gang, taking him to a coastal plantation to pick cotton as a powerful moral lesson. Another sent a daughter to relatives living in a different state, in order to encourage her to give her attention to school rather than to friends who were a bad influence. Increasing numbers of Maya families have pooled enough money to relocate to south-central Los Angeles or even to suburban neighborhoods, where they rent small houses that are both safer and more spacious than the tenements they leave behind.

Whether single, in the process of creating families, or part of more mature families, Maya in Los Angeles are clearly involved in a set of both visible and invisible strategies involving intersecting worlds of work, community, and family activities. Social networks are at least as critical as self-help efforts in these strategies. In the face of numerous urban environmental risks and economic demands, the resilience exhibited by Maya immigrants represents substantial funds of knowledge, rooted in struggle and survival in Central America and tested and tempered in the tremendous flux of migration and settlement in the urban United States.

CONCLUSION

The Maya experience of both cultural and physical estrangement in Los Angeles, along with their resourcefulness in responding to multiple needs and crises relating to employment, housing, and child welfare, helps expand our understanding of the dimensions of uprooting and settlement. The ways in which Maya individuals and families have adjusted to new urban realities, while simultaneously changing the neighborhoods and society in which they live and work, can largely be attributed to their prior socialization for and adjustment to situations of poverty and discrimination, including the necessity of hard work to ensure survival.

The outcome of the many changes required by urban life is not entirely clear, although flexibility and movement on many levels—physical, social, psychological—are occurring and are certain to continue. With lengthening geographic and temporal distance from highland Guatemala, the increased mobility of the Maya across the continent contributes to a growing sense of isolation from, and dissolution of, traditional communities. Identities long associated with distinctive hometowns may also be giving way to previously de-emphasized regional identification as "Guatemalan" or "Central American," while perhaps also coexisting with new affiliations, such as "Latino" culture. Nevertheless, new forms of community are constantly developing, with people drawing their sense of place and humanity from different sources, including from transnational links afforded by legal status and improvements in transportation and communications between sending and migrant communities (Kearney 1996). In Los Angeles, as the Maya generational, gender, and cultural roles shift, and as those traditional Maya roles learned in Guatemala become increasingly de-emphasized or even anachronistic in the urban United States, the next generation's adaptations and endurance will hold the key to the prospects for this community in the future.

MARILYN M. MOORS

16 Conclusion: The Maya Diaspora Experience

THE TRAUMA OF THE DIASPORA

WHILE MOST of the participants in the Maya diaspora have come from northwestern Guatemala and from a background of farming or agricultural work, the whole diaspora stream contains people from many localities, with differing work, skill, and education histories. Two major factors compelled the movement out of the highlands: terror of war and fear for one's life, and pervasive poverty, caused largely by the shortage of land and consequent limits to economic options, especially for wage labor. Following the distinctions made by Antonella Fabri in Chapter 4, the first of these people we have been calling "refugees," the second "migrants." Refugees fled usually in families or in community groups, especially to Mexico, but migrants generally traveled longer distances with few others, seeking safety and avoiding border problems in smaller numbers. For both groups, the process of movement was expensive and involved many hardships, and it was usually accompanied by the trauma of loss and separation.

Maya refugees found individual and family safety in flight, but the personal costs were very high, probably higher than we yet know. The violence itself and the fear it engendered, the long trek to safety, the loss of children and loved ones, the necessity of relinquishing one's identity in order to survive, all these costs were born by the diaspora refugees. Whether they sought safety in the anonymity of Guatemala City or Mexico City, whether they exchanged the role of peasant farmer for that of camp refugee, whether they migrated further to start again in a new place, all refugees bore the weight of physical and psychological suffering. Those who acted together were able to help sustain each other, as in the refugee camps in Mexico. Those who acted alone sought kin and fellow townspeople whenever possible in order not to bear the pain alone.

Maya migrants carried similar burdens. Both the physical and economic costs of being smuggled into the United States are high. The debt incurred to the *coyote* who led them to the border had to be paid back. Recent changes in U.S. and Mexican Border Patrol policies have made the migration from Guatemala even more dangerous than it was in the 1980s. Intense patrolling of frequent crossing points has forced the coyotes to travel through rugged, arid country where exhaustion and dehydration are likely. The experience is always harrowing and sometimes deadly. Three hundred-fifty migrants, mostly Mexicans, died from starvation, thirst, or exhaustion while attempting to cross the border in 1998. The United States has also put pressure on the Mexican government to interdict the migrant flow from Central America at the Chiapas border (Swedish 1999).

In two cases, in Los Angeles and south Florida, the Maya have again found themselves living in situations of personal danger. The crime and violence of the ghetto/barrio or of the rural south have affected their ability to live, work, and raise their families in peace.

In leaving Guatemala, migrants give up their traditional homes and family ties, and those losses are an additional burden. And like the refugees, they live with an uncertain future and with doubts about the rightness of their decision to leave. As networks developed for others to leave home villages and migrate to relatives in receiving areas, these problems lessened some. Young, unattached males without kin or village friends seem to have had the most difficult time, especially in Florida, where problems with alcoholism, drugs, and automobile accidents indicated the instability of their new lives.

FROM REFUGEE TO MIGRANT TO WORKER

With the exception of those who remained in the camps in Chiapas and the Yucatán, most of the refugees in this book were unable to avoid the basic transition to migrant status. To be a migrant meant making a positive decision to be somewhere else, to be on one's own, to make a life in a new land. For these people, we can clearly see the end of Maya farming as a subsistence activity, and with it the sense of self-sufficiency and authority that comes from having land, making one's own decisions, and being in control of one's life. Migrants, whether economic or political, have no choice but to move into the wage-labor markets of the areas where they establish themselves. In Florida, Houston, Los Angeles, and Morganton, Mayas could not replicate the economic strategies that had supported them for generations in the highlands. They had to give up any presumption of self-sufficiency and become full members of the working class. Their limited job skills and language restrictions initially placed them at the lowest point in that class. Their courage, their persistence, their networks, and their sense of community form the backbone of the advancement they have made.

While most began at the bottom, Maya have creatively sought work in niche environments, moving in Florida, for example, from general agricultural labor (mostly picking crops) to more specialized work in greenhouses, nurseries, and golf courses. When job opportunities are available, relatives and friends are notified, so that the population of a receiving work area comes to duplicate the ethnic makeup of the sending area. This is clearly the case in Houston and Morganton. Both Florida and Los Angeles are larger receiving areas and more open to various Maya streams.

Two exceptions to this process of movement away from the land and into the working class are the Maya who fled to Belize, where the availability of land is again a major issue, and those refugees who returned to Guatemala, including the people of Santa María Tzejá, where subsistence farming again became the central pattern of their lives.

ADAPTING TO NEW SITUATIONS

After finding jobs in markets often crowded with migrants from other areas (Caribbean natives in Florida, Asians in Los Angeles, Mexicans in Houston), the problem of housing had to be resolved. Generally, both the quality and the quantity of housing available for migrants ranges from truly awful to barely passable. Where the housing supply is tight or where there are many young unattached men, as in Florida, individuals and families make do with minimal space, crowding into whatever shelter is handy, taking in relatives until there is no room left for sleeping. When housing is more readily available, as in Houston, they tend to live close to each other, taking over apartments in the same complex as they become available.

Legal status in their new countries remains questionable for many of the migrants. Some of the first refugees to arrive in the United States received political asylum, which allowed them to seek work legally. More benefited from the lawsuit filed by the American Baptist Church (ABC) against the Immigration and Naturalization Service (INS), which reopened asylum cases previously denied and mandated fairer action on cases still pending. Again in the United States, a general amnesty for Central Americans in the 1990s made legal status possible for others. But many continue to work in the United States without documentation. The hardships of work here will grow worse as the INS intensifies its present policy, "Operation Vanguard," an attack on the undocumented workers in Midwestern meat-processing plants, particularly in those plants where union activity is taking place. The INS, in collusion with the meat-packing industry, is targeting one sector of the job market for undocumented workers at a time, making it impossible for migrants with or without papers to work in these plants. The ultimate goal is to pressure Congress to initiate a new *bracero* or guestworker program, whereby workers can be imported when needed and exported when the need no longer exists, and under which they will have little say over wages or working conditions (Bacon 1999). Mayas persist in seeking work under these difficult conditions and they counter the prospect of arrest and deportation by becoming as invisible as possible, as did the refugees in Guatemala City in the 1980s.

They have come to understand and make their place in more complex systems of discrimination. They have found jobs and housing in competition with others, equally marginalized, equally migrant, and equally discriminated against. They have learned to cope with and to counter different forms of violence and racism and both gross and subtle systems of exploitation similar to those of their homeland. They watch their children coping with learning to speak and being schooled in English, and they know that they risk the loss of their mother tongue.

While individual Mayas often found solutions to these problems, they did not always have to act alone. Those in the refugee camps in Chiapas had the personnel of the UNHCR, the Catholic Diocese of San Cristóbal, COMAR, and whatever international solidarity workers COMAR permitted in the camp area. As migrants moved farther north, they were aided by church people, those in the sanctuary movement, solidarity workers, legal assistance personnel, and anthropologists and their students. But most commonly and most comfortingly, they had each other. The bonds of community forged in the Guatemalan highlands held strong for the migrants and often stretched to include other Maya, not always from the same communities.

As migrant communities, rather than as individuals, another series of problems needed resolution. After finding work and housing, people began to seek ways to help each other re-create the social support networks they needed in their new homes. They formed their own community organizations and sought the resources—churches, soccer teams, soccer fields—necessary for community activities. They answered racism and exploitation by forming unions, and they learned to seek help to cope with the local boss, local police, or the INS. Local Maya community groups like CornMaya and IXIM helped the migrants make sense of life in this new land.

These same community groups helped to create new bonds with home communities by reproducing patron saint festivals and collecting funds to send the dead home for burial. Newer technologies added links of audio- and videotape to the telephone system. Safe methods have also been developed for sending money and consumer goods to relatives at home. New trucks, chain saws, and cinder-block houses with tin roofing have replaced donkeys, hand tools, and adobe and thatch houses. Television sets, VCRs, refrigerators, and other consumer goods now heighten the differences between families with migrant workers abroad and those without. Migration networks were established to provide channels for those in trouble or looking for work to join established migrant communities. Today, throughout the northwest highlands, a façade of prosperity created by money sent from relatives in the United States covers the underlying poverty of the still land-poor Guatemalan Maya.

Throughout the entire process, Mayas, both as individuals and as groups, have demonstrated that they are not perpetually victimized by horrible events beyond their control but can act for themselves. They made decisions based on available options, and when the options were insufficient, they creatively expanded the possibilities open to them. Their organization in the Chiapas camps to take part in the negotiations regarding their return is an illustration of their effective participation in their own lives and futures.

THE TAPESTRY OF IDENTITY

In the year 2000, U.S. census takers probably counted Mayas as "hispanics," grouping them with other Guatemalan, Mexican, and Central and South American migrants. They could just as accurately be counted as "Native Americans," although as such they would not have the treaty-defined and bound relationship with the U.S. or Canadian government that holds these native groups in thrall to their governments. In this book the people of the diaspora have been called "Maya," but this designation obscures subtle differences that are nevertheless important to them.

Questions of identity have received more theoretical and practical attention of late, particularly as the Maya people in Guatemala adapt, build, and transform their identities in the postwar period. In theoretical terms, the concept of "identity" is currently viewed as a multifaceted, malleable process rather than as a fixed or static entity. In Guatemala, prewar studies of identity by anthropologists and others were based on "not this—therefore that" constructions. The "ladino" was identified by one set of characteristics, the "indigenous" by the opposite characteristics. In Guatemala since the Peace Accords, however, newer investigations of identity seek to understand the processes by which it is made and remade by each generation, reflecting the personal and political issues surrounding and constricting one's choices (Warren 1998; Wilson 1995).

Prior to the war, most highland Maya identified themselves with their community (Tax 1937; Smith 1990b). The village was the unit to which they gave their loyalty. They recognized that other Maya spoke the same or similar languages, but a person identified him or herself as being from a particular community. This identity was reinforced by the *traje* or traditional clothing of the community, more often worn by women than men.

The common experience of flight or migration, which displaced them from their fixed locations ("where our placentas are buried"), and uprooted them from their language communities, has led to a reassessment of those identity markers. While community ties remain strong and can be seen in the continuation of saint's day fiestas in the United States and in the recruiting networks and support for incoming migrants, they are no longer the only threads in the Maya tapestry of identity. A common experience of loss, suffering, and survival has extended "we-ness" to those speaking the same language but from different towns. Language names—Q'anjob'ales, K'iche's, Mames—are given as referents of identity, especially in the larger Maya communities in Los Angeles and Florida.

And increasingly, as in Guatemala where the pan-Maya movement seeks to give political impetus to cultural issues, the term "Maya," crosscutting individual languages to incorporate the entire population of Mayan speakers, is the preferred identity. For migrants, "Maya" is not, for the most part, interchangeable with "Guatemalan," an identity the Maya often seek to avoid unless it can aid their chances in an immigration hearing. If one is to be deported, for instance, it is better to claim to be a Mexican and be driven over the border than to be flown back to Guatemala City. For the refugees, however, "Guatemalan" was the identity of choice, tying together Mayas and ladinos and stressing their rights as citizens of Guatemala. The Maya in Belize stress their rights as Maya, the original inhabitants of that land and the identity most likely to gain them some little political or economic advantage. But, as Warren (1998:191–93) reminds us, each individual's choice of identity is built on the process of resolving some of the contradictions inherent in the construction of identity by the previous generation. This generation of Maya migrants has lived in exceedingly contradictory times, and its experience encompasses the contradictions between land or wage work; legal or illegal status; loyalty to town or country; English or Spanish or Mayan as a primary language. Resolution of these contradictions awaits the next generation of young Maya-Americans or Maya-Canadians now attending school and learning in English rather than in Spanish. In reshaping their identities, Mayas both open and close doors to the future.

THEIR FUTURE AND OURS

Now that the Peace Accords have been signed and a tremulous peace is at hand, some Maya have returned to Guatemala. But more will stay in the diaspora, making their homes here and returning to Guatemala only for visits. Maya communities in the United States and Canada are taking hold, settling in. The April 1999 issue of *El Maya Católico*, the newsletter of the Proyecto Pastoral Maya in Arizona, lists twenty communities in the United States where its program has coordinators—six in California, five in Florida, three in Nebraska, and one each in Arizona, Colorado, Georgia, Ohio, North Carolina, and South Carolina. In March 1999, under the auspices of the Archdiocese of Los Angeles, the Proyecto Pastoral Maya held its first national meeting with seventy participants. Its newsletter now includes a column in English addressed to Maya teens who are more comfortable with English than with Spanish. And the Proyecto Pastoral Maya is only one of many pan-Maya groups working to make these linkages and to address Maya concerns in the diaspora.

As social scientists we are obligated to ask questions about the long-term processes of Maya assimilation and Maya integration, both on return to their homeland and into North American societies. Like other ethnic groups of past diasporas, the Maya arrived to find themselves on the economic bottom. Will their persistence and courage, their adaptability, their community-centered ethic, their ties to language and homeland, make them different from those who have preceded them? Can they, through home and community, maintain Mayaness not only in the face of racism and discrimination but more importantly against the hegemonic North American culture of television, commodities, and consumption? What future awaits these hardworking and courageous people who sought new lives in strange lands? The answers are in their hands, as they are in ours. Can we as North Americans change our cultural institutions, particularly our immigration and labor laws, to be more supportive of their struggles? Can we together temper the driving imperative of consumer capitalism to their benefit as well as our own? In their strength born of struggle, can they help us weave our way to a better society for all of us, one that respects differences and values family and community? It is fervently to be hoped.

Víctor D. Montejo

Epilogue: Elilal/Exilio

Salí trémulo de mi país
perseguido por toros negros
y rabiosos mastines pintos.
He rodado por el mundo solo
arrastrando mis penas
y mi sombra sin descansar.

Ahora quiero regresar
en busca del cordón umbilical,
sembrado junto a la fuente
de agua fresca y pura
donde bebe mi tonal;
¡pues, esa es mi raíz!

He estado ausente mucho tiempo
y mis maletas están sin abrir,
siempre quise regresar mañana
pasado mañana, al día siguiente;
pero los días se han ido
dejando sus duras huellas en mí.

He reposado mi cabeza triste
en la almohada de muchos pueblos
que me han dado asilo y descanso,
y aun así me siento un ser errante
un ser solo y sonámbulo
en busca se la aurora más brillante.

He aprendido varios idiomas
y ahora me siento más confuso
que los mismos arquitectos
de la Torre de Babel.
Soy de allá y soy de aquí,
mi identidad es ya universal.

El mundo que me rodea
también se ha globalizado tanto
y puedo ver paisanos en Roma,
Nueva York y en Vancouver;
cruelmente el mundo se ha achicado
agigantando de paso mis penas.

Ahora que el tiempo del retorno
ha llegado a tocarme las puertas,
he deshecho mis maletas,
ya no puedo volver como lo quise antes;
pues mis raíces se han multiplicado
en los hijos que traje a este país.

Eso sí, a donde quiera que voy
veo el rostro de mi bello país;
y ya no me atemorizan los policías,
los agentes de migración
y los que me han visto como vagabundo
trotando por el camino sin retorno.

Se me han secado las lágrimas
y ahora mi dolor es alegría,
puedo volar por los aires, viajar,
ir y regresar de los dos mundos
que ahora son mi hogar;
¡divinos suelos donde puedo respirar!

Pero mis años mozos se han ido
y empiezo a encorvarme poco a poco.
¡Ay! mis batallas con la soledad;
solo mis huellas han quedado allí
junto a mi nombre, Víctor,
grabadas en la avenida gris del exilo.

EXILO/EXILE
Translation by Susan Rascon

I left my country in fear,
pursued by black bulls
and rabid camouflaged dogs.
I have wandered the world alone
dragging my sorrows
and my shadow, without rest.

Now I wish to return
in search of the umbilical cord
sown near the fountain
of cool, clear water
where my *tonal* drinks;
those are my roots!

I have been away a long time
my bags still unopened;
I always wished to return tomorrow
the day after, the following day;
but the days have passed
leaving their harsh traces in me.

I have rested my sorrowful head
on the pillows of many towns
that have given me rest and refuge,
but even so I feel like a nomad,
lonely, walking in my sleep
in search of the brighter dawn.

I have learned several languages
and now I feel more confused
than the very architects
of the Tower of Babel.
I'm from there and I'm from here;
my identity is now universal.

The world around me
has also globalized so much
and I can find my compatriots in Rome,
New York and Vancouver;
cruelly, the world has grown smaller,
magnifying my sorrows along the way.

Now that the moment of the return
has come and knocked on my door,
I have unpacked my bags;
I can no longer return as I wished before;
my roots have multiplied
in the children I brought to this country.

But wherever I go
I see the face of my beautiful country;
and I am no longer terrified by police,
immigration agents
or those who saw me as a wanderer
hurrying down the path of no return.

My tears have now dried
and my pain become joy;
I can fly through the skies, travel,
come and go between the two worlds
which are now my home,
glorious lands where I can breathe!

But my youthful years have gone
and I have begun to bend with age
Ah! My battles with loneliness;
only my footprints are left
next to my name, Victor,
etched on the gray avenue of exile.

References

ACNUR (Alto Comisionado de las Naciones Unidas para los Refugiados/ United Nations High Commissioner for Refugees). 1998a. *Returnee Map*. Guatemala: ACNUR, November.

————. 1998b. *Ubicación de Comunidades de Retornados*. Guatemala: ACNUR, December.

Adams, Richard. 1959. "La Ladinización en Guatemala." *Integración social en Guatemala* 2 (6): 123–37. Guatemala City: Seminario de Integración Social Guatemalteca.

Aguayo, Sergio. 1986. "Refugees: Another Piece in the Central American Quagmire." In *Fleeing the Maelstrom: Central American Refugees*, ed. Patricia Weiss Fagen and Sergio Aguayo, 95–176. Baltimore: Johns Hopkins University Press.

————. 1987a. "Las Poblaciones Desplazadas en la Recuperación y el Desarrollo Centroamericano." Paper presented at the meeting of the Comisión Internacional para la Recuperación y el Desarrollo Latinoamericano, San José, Costa Rica.

————. 1987b. "Chiapas: Las Amenazas a la Seguridad Nacional." Serie: Estudios del CLEE, EST–006–86, Mexico, D.F.: Centro Latinoamericano de Estudios Estratégicos, A.C.

Anaya, S. James. 1998. "Maya Aboriginal Land and Resource Rights and the Conflict over Logging in Southern Belize." *Yale Human Rights and Development Law Journal* 10 (1); <http://diana.law.yale.edu/yhrdlj/vol0/iss01/anaya_james_article.htm>

Anderson, Benedict. 1991. *Imagined Communities: Reflections on the Origin and Spread of Nationalism*. Rev. ed. London: Verso.

Anderson, Kenneth, and Jean-Marie Simon. 1987. "Permanent Counterinsurgency in Guatemala." *Telos* 73: 9–46.

Anderson, Marilyn, and Jonathan Garlock. 1988. *Granddaughters of Corn: Portraits of Guatemalan Women*. Willimantic, Conn.: Curbstone Press.

Anderson, Sarah. 1995. "OSHA under Siege." *The Progressive*, December 1995: 26–28.

Anfuso, Joseph, and David Sczepanski. 1983. *Efraín Ríos Montt, Servant or Dictator: The Real Story of Guatemala's Controversial Born-again President*. Ventura, Calif.: Vision House.

Arizona Republic. Tuesday, 10 January 1995: B-1.

Arturo, Julian. 1994. "In Purgatory: Mayan Immigrants in Indiantown and West Palm Beach, South Florida." Ph.D. diss., University of Florida, Gainesville.

Ashabranner, Brent. 1986. *Children of the Mayas, a Guatemalan Indian Odyssey.* New York: Dodd, Mead.

Aslam, Abid. 1996. "Environment-Belize: Indigenous People Question Highway Project." Washington, D.C.: InterPress Service, 7 November. Gaia Forest Conservation Archives: <http://www.forests.org>.

AVANCSO (Asociación Para el Avance de Ciencias Sociales en Guatemala). 1990. *Política institucional hacia el desplazado interno en Guatemala.* Cuadernos de Investigación no. 6. Guatemala: Inforpress Centroamericana.

———. 1992. *Donde está el futuro: Procesos de reintegración en comunidades de retornados.* Cuadernos de Investigación no. 8. Guatemala: Inforpress Centroamericana.

Bacon, David. 1999. "INS Declares War on Labor." *The Nation,* 25 October: 18–33.

Barker, Hubert. 1985. *1980–1981 Population Census of the Commonwealth Caribbean.* Kingston: Statistical Institute of Jamaica.

Bastos, Santiago, and Manuela Camus. 1991. *Diagnóstico socioeconómico de la Colónia Belén Mixco.* Guatemala: FLACSO.

Baudrillard, Jean. 1988. "The Masses: The Implosion of the Social in the Media." In *Selected Writings,* ed. M. Poster, 207–19. Stanford: Stanford University Press.

Bayón, M. 1997. "Las Lecciones de la selva." *El Pais* (Edición Internacional), 7 July, no. 6.

Becker, David. 1994. "Trauma, Duelo e Identidad: Una Reflexión Conceptual." In *Trauma Psicosocial y Adolescentes Latinoamericanos: Formas de Acción Grupal,* ed. David Becker, Germán Morales, and María Inés Aguilar. Santiago: Instituto Latinamericano de Salud Mental y Derechos Humanos.

Belize Times. 1994. "Minister Sells Out Toledo." 24 February.

Benz, Stephen Connely. 1996. *Guatemalan Journey.* Austin: University of Texas Press.

Billings, Deborah Lynn. 1995. "Identities, Consciousness and Organizing in Exile: Guatemalan Refugee Women in the Camps of Southern Mexico." Ph.D. diss, University of Michigan.

Bjerklie, Steve. 1995. "On the Horns of a Dilemma: The U.S. Meat and Poultry Industry." In *Any Way You Cut It: Meat Processing and Small-Town America,* ed. Donald D. Stull, Michael J. Broadway, and David Griffith, 41–60. Lawrence: University Press of Kansas.

Black, George. 1985. "Under the Gun." *NACLA Report on the Americas* 19 (November–December): 10–23.

Black, George, with Milton Jamail and Norma Stoltz Chinchilla. 1984. *Garrison Guatemala.* New York: Monthly Review Press.

Bogin, Barry, and James Loucky. 1997. "Plasticity, Political Economy, and Physical Growth Status of Guatemala Maya Children Living in the United States." *American Journal of Physical Anthropology* 102: 17–32.

Bowen, F.C.P. 1933. *Census of British Honduras, 1931.* Belize: Government Printer.

Brintnall, Douglas E. 1979. *Revolt against the Dead: The Modernization of a Mayan Community in the Highlands of Guatemala.* New York: Gordon and Breach.

Brow, James. 1988. "In Pursuit of Hegemony: Representations of Authority and Justice in a Sri Lankan Village." *American Ethnologist* 15: 311–27.

Burns, Allan F. 1988. "Resettlement in the U.S.: Kanjobal Maya in Indiantown, Florida." *Cultural Survival Quarterly* 12 (4): 41–45.

―――. 1989a. *Immigration, Ethnicity and Work in Indiantown, Florida.* Gainesville: University of Florida Center for Latin American Studies.

―――. 1989b. "Internal and External Identity among Kanjobal Refugees in Florida." In *Conflict, Migration, and the Expression of Ethnicity,* ed. Nancy Gonzalez and C. McCommon, 46–59. Boulder: Westview Press.

―――. 1993a. *Maya in Exile: Guatemalans in Florida.* Philadelphia: Temple University Press.

―――. 1993b. "Everybody's a Critic: Video Production and Applied Anthropology with Guatemalan Refugees." In *Anthropological Film and Video in the 1990s,* ed. Jack Rollwagen, 105–29. Brockport, N.Y.: Dual Printing.

Camposeco, Jerónimo. 1993. "Introduction." In Allan F. Burns, *Maya in Exile, Guatemalans in Florida,* ix–xii. Philadelphia: Temple University Press.

Carmack, Robert M. 1981. *The Quiché Mayas of Utatlán: The Evolution of a Highland Guatemala Kingdom.* Norman: University of Oklahoma Press.

―――. 1995. *Rebels of Highland Guatemala: The Quiché Mayas of Momostenango.* Norman: University of Oklahoma Press.

―――, ed. 1988. *Harvest of Violence: The Mayan Indians and the Guatemalan Crisis.* Norman: University of Oklahoma Press.

Castañeda, C. 1998. *Lucha por la Tierra, Retornados y Medio Ambiente en Huehuetenango.* Guatemala: Facultad Latinoamericana de Ciencias Sociales.

Castellanos Cambranes, Julio. 1985. *Café y campesinos en Guatemala, 1853–1897.* Vol. 12. Editorial Universitaria de Guatemala, Universidad de San Carlos de Guatemala.

CCPP (Comisiones Permanentes). 1992. "Acuerdos de la Negociación para el Retorno Colectivo y Organizado." Texto Integro. Pamphlet published for the Refugee Population by the CCPPs.

CEH (Comisión de Esclaramiento Histórico). 1999. *Guatemala: Memory of Silence (Tz'inil Na 'Tab'al): Report of the Commission for Historical Clarification, Conclusions and Recommendations.* Guatemala: CEH.

Central Statistical Office, Government of Belize. 1991. *1991 Population Census: Major Findings.* Belmopan: Central Statistical Office.

Centro de Investigaciones y Estudios Superiores en Antropología Social. 1991. *Los Refugiados Guatemaltecos y Los Derechos Humanos: Cuaderno para los refugiados Guatemaltecos.* Tuxtla Gutiérrez, Chiapas: Instituto Chiapaneco de Cultura.

CERIGUA Weekly Briefs (Guatemala news agency). 1996. 23 December, electronic mail.

―――. 1998a. "Refugee Returns Pick Up Steam." No. 29, 6 August.

―――. 1998b. "Refugees Return to Start New Life." No. 41, 23 October.

———. 1998c. "CPRs and Refugees Travel to New Home." No. 45, 19 November.

———. 1999. "Return of Refugees Officially Ends." No. 2, 14 January.

Chance, John K. 1978. *Race and Class in Colonial Oaxaca*. Stanford: Stanford University Press.

Chapin, Mac. 1995. "La Lucha por la tierra en la ultima frontera de Centroamérica." *Mesoamérica* 29: xv–xxviii.

Chavez, Leo. 1992. *Shadowed Lives: Undocumented Immigrants in American Society*. Fort Worth: Holt, Rinehart, and Winston.

Chinchilla, Norma, Nora Hamilton, and James Loucky. 1993. "Central Americans in Los Angeles: An Immigrant Community in Transition." In *In the Barrios: Latinos and the Underclass Debate*, ed. Joan Moore and Raquel Pinderhughes, 51–78. New York: Russell Sage Foundation.

Ch'oc, Gregory. 1996. "Land, Value and Economic Development in Toledo (A Maya Perspective)." Washington, D.C.: InterPress Service, 28 May, posted to PeaceNet: <peacenet-info@igc.apc.org>.

CHRLA (Center for Human Rights Legal Action). 1993. "Second On-Site Report on the First Collective Return of Refugees to Guatemala, Comunidad Victoria 20 de enero, Ixcán." March–April. Washington, D.C.: CHRLA.

Cieza de León, Pedro de. 1998 (1553). *The Discovery and Conquest of Peru: Chronicles of the New World Encounter*. Ed. and trans. by Alexandra Parma Cook and Noble David Cook. Durham: Duke University Press.

CIREFCA (International Conference on Central American Refugees). 1992a. "Progress Report on the Implementation of the Concerted Plan of Action for Refugees, Returnees and Displaced Persons in Central America." Second International Meeting of the Follow-Up Committee, CIREFCA/CS/92/6, United Nations.

———. 1992b. *Questions and Answers about CIREFCA*. San José, Costa Rica: United Nations High Commissioner for Refugees.

Cojtí Cuxil, Demetrio. 1991. *Configuración del pensamiento político del pueblo Maya*. Quezaltenango, Guatemala: El Estudiante.

Collymore, Yvette. 1996. "Maya Try to Fend Off Malayasian Timber Barons." Washington, D.C.: InterPress Service, 6 December, posted to PeaceNet: <peacenet-info@igc.apc.org>.

Conchoá Chet, Hector Aurelio. N.d. "El concepto del montañes entre los kaqchikeles de San Juan Sacatepéquez, 1524–1700." N.p.

CONGCOOP (Coordinación de Organizaciones No Gubernamentales y Cooperativas para el Acompañamiento de la Población Damnificada por el Conflicto Armado Interno). 1996. "The History and Future of the Return of Guatemalan Refugees." *Reunion* 2 (6): 8.

———. 1998. "Dispersed Refugees Return from Mexico to Guatemala." *Reunion* 4 (3): 7.

Conover, Ted. 1987. *Coyotes*. New York: Vintage Press.

Craig, Alan K. 1969. "Logwood as a Factor in the Settlement of British Honduras." *Caribbean Studies* 9: 53–62.

Craig, Colette. 1977. *The Structure of Jacaltec.* Austin: University of Texas Press.

Cultural Survival, Inc., and the Anthropology Resource Center. 1983. *Voices of the Survivors: The Massacre at Finca San Francisco, Guatemala.* Peterborough, N.H.: Transcript Printing.

Current Biography Yearbook, ed. Charles Moritz. 1983. "Ríos Montt," 321–25. New York: H. H. Wilson Co.

Dakin, Karen, and Christopher H. Lutz, eds. 1996. *Nuestro pesar; Nuestra aflicción: Memorias en lengua Náhuatl enviadas a Felipe II por indígenas del valle de Guatemala hacia 1572.* No. 7. Mexico City and Antigua, Guatemala: Facsímiles de Lingüística y Filología Nahuas and Instituto de Investigaciones Históricas/UNAM and CIRMA.

Davis, Shelton H. 1970. "Land of Our Ancestors: A Study of Land Tenure and Inheritance in the Highlands of Guatemala." Ph.D. diss., Harvard University.

———. 1983. "The Social Roots of Political Violence in Guatemala." *Cultural Survival Quarterly* 7 (1): 32–35.

———. 1988. "Introduction: Sowing the Seeds of Violence." In *Harvest of Violence: The Maya Indians and the Guatemalan Crisis,* ed. Robert M. Carmack, 3–36. Norman: University of Oklahoma Press.

———. 1997 (1970). *La tierra de nuestros antepasados: Estudio de la herencia y la tierra en el altiplano de Guatemala.* Trans. C. Margarita Cruz Valladares. Antigua, Guatemala and South Woodstock, Vt.: CIRMA and Plumsock Mesoamerican Studies.

Davis, Shelton H., and Julie Hodson. 1983. *Witness to Political Violence in Guatemala: The Suppression of a Rural Development Movement.* Boston: Oxfam America.

De Certeau, Michel. 1986. "Montaigne's 'Of Cannibals': the Savage 'I.'" In *Heterologies: Discourse on the Other,* 67–79. Minneapolis: University of Minnesota Press.

de las Casas, Bartolomé. 1992 (1552). *The Devastation of the Indies: A Brief Account.* Baltimore: Johns Hopkins University Press.

Dorman, Sherri. 1986. "Applied Anthropology with Haitian Immigrants." Non-Thesis Report, Department of Anthropology. Gainesville: University Press of Florida.

Douglas, Mary. 1966. *Purity and Danger.* London: Routledge and Kegan Paul.

Dunk, Herbert. 1921. *British Honduras: Report on the Census of 1921.* Belize: Government Printing Office.

Earle, Duncan M. 1988. "Mayas Aiding Mayas: Guatemalan Refugees in Chiapas, Mexico." In *Harvest of Violence: The Maya Indians and the Guatemalan Crisis,* ed. Robert M. Carmack, 256–73. Norman: University of Oklahoma Press.

Early, John D. 1982. *The Demographic Structure and Evolution of a Peasant System: The Guatemalan Population.* Gainesville: University Press of Florida.

Eliade, Mircea. 1959. *The Sacred and the Profane.* New York: Harcourt Brace & Co.

Fabri, Antonella. 1990. "Tactics of Resistance of Maya Women in Guatemala."

Paper presented on the panel "Maya Women and Women Anthropologists" at the American Anthropology Association Meeting, New Orleans.

———. 1991. "Violence, Identity and the Self: Strategies and Tactics of Violence in the Representation of Identity among Maya Migrants." Dissertation Proposal, State University of New York at Albany.

———. 1994. "Re-composing the Nation." Ph.D. diss., State University of New York, Albany.

———. 1999. "Silence, Invisibility, and Isolation: Mayan Women's Strategies for Defense and Survival in Guatemala." In *Women and War in the Twentieth Century*, ed. Nicole Ann Dombrowski. New York: Garland.

Falla, Ricardo. 1992. *Masacres del la Selva: Ixcán, Guatemala (1975–1982)*. Guatemala: Editorial Universitaria.

———. 1994. *Massacres in the Jungle: Ixcán, Guatemala, 1975–1982*. Boulder: Westview Press.

Farriss, Nancy M. 1978. "Nucleation versus Dispersal: The Dynamics of Population Movement in Colonial Yucatán." *Hispanic American Historical Review* 58 (2): 187–216.

———. 1983. "Indians in Colonial Yucatán: Three Perspectives." In *Spaniards and Indians in Southeastern Mesoamerica: Essays on the History of Ethnic Relations*, ed. Murdo J. MacLeod and Robert Wasserstrom, 1–39. Lincoln: University of Nebraska Press.

———. 1984. *Maya Society under Colonial Rule: The Collective Enterprise of Survival*. Princeton: Princeton University Press.

Ferris, Elizabeth. 1987. *The Central American Refugees*. New York: Praeger.

Foucault, Michel. 1979. *Discipline and Punish: The Birth of the Prison*. New York: Vintage Press.

Francis, O. C. 1964. *Census of British Honduras, 7th April 1960*. Kingston: Jamaica Tabulation Center.

Franco, René. 1993. Clínica Caminante meeting agenda for 8 April 1993. Chandler, Ariz.: Chandler Regional Hospital.

Freire, Paulo. 1970. *Pedagogy of the Oppressed*. New York: Continuum Press.

Fuentes, Carlos. 1983. *Latin America: At War with The Past*. Toronto: CBC Enterprises.

Galeano, Eduardo. 1990. "Language, Lies, and Latin Democracy." *Harper's Magazine*, February: 19–22.

Gall, Francis. 1966. *Diccionario geográfico de Guatemala*. Vol. 1. Guatemala City: Editorial José de Pineda Ibarra.

Gallardo, Eugenia, and José Roberto López. 1986. *Centroamérica: la crisis en cifras*. San José, Costa Rica: Instituto Interamericano de Cooperación para la Agricultura y Facultad Latinoamericana de Ciencias Sociales.

García, Ana Isabel, and Enrique Gomaríz. 1989. *Mujeres centroamericanas: Tomos I & II Efectos del conflicto*. San José, Costa Rica: Facultad Latinoamericana de Ciencias Sociales.

Gasco, Janine. 1991. "Indian Survival and Ladinoization in Colonial Soconusco." In *Columbian Consequences: The Spanish Borderlands in Pan-American*

Perspective, ed. David Hurst Thomas, vol. 3, 301–18. Washington, D.C.: Smithsonian Institution Press.

GHRSP (Guatemala Health Rights Support Project, USA). 1992. "Unfinished Stories: Guatemalan Refugees in Mexico." Issue Brief. Washington, D.C.: GHRSP.

Gilbreth, Christopher. 1999. "The Refugee Return Process: As One Journey Ends Another Begins." *Report on Guatemala* 20 (1): 10–13.

Gleijeses, Piero. 1989. "The Agrarian Reform of Jacobo Arbenz." *Journal of Latin American Studies* 21: 453–80.

———. 1991. *Shattered Hope: The Guatemalan Revolution and the United States, 1944–1954*. Princeton: Princeton University Press.

GOB (Government of Belize). 1991. *1991 Population Census: Major Findings*. Belmopan: Central Statistical Office.

GOBH (Government of British Honduras). 1891. *British Honduras Blue Book*. Belize City: Government Printer.

Golden, Renny, and Michael McConnell. 1986. *Sanctuary: The New Underground Railroad*. Maryknoll, N.Y.: Orbis Press.

González de la Rocha, Mercedes. 1994. *The Resources of Poverty: Women and Survival in a Mexican City*. Oxford: Blackwell.

Gordon, Edmund T., and Mark Anderson. 1999. "The African Diaspora: Toward an Ethnography of Diasporic Identification." *Journal of American Folklore* 112 (445): 282–96.

GRICAR (Grupo Internacional de Apoyo al Retorno). 1996. *Situation Report #44, 20 December 1996*. Guatemala: GRICAR.

Griffith, David. 1993. *Jones's Minimal: Low-Wage Labor in the United States*. Albany: State University of New York Press.

———. 1995. "*Hay Trabajo*: Poultry Processing, Rural Industrialization and the Latinization of Low-Wage Labor." In *Any Way You Cut It: Meat Processing and Small-Town America*, ed. Donald D. Stull, Michael J. Broadway, and David Griffith, 129–51. Lawrence: University Press of Kansas.

Gruhn, Ruth, and Alan Lyle Bryan. 1976. "An Archaeological Survey of the Chichicastenango Area of Highland Guatemala." *Cerámica de Cultura Maya* 9: 75–119.

Guatemala. 1880. *Censo General de la República de Guatemala levantado el año de 1880*. Guatemala: Establecimiento Tipográfico.

Gutman, Herbert G. 1976. *Work, Culture and Society in Industrializing America: Essays in American Working-Class and Social History*. New York: Knopf.

Hagan, Jacqueline Maria. 1994. *Deciding to Be Legal: A Maya Community in Houston*. Philadelphia: Temple University Press.

Hagan, Jacqueline Maria, and Susan Gonzalez Baker. 1993. "Implementing the U.S. Legalization Program: The Influence of Immigrant Communities and Local Agencies in Immigration Policy Reform." *International Migration Review* 27 (3): 513–36.

Hamilton, Nora, and Norma Stolz Chinchilla. 1991. "Central America Migration: A Framework for Analysis." *Latin American Research Review* 6 (1): 75–110.

Handy, Jim. 1984. *Gift of the Devil: A History of Guatemala*. Boston: South End Press.

―――. 1990. "The Corporate Community, Campesino Organizations, and Agrarian Reform: 1950–1954." In *Guatemalan Indians and the State, 1540 to 1988*, ed. Carol A. Smith. Austin: University of Texas Press.

―――. 1994. *Revolution in the Countryside: Rural Conflict and Agrarian Reform in Guatemala, 1944–1954*. Chapel Hill: University of North Carolina Press.

Henderson, John S. 1981. *The World of Ancient Maya*. Ithaca: Cornell University Press.

Hernandez Castillo, Rosalva Aida. 1988. "Mecanismos de Producción Social y Cultural de los Indígenas Q'anjob'ales Refugiados en Chiapas," Ph.D. diss., Escuela Nacional de Antropoloía e Historia, Mexico City.

Hobsbawm, E. J. 1965. *Primitive Rebels: Studies in Archaic Forms of Social Movement in the Nineteenth and Twentieth Centuries*. New York: Norton.

Hopkins, L. G. 1948. *Census of British Honduras, 9th April 1946*. Belize: Government Printer.

Horowitz, Roger, and Mark J. Miller. 1997. "Immigrants in the Delmarva Poultry Processing Industry: The Changing Face of Georgetown, Delaware and Environs." Paper presented at the conference on "The Changing Face of Delmarva," University of Delaware, 11–13 September.

House, Krista L. 1999. *"Absent Ones Who Are Always Present": Migration, Remittances and Household Survival Strategies in Guatemala*. Master's thesis, Queen's University, Kingston, Ontario.

ICVA/GRICAR (International Council of Voluntary Agencies). 1996. *Report No. 28*, 13 November 1996. Guatemala: ICVA/GRICAR.

IGE (Guatemalan Church in Exile). 1989. *Guatemala: Security, Development, and Democracy*. Managua, Nicaragua: IGE.

ILRC (Indian Law Resource Center). 1996. "Massive Logging in 'Environmentally Friendly' Belize." Helena: ILRC.

―――. 1998. "Maya Atlas Released." *Indian Rights—Human Rights* 5 (1). <http://www.indianlaw.org/newsltrs/news98sp.htm#Maya_Atlas_Released>.

InterPress Service. 1996. "Mayans Go to Washington to Oppose Logging Concessions." 4 December, posted to PeaceNet: <peacenet-info@igc.apc.org>.

Jonas, Susanne. 1991. *The Battle for Guatemala: Rebels, Death Squads, and U.S. Power*. Boulder: Westview Press.

―――. 1995. "Transnational Realities and Anti-Immigrant State Policies: Issues Raised by the Experience of Central American Immigrants and Refugees in a Transnational Region." *Estudios Internacionales* 6 (11): 17–29.

―――. 1996a. "National Security, Regional Development and Citizenship in U.S. Immigration Policy: Reflections from the Case of Central American Immigrants and Refugees." In *Transnational Realities and Nation-States: Trends in International Migration and Immigration Policy in the Americas*, ed. M. Castro. Miami: North-South Center.

―――. 1996b. "Transnational Realities and Anti-Immigrant State Policies: Issues Raised by the Experience of Central American Immigrants and Refugees in a

Transnational Region." In *Latin America and the World Economy*, ed. R. Korzeniewietz and W. Smith, 117–32. Westport, Conn.: Greenwood Press.

Jones, Chester Lloyd. 1940. *Guatemala: Past and Present*. Minneapolis: University of Minnesota Press.

Jones, Grant D. 1989. *Maya Resistance to Spanish Rule: Time and History on a Colonial Frontier*. Albuquerque: University of New Mexico Press.

Jopling, Carol F. 1994. *Indios y negros en Panamá en los siglos XVI y XVII: selecciones de los documentos del Archivo General de Indias*. Antigua, Guatemala and South Woodstock, Vt.: CIRMA and Plumsock Mesoamerican Studies.

Joseph, Gilbert M. 1987. "The Logwood Trade and Its Settlements." In *Readings in Belizean History*, 2d ed., ed. Lita Hunter Krohn, 32–47. Belize City: St. John's College.

Kaufman, Terence. 1976. *Proyecto de alfabetos y ortographías para hablar las lenguas mayances*. Guatemala: Proyecto Lingüístico Francisco Marroquin, Editorial José de Pineda Ibarra.

Kearney, Michael. 1996. *Reconceptualizing the Peasantry*. Boulder: Westview Press.

Kramer, Wendy Jill. 1990a. Personal communication.

———. 1990b. "The Politics of Encomienda Distribution in Early Spanish Guatemala, 1524–1544." Ph.D. diss., University of Warwick.

———. 1994. *Encomienda Politics in Early Colonial Guatemala, 1524–1544: Dividing the Spoils*. Dellplain Latin American Studies Series, No. 31. Boulder: Westview Press.

Kramer, Wendy Jill, W. George Lovell, and Christopher H. Lutz. 1991. "Fire in the Mountains: Juan de Espinar and the Indians of Huehuetenango, 1525–1560." In *Columbian Consequences*, vol. 3, ed. David Hurst Thomas, 263–82. Washington, D.C.: Smithsonian Institution Press.

La Cecla, Franco. 1988. *Perdersi: L'uomo Senza Ambiente*. Florence: Laterza.

La Hora. 1996. 31 December. Internet site: <http://www.lahora.com.gt/p1996.htm>.

Levenson-Estrada, Deborah. 1994. *Trade Unionists against Terror: Guatemala City 1945–1985*. Chapel Hill: University of North Carolina Press.

Lira, Elizabeth, and María Isabel Castillo. 1991. *Psicología de la Amenaza Política y del Miedo*. Santiago: Instituto Latinamericano de Salud Mental y Derechos Humanos.

Lockhart, James. 1968. *Spanish Peru, 1532–1560: A Colonial Society*. Madison: University of Wisconsin Press.

Loftis, Randy Lee. 1996a. "Protecting Their Roots: Mayan Villagers Fight to Save Belize Forests from Logging." *Dallas Morning News*, 15 September: 1A.

———. 1996b. "Southeast Asia Invests in Tropics." *Dallas Morning News*, 15 September: 33A.

Loucky, James. 1987. "Central American Refugees and the Right to Life in Family Perspective." *Pacific Coast Council on Latin American Studies* 14 (1): 15–24.

———. 1992. "Central American Refugees: Learning New Skills in the U.S.A." In *Anthropology: Understanding Human Adaptation*, ed. Michael C. Howard and Janet Dunaif-Hattis, 485–87. New York: Harper Collins.

Loucky, James, et al. 1994. "Immigrant Enterprise and Labor in the Los Angeles Garment Industry." In *The Globalization of the Apparel Industry in the Pacific Rim*, ed. Edna Bonacich, 345–61. Philadelphia: Temple University Press.

Lovell, W. George. 1988. "Surviving Conquest: The Maya of Guatemala in Historical Perspective." *Latin American Research Review* 23 (2): 25–57.

———. 1990. *Conquista y cambio cultural: La sierra de los Chuchumatanes de Guatemala 1500–1821.* Antigua, Guatemala and South Woodstock, Vt.: CIRMA and Plumsock Mesoamerican Studies.

———. 1995. *A Beauty That Hurts: Life and Death in Guatemala.* Toronto: Between the Lines.

———. 1996. "The Century after Independence: Land and Life in Guatemala." *Canadian Journal of Latin American and Caribbean Studies*, 19 (37–38): 243–62.

Lovell, W. George, and Christopher Lutz. 1995. *Demography and Empire: A Guide to the Population History of Spanish Central America, 1500–1821.* Dellplain Latin American Studies Series, No. 33. Boulder: Westview Press.

Lovell, W. George, Christopher Lutz, and William R. Swezey. 1990. "Indian Migration and Community Formation: An Analysis of Congregación in Colonial Guatemala." In *Migration in Colonial Spanish America*, ed. David J. Robinson, 18–40. Cambridge: Cambridge University Press.

Lutz, Christopher H. 1982. *Historia sociodemográfica de Santiago de Guatemala, 1541–1773.* Antigua, Guatemala: CIRMA.

———. 1993. "The Late Nineteenth-Century Guatemalan Maya in Historical Context: Past and Future Research." In Margot Schevill, *Maya Textiles of Guatemala: The Gustavus A. Eisen Collection, 1902,* 43–53. Austin: University of Texas Press.

———. 1994a. *Santiago de Guatemala, 1571–1773: City, Caste and the Colonial Experience.* Norman: University of Oklahoma Press.

———. 1994b. "Santiago de Guatemala, 1700–1773." In *Siglo XVIII hasta la Independencia*, ed. Cristina Zilbermann de Luján, 185–98. Vol. 3 of *Historia general de Guatemala*, ed. Joge Luján Muñoz. Guatemala: Asociación de Amigos del País, Fundación para la Cultura y el Desarrollo.

———. 1996. "Introducción histórica." In *Nuestro pesar; Nuestra aflicción: Memorias en lengua Náhuatl enviadas a Felipe II por indígenas del valle de Guatemala hacia 1572*, ed. Karen Dakin and Christopher H. Lutz, xi–1. Mexico City and Antigua, Guatemala: Facsímiles de Lingüística y Filología Nahuas and Instituto de Investigaciones Históricas/UNAM and CIRMA.

Lutz, Christopher H., and W. George Lovell. 1990. "Core and Periphery in Colonial Guatemala." In *Guatemalan Indians and the State: 1540 to 1988*, ed. Carol A. Smith, 35–51. Austin: University of Texas Press.

MacLeod, Murdo J. 1973. *Spanish Central America: A Socioeconomic History, 1520–1720.* Berkeley: University of California Press.

———. 1983. "Ethnic Relations and Indian Society in the Province of Guatemala, ca. 1620–ca. 1800." In *Spaniards and Indians in Southeastern Mesoamerica: Essays on the History of Ethnic Relations*, ed. Murdo J. MacLeod and Robert Wasserstrom, 189–214. Lincoln: University of Nebraska Press.

Malkki, Liisa. 1990. "Context and Consciousness: Local Conditions for the Production of Historical and National Thought among Hutu Refugees in Tanzania." In *Nationalist Ideologies and the Production of National Culture*, ed. Richard G. Fox. Washington, D.C.: American Ethnological Society Monograph Series, no. 2.

Mamá Maquín. 1993a. "Refugee Women: Participation and Organization." Conference Papers, vol. 2. *Gender Issues and Refugees: Development Implications.* Paper given at a conference at York University, Toronto.

———. 1993b. "Mensaje de Mamá Maquín a las Mujeres: Abriendo Nuevos Caminos por la Dignidad e Igualdad de la Mujer Guatemalteca." Boletín No. Agosto.

———. 1994. *De Refugiadas a Retornadas: Memorial de Experiencias Organizativas de las Mujeres Refugiadas en Chiapas.* Chiapas, Mexico: United Nations.

Manz, Beatriz. 1988a. *Refugees of a Hidden War.* Albany: State University of New York Press.

———. 1988b. *Repatriation and Reintegration: An Arduous Process in Guatemala.* Washington, D.C.: Center for Immigration Policy and Refugee Assistance (CIPRA), Georgetown University.

———. 1989. "Issues of Central American Return and Reintegration." Washington, D.C.: Center for Immigration Policy and Refugee Assistance (CIPRA), Georgetown University.

———. 1994. "Epilogue: Exodus, Resistance, and Readjustment in the Aftermath of Massacres." In Ricardo Falla, *Massacres in the Jungle: Ixcán, Guatemala, 1975–1982,* 191–211. Boulder: Westview Press.

Massey, Douglas, et al. 1987. *Return to Aztlan: The Social Process of International Migration from Western Mexico.* Berkeley: University of California Press.

McCreery, David J. 1983. "Debt Servitude in Rural Guatemala, 1876–1936." *Hispanic American Historical Review* 63: 735–59.

———. 1994. *Rural Guatemala, 1760–1940.* Stanford: Stanford University Press.

Medina, Laurie Kroshus. 1997. "Development Policies and Identity Politics: Class and Collectivity in Belize." *American Ethnologist* 24 (1): 148–69.

———. 1998. "History, Culture and Place-Making: 'Native' Status and Maya Identity in Belize." *Journal of Latin American Anthropology* 4 (1): 134–65.

Mendelson, E. Michael. 1965. *Los escandalos de Maximón: un estudio sobre la religión y la visión del mundo en Santiago Atitlán.* Guatemala: Tipografía Nacional, for Seminario de Integración Social Guatemalteca, Publicación no. 19.

Ministerio de Economía. 1984. *Censo Nacionales: IV Habitación-IX Población, 1981.* Guatemala City: Republica de Guatemala, Dirección General de Estadística, febrero.

Mintz, Sidney W. 1989 (1974). *Caribbean Transformations.* New York: Columbia University Press.

Miralles, Maria A. 1987. "Some Observations of the Food Habits of Guatemalan Refugees in South Florida." *Florida Journal of Anthropology* 12 (2): 11–27.

Moberg, Mark. 1997. *Myths of Ethnicity and Nation: Immigration, Work and Identity in the Belize Banana Industry.* Knoxville: University of Tennessee Press.

Montejo, Victor. 1987. *Testimony: Death of a Guatemalan Village*. Willimantic, Conn.: Curbstone Press.

Morrison, Andrew R., and Rachel A. May. 1994. "Escape from Terror: Violence and Migration in Post-Revolutionary Guatemala." *Latin American Research Review* 29 (2): 111–32.

Mosquera Aguilar, Antonio. 1990. *Los Trabajadores Guatemaltecos en México*. Guatemala: Tiempos Modernos.

Nairn, Allan. 1992. "The Roots of Torture: U.S. Complicity and the Need for Change." Keynote presentation at "Confronting the Heart of Darkness: An International Symposium on Torture in Guatemala" a symposium of the Guatemala Human Rights Commission, Washington, D.C., 13–15 November.

Nash, June. 1994. "Judas Transformed." *Natural History* 103 (3): 47–52.

Nash, Manning. 1989. *The Cauldron of Ethnicity in the Modern World*. Chicago: University of Chicago Press.

New York Times, 10 February 1998.

News and Observer, Raleigh, N.C., 30 November 1996.

News Herald, Morgantown, N.C., 15–18 May 1995.

Newson, Linda. 1986. *The Cost of Conquest: Indian Decline in Honduras under Spanish Rule*. Dellplain Latin American Studies Series, No. 20. Boulder: Westview Press.

———. 1987. *Indian Survival in Colonial Nicaragua*. Norman: University of Oklahoma Press.

Nolasco, José Carlos. 1989. "Campamentos: Los Refugiados Guatemaltecos en la Frontera Sur de México." Unpublished paper prepared for the Latin American Studies Association Conference, San Juan, Puerto Rico.

Nolin Hanlon, Catherine L. 1995. *Flight, Exile, and Return: Place and Identity among Guatemalan Maya Refugees*. Master's thesis, Queen's University, Kingston, Ontario.

———. 1998. "Transnational Connections: Challenges of Place-making for Guatemalan Refugees and Immigrants in Toronto, Canada." Paper presented at the Annual Meeting of the American Anthropological Association, Philadelphia, 5 December 1998.

Nolin Hanlon, Catherine L., and W. George Lovell. 1997. "Huida, exilio, repatriación y retorno: Escenas de los refugiados guatemaltecos, 1081–1997." *Mesoamérica* 34: 559–82.

Noticias de Guatemala. 1991. 13 Junio, no. 189.

Observer, Charlotte, N.C., 15 May 1995.

ODHA (Oficina de Derechos Humanos del Arzobispo). 1998. "Guatemala Nunca Mas." Summary version in *Prensa Libre*, 6 June: 35, 58.

O'Docherty Madraza, Laura. 1988. "The Hidden Face of War in Central America." *Current Sociology* 36 (2): 93–106.

———. 1989. *Central Americans in Mexico City: Uprooted and Silenced*. Washington, D.C.: Center for Immigration Policy and Refugee Assistance (CIPRA), Georgetown University.

Payne, Anthony J. 1990. "The Belize Triangle: Relations with Britain,

Guatemala, and the United States." *Journal of Interamerican Studies and World Affairs* 32 (1): 119–35.

Pellett, Lea B. 1994. "Still Sons of the Shaking Earth: Mexicans and Guatemalans in the East Coast Labor Stream." *Migration World* 22 (2/3): 22–31.

Percheron, Nicole. 1990. "Producción agrícola y comercio de la Verapaz en la época colonial." *Mesoamérica* 20 (diciembre): 231–48.

Pérez Brignoli, Héctor. 1990. *Breve historia de Centroamérica*. Madrid: Alianza Editorial.

Phillips, H. Denbigh. 1912. *Report on the 1911 Census of the Colony of British Honduras*. Belize: Angelus.

Pinto Soria, Julio César. 1989. "Apuntes históricos sobre la estructura agraria y asentamiento en la Capitanía General de Guatemala." In *La sociedad colonial en Guatemala: estudios regionales y locales*, ed. Stephen Webre, 109–40. Antigua, Guatemala, and South Woodstock, Vt.: CIRMA and Plumsock Mesoamerican Studies.

Portes, Alejandro. 1985. *Latin Journey: Cuban and Mexican Immigrants in the U.S.* Berkeley: University of California Press.

——. 1989. "Latin American Urbanization during the Years of the Crisis." *Latin American Research Review* 24 (3): 7–44.

Pratt, Mary Louise. 1992. *Imperial Eyes: Travel Writing and Transculturation*. London: Routledge.

Project Accompaniment. 1996. *Report on the Situation in the Refugee Camps in Mexico*. Unpublished report, January–May.

——. 1997. Personal communication, 20 February 1997.

——. 1998a. *Project Accompaniment Basic Fact Sheet*. 30 December.

——. 1998b. "Returnees Ready for Next Step." *Projecto A: Newsletter of Canadian Accompaniment in Guatemala*. 5 February.

——. 1998c. "Return Watch 1998." *Projecto A: Newsletter of Canadian Accompaniment in Guatemala*. 7 May.

——. 1998d. "Return Watch 1998: An End in Sight." *Projecto A: Newsletter of Canadian Accompaniment in Guatemala*. 5 July.

——. 1998e. "Return Watch and Impact of Hurricane Mitch." *Projecto A: Newsletter of Canadian Accompaniment in Guatemala*. 5 November.

Recopilación de Leyes de los Reynos de las Indias. 1973. Madrid: Ediciones de Cultura Hispánica.

Redfield, Robert. 1934. "Folk Ways and City Ways." In *Human Nature and the Study of Society: The Papers of Robert Redfield*, ed. M. P. Redfield, vol. 1, 172–82. Chicago: University of Chicago Press.

Roberts, G. W. 1976. *1970 Population Census of the Commonwealth Caribbean*. Kingston: Census Research Programme.

Robinson, David J. 1990. "Introduction: Towards a Typology of Migration in Colonial Spanish America." In *Migration in Colonial Spanish America*, ed. David J. Robinson, 1–17. Cambridge: Cambridge University Press.

Rodríguez, Nestor P. 1987. "Undocumented Central Americans in Houston: Diverse Populations." *International Migration Review* 21 (1): 4–26.

Rodríguez, Nestor P., and Jacqueline Maria Hagan. 1992. "Apartment Restructuring and Immigrant Tenant Struggles: A Case Study of Human Agency." *Comparative Urban and Community Research* 4: 164–80.

Rosaldo, Renato. 1993 (1989). *Culture and Truth: The Remaking of Social Analysis.* Boston: Beacon Press.

Salvadó, Luis Raul. 1988. *The Other Refugees: A Study of Nonrecognized Guatemalan Refugees in Chiapas, Mexico.* Washington, D.C.: Center for Immigration Policy and Refugee Assistance (CIPRA), Georgetown University.

Sandal, Inger. 1996. "Field of Dreams." *Mesa Tribune,* 7 January 1996: A1.

Santoli, Anthony. 1988. *New Americans: An Oral History.* New York: Viking.

Scarry, Elaine. 1985. *The Body in Pain: The Making and Unmaking of the World.* New York: Oxford University Press.

Schirmer, Jennifer. 1998. *The Guatemalan Military Project: A Violence Called Democracy.* Philadelphia: University of Pennsylvania Press.

Scott, Allen J., and Edward W. Soja, eds. 1997. *Los Angeles and Urban Theory at the End of the Twentieth Century.* Berkeley: University of California Press.

Scott, James C. 1998. *Seeing Like a State: How Certain Schemes To Improve the Human Condition Have Failed.* New Haven: Yale University Press.

Scott, Jeffrey D. 1994. "Hands That Pick the Fruit." *St. Anthony Messenger,* October: 22–27.

Shapiro, Michael. 1988. *The Politics of Representation: Writing Practices in Biography, Photography, and Policy Analysis.* Madison: University of Wisconsin Press.

Sherman, William L. 1979. *Forced Native Labor in Sixteenth-Century Central America.* Lincoln: University of Nebraska Press.

Siglo News. 1997. "Seven Month Hiatus in Refugee Returns Ends." 9 July.

———. 1999. "This Week in Guatemala." 27 July.

Simpson, Lesley Byrd. 1934. *Studies in the Administration of the Indians in New Spain.* Ibero-Americana Series (7). Berkeley: University of California Press.

———. 1966. *The Encomienda in New Spain: The Beginnings of Spanish Mexico.* Berkeley: University of California Press.

Smith, Carol A. 1987. "Culture and Community: The Language of Class in Guatemala." In *The Year Left: An American Socialist Yearbook,* ed. M. Davis et al., 197–217. London: Verso.

———. 1988. "Destruction of the Material Bases for Indian Culture." In *Harvest of Violence,* ed. Robert M. Carmack, 206–34. Norman: University of Oklahoma Press.

———. 1990a. "Introduction: Social Relations in Guatemala over Time and Space." In *Guatemalan Indians and the State, 1540 to 1988,* ed. Carol A. Smith, 1–34. Austin: University of Texas Press.

———. 1990b. "Class Position and Class Consciousness in an Indian Community." In *Guatemalan Indians and the State, 1540 to 1988,* ed. Carol A. Smith, 205–29. Austin: University of Texas Press.

Spence, Jack, et al. 1998. *Promise and Reality.* Cambridge, Mass.: Hemisphere Initiatives.

Stepputat, Finn. 1994. "The Imagined Return Community of Guatemalan Refugees." *Refuge* 13 (10): 13–15.

Stoll, David. 1993. *Between Two Armies in the Ixil Towns of Guatemala*. New York: Columbia University Press.

———. 1999. *Rigoberta Menchú and the Story of All Poor Guatemalans*. Boulder: Westview Press.

Stone, Michael C. 1995. "La política cultural de la identidad maya en Belice." *Mesoamérica* 29: 167–214.

Suárez-Orozco, Carola, and Marcelo Suárez-Orozco. 1995. *Transformations: Migration, Family Life, and Achievement Motivation among Latino Adolescents*. Stanford: Stanford University Press.

Swedish, Margaret. 1999. "Border Deaths Expected to Rise." *Central America/Mexico Report*, September 1999: 2.

Taylor, Clark. 1998. *Return of Guatemala's Refugees: Reweaving the Torn*. Philadelphia: Temple University Press.

Tax, Sol. 1937. "The Municipios of the Midwestern Highlands of Guatemala." *American Anthropologist* 39 (3): 423–44.

Tenbruck, Friedrich H. 1990. "The Dream of a Secular Ecumene: The Meaning and Limits of Policies of Development." In *Global Culture: Nationalism, Globalization and Modernity*, ed. Mike Featherstone, 193–206. London: Sage Publications.

Thorndike, A. E. 1978. "Belize among Her Neighbors: An Analysis of the Guatemala-Belize Dispute." *Caribbean Review* 8 (2): 13–19.

Turner, Victor. 1972. "The Center Out There: Pilgrim's Goal." *History of Religions* 12: 191–230.

Turner, Victor, and E. Turner. 1978. *Image and Pilgrimage in Christian Culture: Anthropological Perspectives*. New York: Columbia University Press.

URNG (Unidad Revolucionaria Nacional Guatemalteca). 1994. "The Guatemala of the Future will be a Pluricultural, Multilingual Nation, with National Unity." Declaration by the URNG General Command. Washington, D.C.: URNG.

USCR (U.S. Committee for Refugees). 1990. *World Refugee Survey: 1989 in Review*. Washington, D.C.: U.S. Committee for Refugees.

———. 1991a. *Running the Gauntlet: The Central American Journey through Mexico*. Washington, D.C.: U.S. Committee for Refugees.

———. 1991b. *World Refugee Survey 1990*. Washington D.C.: U.S. Committee for Refugees.

———. 1993. *El Retorno: Guatemalans' Risky Repatriation Begins*. Washington, D.C.: U.S. Committee for Refugees.

Virilio, Paul. 1986. *Speed and Politics*. Semiotext(e) Series. New York: Columbia University Press.

Vlach, Norita. 1992. *The Quetzal in Flight: Guatemalan Refugee Families in the United States*. Westport, Conn.: Praeger.

Voorhies, Barbara. 1989. *Ancient Trade and Tribute: Economies of the Soconusco Region of Mesoamérica*. Salt Lake City: University of Utah Press.

Warren, Kay B. 1978. *The Symbolism of Subordination: Indian Identity in a Guatemalan Town*. Austin: University of Texas Press.

———. 1998. *Indigenous Movements and Their Critics: Pan-Maya Activism in Guatemala*. Princeton: Princeton University Press.

Wasserstrom, Robert. 1983. *Class and Society in Central Chiapas*. Berkeley: University of California Press.

Watanabe, John M. 1990. "Enduring Yet Ineffable Community in the Western Periphery of Guatemala." In *Guatemalan Indians and the State, 1540 to 1988*, ed. Carol A. Smith, 183–204. Austin: University of Texas Press.

Webre, Stephen. 1986. "El trabajo forzoso de indígenas en la política colonial guatemalteca, siglo XVII." Paper presented at symposium on "Sociedad Colonial en Mesoamérica y el Caribe," San José, Costa Rica, 1–5 December.

Wellmeier, Nancy J. 1998. *Rituals of Resettlement*. New York: Garland.

Whetten, Nathan L. 1961. *Guatemala: The Land and the People*. New Haven: Yale University Press.

Wilk, Richard. 1987. "The Kekchi and the Settlement of the Toledo District." *Belizean Studies* 15 (3): 33–50.

———. 1991. *Household Ecology: Change and Domestic Life among the Kekchi Maya of Belize*. Tucson: University of Arizona Press.

Williams, Robert G. 1986. *Export Agriculture and the Crisis in Central America*. Chapel Hill: University of North Carolina Press.

Wilson, Arthur M. 1936. "The Logwood Trade in the 17th and 18th Centuries." In *Essays in the History of Modern Europe*, ed. Donald McKay, 1–15. New York: Harper.

Wilson, Richard. 1995. *Maya Resurgence in Guatemala: Q'eqchi' Experiences*. Norman: University of Oklahoma Press.

WOLA (Washington Office on Latin America). 1989. *Uncertain Return: Refugees and Reconciliation in Guatemala*. Washington, D.C.: Washington Office on Latin America.

Wolf, Eric R. 1957. "Closed Corporate Peasant Communities in Mesoamérica and Central Java." *Southwestern Journal of Anthropology* 13 (1): 1–18.

———. 1982. *Europe and the People without History*. Berkeley: University of California Press.

Woodward, Ralph Lee, Jr. 1983. "Population and Development in Guatemala, 1840–1879." *Annals of the Southern Council on Latin American Studies* (SECOLAS) 13: 5–18.

———. 1993. *Rafael Carrera and the Emergence of the Republic of Guatemala, 1821–1871*. Athens: University of Georgia Press.

Woost, Michael D. 1993. "Nationalizing the Local Past in Sri Lanka: Histories of Nation and Development in a Sinhalese Village." *American Ethnologist* 20 (3): 502–21.

WCC/GRICAR (World Council of Churches/Grupo Internacional de Apoyo al Retorno). 1996. *Situation Report* #44, 20 December. Guatemala: GRICAR.

———. 1999. *Situation Report* #56, 19 January. Guatemala: GRICAR.

Wright, Ronald. 1993. "The Death-List People." In Ronald Wright, *Home and Away*, 63–84. Toronto: Knopf Canada.

Young, A. K. 1901. *Report on the Result of the Census of the Colony of British Honduras*. Belize: Angelus Press.

Young, Alma Harrington, and Dennis Young. 1988. "The Impact of the Anglo-Guatemalan Dispute on the Internal Politics of Belize." *Latin American Perspectives* 15 (2): 6–30.

Zetter, Roger. 1988. "Refugees and Refugee Studies: A Label and An Agenda." *Refugee Studies* 1: 1–6.

About the Contributors

DEBORAH L. BILLINGS received her Ph.D. in sociology from the University of Michigan and currently works as a researcher in the Health Systems Research Division of Ipas, an international reproductive health organization, and as an adjunct assistant professor in the Department of Health Behavior and Health Education at the University of North Carolina, Chapel Hill. She conducted her field research with Guatemalan refugee women in southern Mexico during 1991 and 1992, and her dissertation focused on women's organizing in exile.

ALLAN F. BURNS is chair of the Anthropology Department at the University of Florida. He works on issues of Maya language and culture in Yucatan, Chiapas, Guatemala, and the United States. In addition to his book *Maya in Exile* (1993), he has published a book on narratives in Yucatec Maya, *An Epoch of Miracles* (1983), as well as numerous articles on oral history, bilingual education, and migration. He directs the Yucatan Exchange program, bringing U.S. students to Mérida and Yucatecan students to the United States.

JERÓNIMO CAMPOSECO continues his work with Mayas in southern Florida. One of the originators of CornMaya, the Maya support group in Indiantown, Florida, he currently works with the Farmworker Child Development Center at the Redlands Christian Migrant Association in Delray, Florida.

ALVIS DUNN is ABD in the Department of History at the University of North Carolina. His concentration is in Latin American history, especially colonial Maya history focusing on identity, race, and resistance. His Ph.D. dissertation deals with the Holy Week uprising in Quezaltenango in 1787. He has taught at Guilford College, Appalachian State University, and the University of North Carolina.

ANTONELLA FABRI earned her undergraduate degree in languages and literature from the University of Rome, Italy, and her Ph.D. in cultural anthropology from the State University of New York, Albany. At present she is an assistant professor at Drew University. Her work with the Maya began in 1989 and has encompassed issues of displacement, violence, and women's organizing. She served with the United Nations Guatemala team, which monitored human rights violations during the negotiation of the peace process.

LEON FINK is professor of history at the University of North Carolina, Chapel Hill. A specialist in American labor history, he is the author most recently of

253

Progressive Intellectuals and the Dilemmas of Democratic Commitment (1998). After years of following Latin American labor and politics from afar, he was delighted when a newspaper story led him to the events in Morganton.

JACQUELINE MARIA HAGAN received her Ph.D. in sociology and demography from the University of Texas at Austin. She is associate professor of sociology and co-director of the Center for Immigration Research at the University of Houston. The author of *Deciding to be Legal: A Maya Community in Houston* (Temple), she is currently conducting a multi-site study with Nestor P. Rodríguez on the effects of the 1996 immigration and welfare initiatives on border communities in Texas and Mexico.

DOMINGO HERNÁNDEZ IXCOY has returned to Guatemala, where he continues to work on Maya community issues. Presently he is working on Maya language, culture, and political issues with *Centro Maya Saqb'e* in Chimaltenango.

JAMES LOUCKY earned his Ph.D. in anthropology from the University of California, Los Angeles, for his work on Maya children's roles in household survival. He has worked with the Maya community in Los Angeles since the mid-1980s. He is a professor teaching anthropology, Latin American Studies, and International Studies at Western Washington University in Bellingham, Washington.

W. GEORGE LOVELL teaches geography at Queen's University, Kingston, Ontario, Canada. His most recent book is *A Beauty That Hurts: Life and Death in Guatemala* (1995), which will be published in a revised U.S. edition. With Christopher H. Lutz he is the co-author of *Demography and Empire: A Guide to the Population History of Spanish Central America, 1500–1821* (1995).

CHRISTOPHER H. LUTZ received his B.A. in history from Antioch College in Yellow Springs, Ohio, and his M.A. and Ph.D. in Latin American History from the University of Wisconsin. Lutz recently retired as the longtime editor of *Mesoamérica*, a semestral Spanish-language regional studies journal co-published by CIRMA in Antigua, Guatemala, and Plumsock Mesoamerican Studies in Vermont. He currently edits a monograph series for PMS/CIRMA and helps to administer the Maya Educational Foundation based in Vermont.

VICTOR D. MONTEJO holds an M.A. in anthropology from the State University of New York at Albany and a Ph.D. in anthropology from the University of Connecticut. He is a Jakaltek Maya who has experienced the diaspora firsthand. He is currently teaching in the Department of Native American Studies at the University of California at Davis. His poetry has been published by Curbstone Press and his first novel was recently published by the Yax Te' Foundation.

MARILYN M. MOORS received an M.A. in anthropology from George Washington University in Washington, D.C. She is professor *emerita* of Montgomery

College and currently adjunct professor teaching anthropology and gender at Frostburg State University in western Maryland. She is the national coordinator of the Guatemala Scholars Network and has been active in Maya issues since the Spanish Embassy fire in 1981.

CATHERINE L. NOLIN HANLON is a doctoral student in the Department of Geography, Queen's University, Kingston, Ontario, Canada, where she completed her Master's degree in 1995. Her doctoral studies focus on the transnational Guatemalan community in Canada and its role in the social transformation of Guatemala through remittance commitments. She is a member of the steering committee of Project Accompaniment Canada, a grassroots network assisting, at their request, the return of refugees from Mexico to Guatemala.

ZOILA RAMIREZ, a Mam weaver, received refugee status from Canada in the mid-1980s. She lives in Vancouver with her husband and four children and is active in the local Maya support network in that area.

NESTOR P. RODRÍGUEZ is associate professor of sociology and co-director of the Center for Immigration Research at the University of Houston. He has been studying Central American immigration in the Houston area since the mid-1980s. His recent work investigates the impact of recent welfare and immigration laws on low-income immigrant communities.

MICHAEL C. STONE holds a Ph.D. in anthropology from the University of Texas at Austin and an M.A. in Latin American Studies from Stanford University. He is assistant professor of anthropology at Hartwick College. His contribution is based on a decade of ethnographic fieldwork among, and archival research on, Mayan-speaking groups in Belize.

CLARK TAYLOR received his Ph D. in urban planning from Rutgers University. He is currently associate professor in the Latin American Studies Program at the College of Public and Community Service, University of Massachusetts, Boston. Through his church community, he has developed a long-term relationship with the village of Santa María Tzejá in the Ixcán. He is author of *Return of Guatemala's Refugees: Reweaving the Torn* (Temple).

NANCY J. WELLMEIER received her Ph.D. in cultural anthropology from Arizona State University. She currently works as a consultant to the Catholic Bishops of the United States in outreach to Maya refugees in the United States.

Index